BUY ME

Buy Me, Boston
ZONE
M.O.B.
The Real Paper
FRANK ROWE

Guaranteed to grab you by the throat!

Compilation and arrangement by Brian Coleman.

Book interior and cover design by Caryn Hirsch

Published in the United States by **Dignified And Old,** Everett, MA

Coleman, Brian
Buy Me, Boston Volume 2: More Local Ads and Flyers, 1960s - 1980s

ISBN 978-0-9903076-7-9

Library of Congress Control Number: 2020915397

Printed and bound in the United States of America

www.BuyMeBoston.com

www.BrianColemanBooks.com

www.Instagram.com/DignifiedAndOld

IMPORTANT NOTE:

Many of the objects and visuals featured in this book were found in defunct publications or handbills without attribution, so many of the creators behind them could not be identified. We believe that this publication constitutes fair use of all materials featured, and is not an infringement of copyright under the Copyright Act, 17 U.S.C. § 107. However, if you have any rights to any of these visuals and do not wish to be included, you have our sincere apologies and we will remove your work from all future printings. Let us know at Hello@GoodRoadGoods.com.

A WORD FROM YOUR CURATOR

When I put out the first volume of *Buy Me, Boston* in 2018 it was an experiment. It was an exploded fanzine, conceptualized at around 100 pages, which quickly grew to 300. I had put out books before, but I had never focused on the town I have called home for most of my life. And so, I presented readers with a stream-of-consciousness, visual-centric yesteryear trip through the wacky maze that we call Boston (and 128 when it's dark outside).

I am happy to say that the experiment worked. And that's less because I am a genius and much more because it was kind of like shooting fish in a barrel – if you want to see any Bostonian swoon, just utter the name of a club or restaurant that they loved but is no longer around. A place where they can still see their late mother or father seated across the booth from them as they got brainfreeze from a childhood milkshake; a haunt they frequented in high school or college that still triggers vivid sense memories; a restaurant where they had a first awkward date with their soulmate... or even ex-soulmate; a VFW hall where they got a black eye in the mosh pit at a hardcore show and still won't shut up about it.

I will repeat one paragraph from the intro to Volume 1 here, because it's the same this time around: The images in this book are scanned from original sources, not from Google Images or any other online shortcut. As a result, some pages jump out in crisp, brilliant color; others are tattered and yellowed with age. Such is the nature of old-ass stuff.

What I endeavor to present in these books is, in a way, a mix of past and present – even if a location is long gone, I like the fact that you can find the address on an ad or a poster and see what stands there today. Inevitably, since Volume 1 we have had more losses – two major ones were The No Name (my personal favorite eatery, going back to visits with my family in the mid-'70s); and another legendary chowda emporium, Durgin Park. As I write these words in the midst of an unprecedented pandemic that has all but outlawed social contact, it will only be a matter of time before more spaces and places, whether celebrated in these pages or not, will fall by the wayside.

Buy Me, Boston is a daydream about a city – whether you grew up here or not – and the people who have made it unique for centuries. As I remarked in the Intro to the first volume, if any establishments in these books are still standing in 2021 they deserve double extra credit, applause and patronage. It's not easy to be a small business of any sort, and those that find a way to give their customers an excuse to return always deserve respect.

The only reason I would dare to attempt a Volume 2 is if I could present an even better product and experience than the last time around. You will be the judge of this claim, but I think I have accomplished it, thanks to many more dozens of digging hours; networking with more generous archival contacts old and new (detailed in the Acknowledgements at the end of the book); scanning; curating; and editing.

Boston isn't always a walk in the park when it comes to thriving, or even just surviving, but I think it's a hell of a place to hang your (Red Sox) hat. And here's to hoping we're all still here – above ground and above water – for at least a couple more decades.

Brian Coleman
Revere, MA

PREFACE

For my entire life, whether I realized it or not, whether I had a day job or not, I was essentially a preservationist, a curator, an archivist. I'm convinced that I worked in a variety of positions in the media worlds not so much for the salary but mainly for the opportunity to collect and save the debris of our culture. The promotional artifacts, the toys and trinkets, the music and pop culture, the flyers and posters, the newspapers, magazines and fanzines. I kept them all, randomly, indiscriminately, totally. I saved the stuff I loved, as well as the marginal detritus.

Among other professional endeavors and projects, while I worked at WBCN, WFNX and the *Boston Phoenix,* I created ads. I did 16- and 24- and 36-page advertorial supplements to newspapers. These sections were essentially nothing but ads... a reader-friendly mix of "editorial" content and hard-sell, self-promotional messages about long-gone radio stations like WBCN and WCOZ, or oral histories of businesses like Newbury Comics and Great Woods (now Xfinity Center).

Two years ago, after a lifetime of generating ads, I was surprised and delighted when Brian Coleman showed me the initial proof of *Buy Me, Boston Volume 1.* Brian had spent months opening boxes in my Archives at the Norwood Space Center, as well as selecting content from other key sources, like Kay Bourne, Chuck White and Wayne Valdez. With Volume 1, and now Volume 2, Brian has assembled a quirky visual history of a semi-forgotten Our Town, Boston – as it once was and will never again be. You can rediscover the city or visit it for the first time through the kaleidoscopic lens of designers and graphic artists of another era.

No periodical, from *Night Life* to *The Noise, Boston Rock* to *New England Teen Scene,* was too obscure. No advertiser, from Captain Freedom Haircuts Ltd to The Mail Box Disco, Spag's to The Old Mole, Café Yana to Rondar The Rent A Magician, was too marginal. For Brian, every unopened box in my Archives was a micro-version of Christmas morning; who could know what spectacular ad was waiting to be liberated and immortalized?

The beauty of Brian's books, beyond the brilliant selections and appealing layouts, is the random placement of the ads. I can open to any page and find a club that I frequented in the 1980s, a type font (probably hand-pressed Letraset rub-on lettering) that was popular in the 1970s, or a store I patronized when I arrived here in the late 1960s.

Back then, as it is now, every ad, every flyer, every ephemera surface was bought and paid for, and represented the hope and dream of a person, a business, an organization, a political movement. Some ads were agency-smart and stylized; others were rudimentary, innocent and hand-crafted Some helped create corporate empires; some didn't generate enough revenue to even cover the cost of the ad itself. Funny, informative, brash, hopeful, enjoyable, and even an occasional, "What were they thinking!?!"

I marvel at the *Buy Me, Boston* books' original source materials; brittle, disposable paper products, flaking off on the edges, but still miraculously intact... 40- and 50-year old editions that were only supposed to have a 7-day or maybe 1-month shelf life. Brian has given the ads within his books a future, a place in history, an unexpected timelessness. He resurrects life as we knew it. Where we came from. What we embraced. How we acted, inappropriately as it might have been. How we got to today.

These books are a mirror, as well as a window to a world that once existed. That world changed very gradually, almost invisibly, vanishing like a vague dream on a warm summer morning. But, now examined between the covers, we can see the cultural shifts in our ways of life.

In my Archives, I have 1960s issues of *Boston After Dark* that are four pages *in total,* sustained by display ads bought by Sack Theatres, Columbia Records and the Paul's Mall/Jazz Workshop music clubs. I also have late-1990s copies of *BAD's* successor publication, the *Boston Phoenix,* that are 440-page behemoths. Lots and lotsa trees died for those newspapers. Ah, the pain of paper cuts while turning the hundreds of pages!

Looking at those old and defunct alt-weeklies now is sort of sad. The last 15 years have seen a steady decline of circulation and advertising for hold-in-your-hands print matter. And that means there are fewer and fewer great, stimulating and curious ads to marinate in the media stew. I'm horrified to open a newspaper or magazine today and calculate the ratio of advertising to editorial content page count. I'll pick up the *Boston Herald* or the *New York Post* with a clever and collectible front page and discover, to my dismay, that in a 40-page edition, there's one page of ads, and that's a tile listing of local area funeral homes, capitalizing on our year of living dangerously with the COVID-19 virus.

I will sum it all up with this: The Rolling Stones once sang the musical question, "Who wants yesterday's papers?" Brian Coleman has answered that question... old ads are new news – elevated, celebrated and venerated.

Keep collecting, keep the landfills empty, keep on the sunny side, and shine on.

See you in Volume 3!

David Bieber
Curator/Archivist
The David Bieber Archives
www.DavidBieberArchives.com

SOURCE ABBREVIATIONS

[BBR]	Blue Bag Records/Chris Guttmacher
[BCA]	Brian Coleman Archives
[CHC]	Cambridge Historical Commission
[CWA]	Chuck White Archives at the David Bieber Archives
[DBA]	David Bieber Archives
[ELA]	Erik Lindgren Archives
[FLYNN]	Mark Flynn/Punkt Data Archives
[GERSHON]	Russ Gershon Archives
[KBA]	Kay Bourne Archives
[LOCO]	Willie "Loco" Alexander Archives
[MHHA]	Massachusetts Hip-Hop Archive
[REEBEE]	Reebee Garofalo Archives
[RIVARD]	Mike Rivard Archives
[THP]	The History Project
[VACCA]	Richard "Dick" Vacca Archives
[VALDEZ]	Wayne Valdez Archives

ROCK
SOUNDS!
aaa recording studios
835 DORCHESTER AVE.
BOSTON, MASS.
CALL
288-2770
thirteen

***New England Teen Scene* magazine** (artist: Ronn Campisi), October 1967 [ELA]

people's
'72
edition
yellow
pages
A Directory of Alternatives:
Free schools
Childcare
Health-Hot lines
Auto repair
Legal aid
Liberation
Political action
Cooperatives
and much more!
also poems,
quotes & illustrations
75ct at many stores
$1.00 by mail from:
Vocations for Social Change
351 Broadway, Cambridge, Ma. 02139
Call 661-1571

Promotional poster, 1972 [Courtesy of Devon Davidson]

GARDEN PARTNERS
BOB the CHEF'S
Home of the Soul Food
604 Columbus Ave.
Boston, Mass. 02118
Open Tues. Thru Sat. 11:00 A.M. to 9:00 P.M.
January
1977
SUN MON TUE WED THU FRI SAT

Calendar, 1977 [DBA]

HEAR!
Dr. MARTIN LUTHER KING
AT
First Baptist Church
Central Square, Cambridge, Massachusetts
Sunday, January 10, 1960 -- 7:30 P. M.
DR. KING
Special music by the Boston University Seminary Singers
Sponsored by the Cambridge Council of Churches

Event poster, January 1960 [CHC]

TOMORROW NIGHT at 8:30 P.M.
AN EVENING WITH
HARRY BELAFONTE
PLUS GUEST ARTIST
SIDNEY POITIER
REMARKS BY
DR. MARTIN LUTHER KING JR.
FOR BENEFIT OF SOUTHERN
CHRISTIAN LEADERSHIP FOUNDATION
BOSTON GARDEN
$7.50, $6.50, $5.50, $4.50
TICKETS AT BOSTON GARDEN BOX OFFICE, Remicks in Quincy, McCarthy in Brockton, Fred Cole in Salem plus other Garden Ticket Outlets.

Boston Globe, October 26, 1967 [BCA]

Equal Rights For Your Ears.

WEEI·FM
STEREO 103

One Hundred and Three Minutes of Uninterrupted Music at Least Once a Day.

Boston Magazine, September 1975 [DBA]

15
The Real Paper/Making the Best of It/Sept. 18 1974
Landlubber clothes are Lodge-ical.
the original and authentic
Landlubber
109 Newbury Street
Boston
662 Belmont Street
Brockton
Bishop's Corner Shopping Center
West Hartford, Conn.
445 Essex Street
Lawrence
THE LODGE
Paramus Park
Paramus, New Jersey
20 Brattle Street
Harvard Square, Cambridge
Northshore Shopping Center
Peabody
Eastfield Mall
Springfield
Russell St., Route 9
Hadley

Real Paper, September 18, 1974 [BCA]

SKIPPY WHITE'S MASS. RECORDS

1820 WASHINGTON ST., BOSTON, MASS. - HI-2-3830

This Old Heart of Mine

SCOOP!

"LITTLE RICHARD" LP
recorded "LIVE" at the
DOMINO CLUB, ATLANTA, GA.

this great LP includes:

1 TUTTI FRUTTI
2 KEEP A KNOCKIN'
3 SATURDAY NIGHT
4 JENNY JENNY
5 BAMA LAMA BAMA LOU
6 LONG TALL SALLY
7 REDDY TEDDY
8 SLIPPIN' AND SLIDDIN'
9 TRUE FINE MAMA
10 BONY MARONIE
11 LUCILLE
12 BRING IT BACK HOME TO ME
13 DO YOU FEEL IT
14 WHOLE LOTTA SHAKIN'

SKIPPY'S "PICK" LP
of the month
MODERN RECORDS

LITTLE RICHARD'S BEST SELLING 45'S

SPECIALTY
561 tutti frutti/I'm just a lonely gay
572 long tall sally/slippin' and sliddin'
579 rip it up/ready teddy
584 she's got it/ heeby-jeebies
591 all around the world/the girl can't help it
598 lucille/send me some lovin'
606 jenny jenny/miss ann
611 keep a knockin'/can't believe you wanna
624 good golly miss molly/hey hey hey
664 kansas city/ lonesome and blue
680 maybe i'm right/whole lotta shakin'
692 bama lama bama lou/annie is back
VEE-JAY
612 whole lotta shakin' goin on/goodnite irene
625 blueberry hill/ cherry red
665 without love/dance what you wanna
652 It ain't whatcha do/cross over
698 I don't know what you've got 1 & 2
OLDIES "45"
194 groovy little suzy/baby face
MYSTIC VALLEY
551 I'm in love again/everynite about this time
MODERN
1018 holy mackeral/baby,don't you want a man
1019 do you feel it, pts. 1 & 2
1022 I'm back/directly from my heart to lyou
OKEH
7251 Poor dog/well

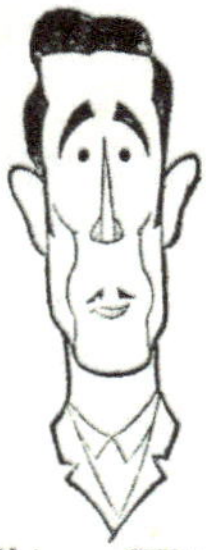

Skippy White

Don't forget . . .

LISTEN TO

SKIPPY WHITE

ON **W-I-L-D** RADIO

Every SUNDAY 4 p.m. to 8:15 p.m.

The ORIGINAL Golden Groove Show

SORRY.....MR. CLEAN
IS ON VACATION.
"Read the soul scene with
MR. CLEAN" will appear in
our next issue.

***Hit Bulletin* newsletter** (Page 4), August 1, 1966 [BCA]

SAT.
MAY 3RD
OPENING AT 8:00
PUNKT DATA GAL.
256 HANOVER
St. 2nd FLOOR OF
SACCO + VANZETTI
BUILDING IN
BOSTONS
NORTH
END
TRIXPAN
NEW EXPOSURES
BY
Philin Phlash

Boston Rock **magazine,** June 1980 [DBA]

66
WVJV-TV
The Beat of Boston

The Beat, June 1986 [BCA]

Mind
over
matter
(give ideas as gifts)
paperback booksmith
Harvard Square (open 24 hours)
751 Boylston (opp. Lord & Taylor)
Dedham Mall
Natick Mall
Coolidge Corner*
Hanover Mall*
*records too

Boston Phoenix, December 1, 1971 [BCA]

TV38
gives you
free checking.
TV38. All fun and games.
The Bruins/Red Sox Station.
ught to you in part by Budweiser Delta N F Dodge Dealers Association, MacDonald's, Eastern Airlines, N.E. Toyota Dealers and Texaco.

Boston Bruins Yearbook, 1974–1975 [BCA]

DMZ
D
M
Z
+ THE RAMONES
APRIL FRI. 15 - SAT 16
Frolics Ballroom
Salisbury Beach
Phone - 465 - 8400
ONE NITE ONLY
The RAT
APRIL 17th

Poster, April 1977 [LOCO]

CALDOR
In Person
TOMMY HEINSOHN
meet him in our
Framingham
Store on Tuesday,
April 6, 1976 from
12 noon to 1:30 p.m.
HEINSOHN
DON'T YOU EVER
SMILE?
THE LIFE AND TIMES OF TOMMY HEINSOHN AND THE BOSTON CELTICS
TOMMY HEINSOHN WITH LEONARD LEWIN
He will autograph purchased copies of "Heinsohn, don't you ever smile"
4 66
Publisher's List 7.95
Tommy Heinsohn and Leonard Lewin's exciting account of Heinsohn's years as Celtic player, and 6 years as their championship coach.
BANKAMERICARD
Charge it 3 ways!
CALDOR CHARGE CARD
master charge
FRAMINGHAM
Route 9
Framingham
SALE: Mon.-Sat.
Mon. thru Fri. 10 a.m. to 9:30 p.m.
Sat. 9 a.m. to 9:30 p.m.

Boston Globe, April 4, 1976 [BCA]

A&P
SEE YOU at the A&P
where young mothers save CASH and
save PLAID STAMPS for wonderful gifts!

Boston College football program, October 27, 1962 [BCA]

Filene's
Date
S. P. NO.
AMT. REC'D.
Price
6995
Dept.
Size
DEPT.
950
Q4
SIZE
16
SKU
1030 3501
BARNEY S
OUR PRICE
$29.99
FILENE'S BASEMENT
3500
952 E2
Dept. 872
IMPORT
12500
Dept. 858
2500
Filene's
BASEMENT
FILENE'S BASEMENT AUTOMATIC MARKDOWN PLAN IS CALCULATED BY USING THE DAYS ON WHICH THIS SELLING LOCATION IS OPEN FOR BUSINESS TO THE GENERAL PUBLIC.
FILENE'S

Various pricetags, 1970s – 1990s [BCA]

Steve's
Steve's
Steve's
Steve's
Steve's

Patches, 1980s [BCA]

Captain Freedom said he'd make me a star.

Maybe you're ready for stardom.
Maybe you're not.
Wherever you want to be, Captain Freedom can put you there.
Anywhere.
From a subtle trim, to stardom.

Captain Freedom Haircuts Ltd.
39 Newbury Street, Boston. Telephone 266-4410.
Hours are 12:00-9:00pm., Monday through Saturday.
Westport, Connecticut.
White Plains, New York.

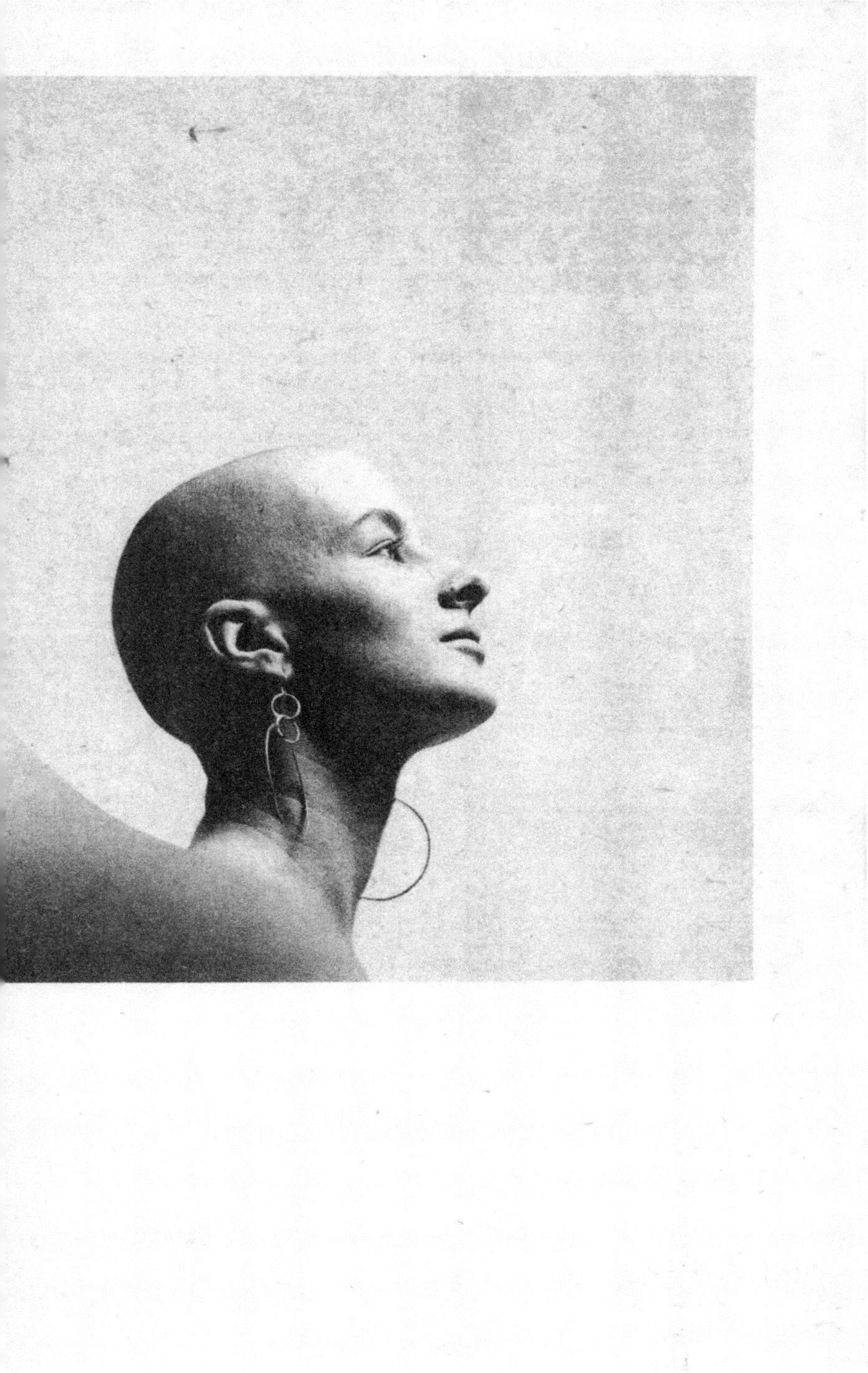

Boston Phoenix, January 19, 1972 [DBA]

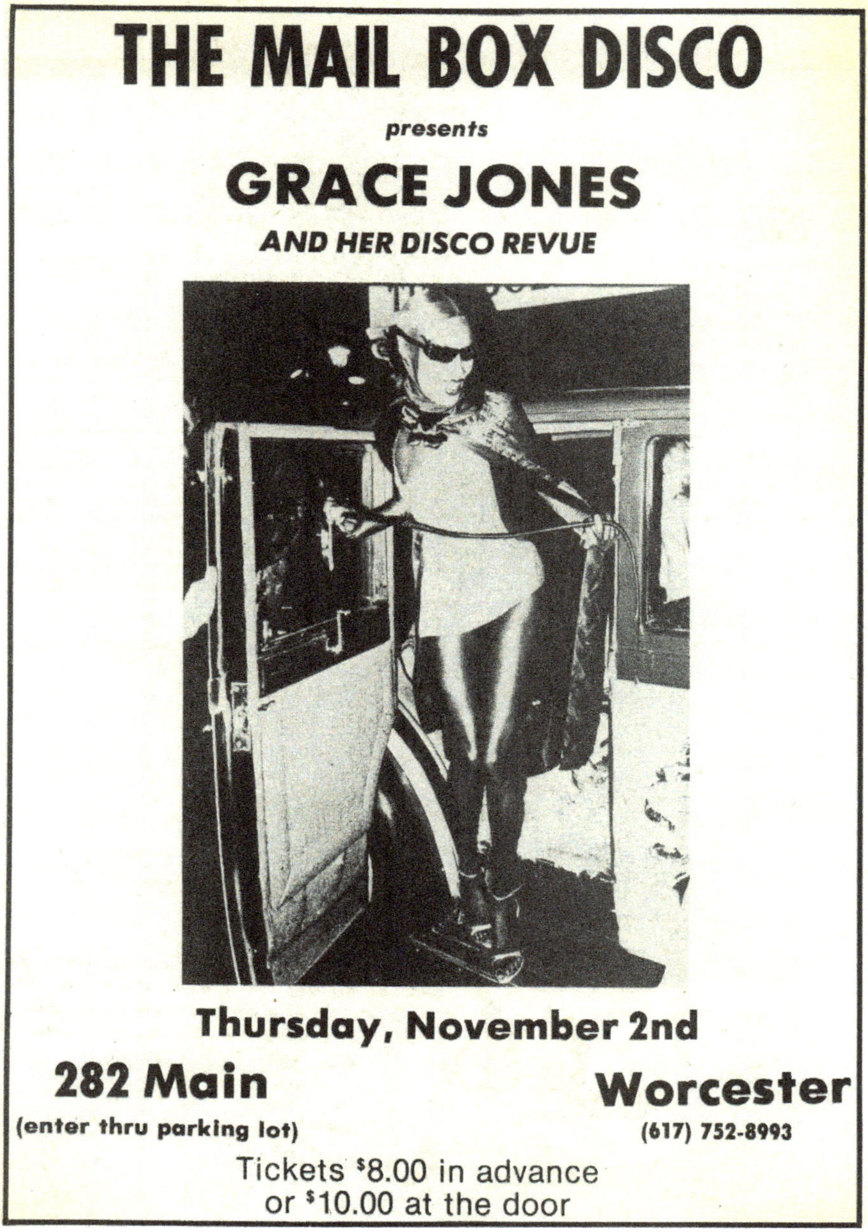
THE MAIL BOX DISCO
presents
GRACE JONES
AND HER DISCO REVUE
Thursday, November 2nd
282 Main
(enter thru parking lot)
Worcester
(617) 752-8993
Tickets $8.00 in advance
or $10.00 at the door

Hit Parade of Boston, November 1978 [DBA]

DRUMS!
E.U.
WURLITZER, INC.
76 BEDFORD ST.
BOSTON, MASS.
426-3897
NEED WE SAY MORE?!!!

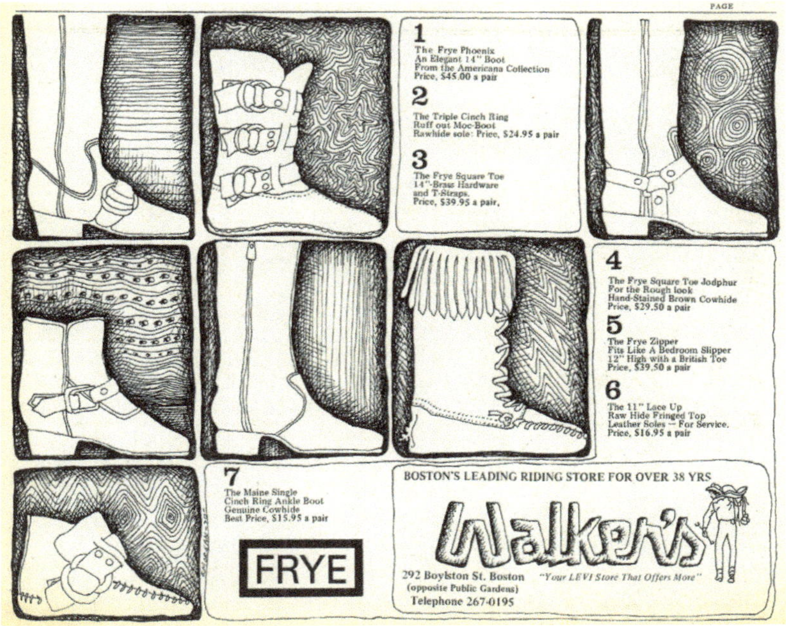
PAGE
1
The Frye Phoenix
An Elegant 14" Boot
From the Americana Collection
Price, $45.00 a pair
2
The Triple Cinch Ring
Ruff out Moc-Boot
Rawhide sole: Price, $24.95 a pair
3
The Frye Square Toe
14"-Brass Hardware
and T-Straps.
Price, $39.95 a pair,
4
The Frye Square Toe Jodphur
For the Rough look
Hand-Stained Brown Cowhide
Price, $29.50 a pair
5
The Frye Zipper
Fits Like A Bedroom Slipper
12" High with a British Toe
Price, $39.50 a pair
6
The 11" Lace Up
Raw Hide Fringed Top
Leather Soles -- For Service.
Price, $16.95 a pair
7
The Maine Single
Cinch Ring Ankle Boot
Genuine Cowhide
Best Price, $15.95 a pair
FRYE
BOSTON'S LEADING RIDING STORE FOR OVER 38 YRS
Walker's
292 Boylston St. Boston
(opposite Public Gardens)
Telephone 267-0195
"Your LEVI Store That Offers More"

TOP: ***Broadside* magazine,** May 24, 1967 [BCA]

BOTTOM: ***Free Paper (Cambridge Phoenix),*** October 14, 1970 [DBA]

THE END OF THE HEALTHY BODY
lose 16 pounds after only 2 visits!
BEFORE 165 LBS
2 WEEKS LATER
check the box for the body you want
Jello Biceps
Darby Crash Chest
Keith Morris Thighs
Dez Neck
only at Newbury Comics

PAC-MAN*
ATARI
PAC-MAN FEVER
BUCKNER & GARCIA
including:
Pac-Man Fever/Froggy's Lament/Hyperspace
Ode To A Centipede/Do The Donkey Kong
RC 37941 Score! With the one and only album of songs inspired by the video game craze. Includes winning Pac-Man patterns on the sleeve!
PAC-MAN FEVER
BUY ATARI'S HOTTEST GAME AND GET A PAC-MAN FEVER ALBUM FREE!
10% OFF OUR ALREADY LOW DISCOUNT PRICES ON ALL OTHER ATARI CARTRIDGES
MOVIES TO GO
VIDEO/COMPUTER CENTER
281 Needham St. Newton, Ma.
(617) 969-1790
FREE PAC-MAN FEVER ALBUM TO THE FIRST 50 CUSTOMERS WHO PURCHASE ATARI PAC-MAN!
(Albums Courtesy of CBS Records)

TOP: ***Boston Rock,*** October 1981 [DBA]
BOTTOM: ***Boston Phoenix,*** May 11, 1982 [DBA]

STRAWBOSS and CHANNEL CONCERTS
in association with MODERN PRODUCTIONS present
KING SUNNY ADÉ
AND THE AFRICAN BEATS
AND SPECIAL GUEST STARS
BLACK UHURU
featuring
SLY DUNBAR
ROBBIE SHAKESPEARE
SUNDAY 7:30 pm
SEPTEMBER 9
GENERAL ADMISSION TICKETS
$15.00 ADVANCE
$16.50 DAY OF SHOW
900 BOYLSTON ST. BOSTON
HYNES AUDITORIUM
Tickets available at all STRAWBERRIES locations, TICKETRON, TELETRON
NEWBURY COMICS, OUT OF TOWN, THE CHANNEL BOX OFFICE or by mail
through MODERN PRODUCTIONS, 19 Perry St. Cambridge, MA. 02139
For further information or group rates, call 451-1050

Boston Phoenix, August 14, 1984 [DBA]

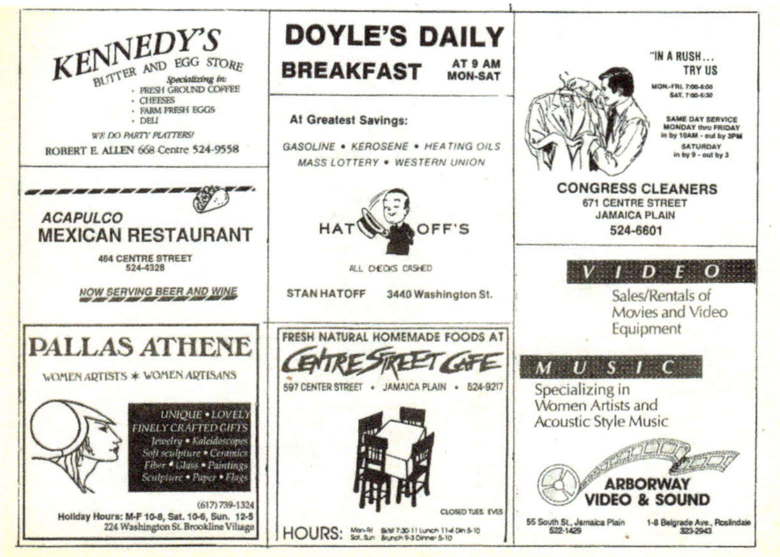
KENNEDY'S
BUTTER AND EGG STORE
Specializing in:
· FRESH GROUND COFFEE
· CHEESES
· FARM FRESH EGGS
· DELI
WE DO PARTY PLATTERS!
ROBERT E. ALLEN 668 Centre 524-9558
DOYLE'S DAILY
BREAKFAST AT 9 AM MON-SAT
At Greatest Savings:
GASOLINE • KEROSENE • HEATING OILS
MASS LOTTERY • WESTERN UNION
HAT OFF'S
ALL CHECKS CASHED
STAN HATOFF 3440 Washington St.
"IN A RUSH... TRY US
MON.-FRI. 7:00-6:00
SAT. 7:00-5:30
SAME DAY SERVICE
MONDAY thru FRIDAY
in by 10AM - out by 3PM
SATURDAY
in by 9 - out by 3
CONGRESS CLEANERS
671 CENTRE STREET
JAMAICA PLAIN
524-6601
ACAPULCO
MEXICAN RESTAURANT
464 CENTRE STREET
524-4328
NOW SERVING BEER AND WINE
PALLAS ATHENE
WOMEN ARTISTS ✱ WOMEN ARTISANS
UNIQUE • LOVELY
FINELY CRAFTED GIFTS
Jewelry • Kaleidoscopes
Soft sculpture • Ceramics
Fiber • Glass • Paintings
Sculpture • Paper • Flags
(617) 739-1324
Holiday Hours: M-F 10-8, Sat. 10-6, Sun. 12-5
224 Washington St. Brookline Village
FRESH NATURAL HOMEMADE FOODS AT
CENTRE STREET CAFE
597 CENTER STREET • JAMAICA PLAIN • 524-9217
CLOSED TUES. EVES
HOURS:
VIDEO
Sales/Rentals of
Movies and Video
Equipment
MUSIC
Specializing in
Women Artists and
Acoustic Style Music
ARBORWAY
VIDEO & SOUND
55 South St., Jamaica Plain
522-1429
1-8 Belgrade Ave., Roslindale
323-2943

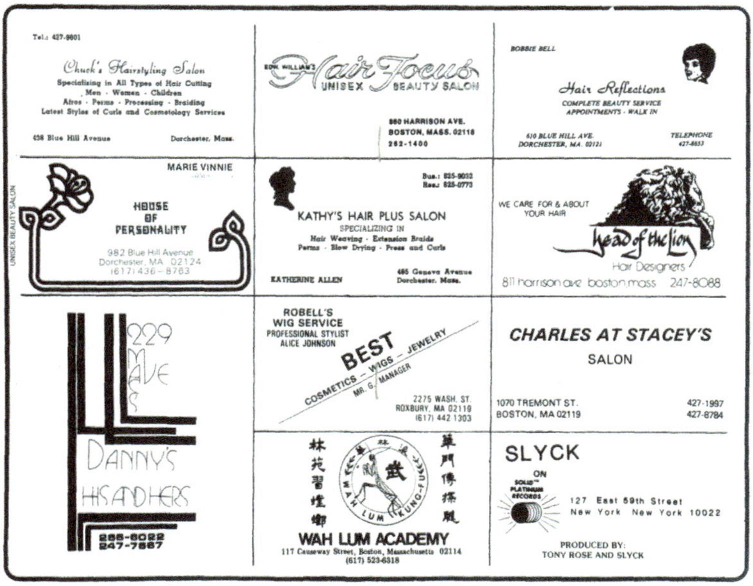
Tel.: 427-9801
Chuck's Hairstyling Salon
Specializing in All Types of Hair Cutting
Men · Women · Children
Afros · Perms · Processing · Braiding
Latest Styles of Curls and Cosmetology Services
438 Blue Hill Avenue Dorchester, Mass.
Hair Focus
UNISEX BEAUTY SALON
880 HARRISON AVE.
BOSTON, MASS. 02118
262-1400
BOBBIE BELL
Hair Reflections
COMPLETE BEAUTY SERVICE
APPOINTMENTS · WALK IN
610 BLUE HILL AVE.
DORCHESTER, MA. 02121
TELEPHONE
MARIE VINNIE
HOUSE
OF
PERSONALITY
982 Blue Hill Avenue
Dorchester, MA 02124
(617) 436-8763
UNISEX BEAUTY SALON
KATHY'S HAIR PLUS SALON
SPECIALIZING IN
Hair Weaving · Extension Braids
Perms · Blow Drying · Press and Curls
KATHERINE ALLEN
485 Geneva Avenue
Dorchester, Mass.
WE CARE FOR & ABOUT
YOUR HAIR
Head of the Lion
Hair Designers
811 harrison ave boston mass 247-8088
229
MAVE
S
DANNY'S
HIS AND HERS
247-7887
ROBELL'S
WIG SERVICE
PROFESSIONAL STYLIST
ALICE JOHNSON
BEST
COSMETICS – WIGS – JEWELRY
MR. G. MANAGER
2275 WASH. ST.
ROXBURY, MA 02119
(617) 442 1303
CHARLES AT STACEY'S
SALON
1070 TREMONT ST.
BOSTON, MA 02119
427-1997
427-8784
WAH LUM KUNG-FU
WAH LUM ACADEMY
117 Causeway Street, Boston, Massachusetts 02114
(617) 523-6318
SLYCK
ON
127 East 59th Street
New York New York 10022
PRODUCED BY:
TONY ROSE AND SLYCK

TOP: ***Jamaica Plain Arts News,*** December 13, 1989 [DBA]

BOTTOM: **Designer's Display Competition event program,** 1982 [KBA]

CHARLES WHITE
3D
RADIO
SATURDAYS – 10:30 – MIDNIGHT
1600 AM
ON YOUR RADIO DIAL

NEW ENGLAND MOBILE BOOK FAIR®
"I only came for one book..."
NEWTON HIGHLANDS, MASSACHUSETTS

TOP: ***Radio show brochure cover,*** 1987 [CWA/DBA]
BOTTOM: ***T-Shirt,*** 1980s or 1990s [DBA]

gozbekian
Leo Gozbekian Photographer 617-899-3627

"Fool around during dinner tonight."
The Medieval Manor™
Theatre-Restaurant
Reservations for knightly nonsense: 262-5144
370 Commonwealth Ave. Boston

TOP: ***Nightfall* magazine,** September 1978 [DBA]
BOTTOM: ***Boston Magazine,*** September 1977 [DBA]

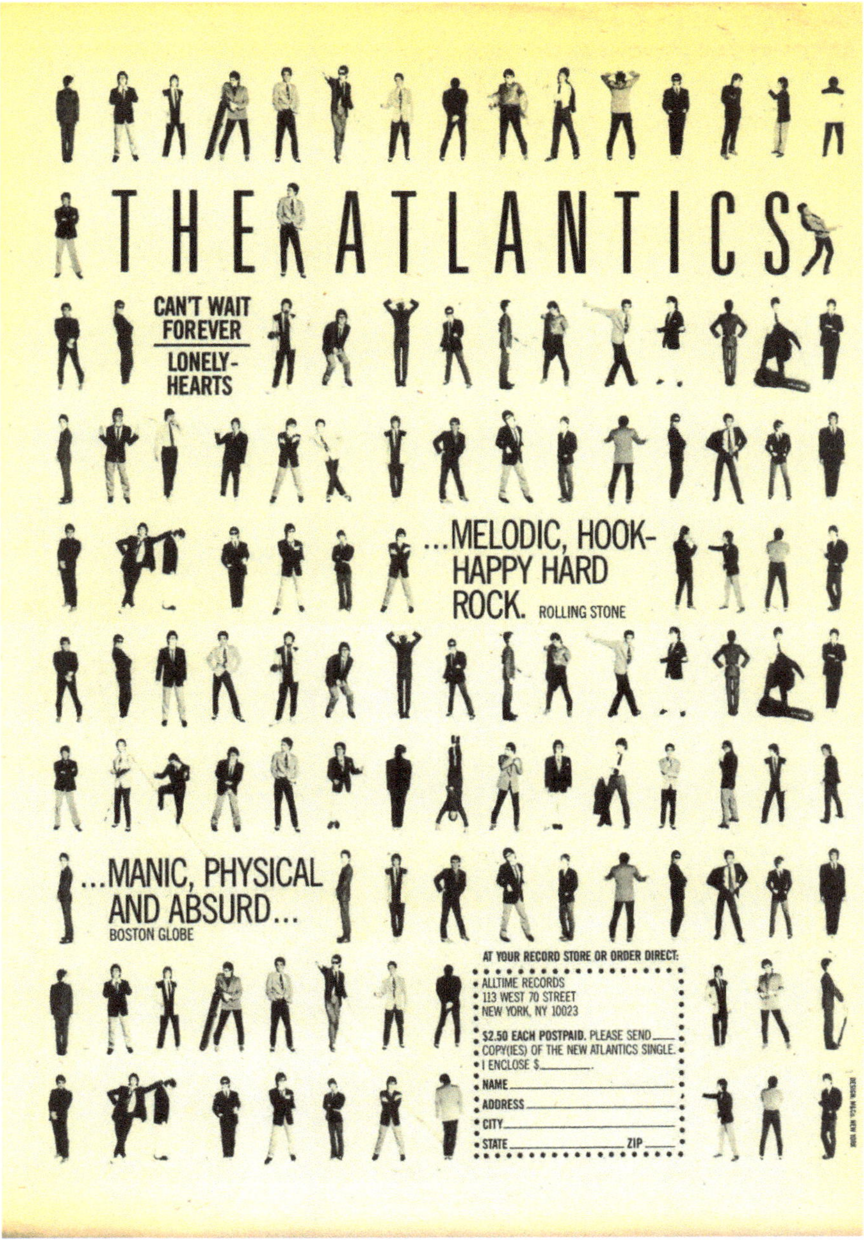
THE ATLANTICS
CAN'T WAIT FOREVER
LONELY-HEARTS
...MELODIC, HOOK-HAPPY HARD ROCK. ROLLING STONE
...MANIC, PHYSICAL AND ABSURD... BOSTON GLOBE
AT YOUR RECORD STORE OR ORDER DIRECT:
ALLTIME RECORDS
113 WEST 70 STREET
NEW YORK, NY 10023
$2.50 EACH POSTPAID. PLEASE SEND ____ COPY(IES) OF THE NEW ATLANTICS SINGLE.
I ENCLOSE $________.
NAME
ADDRESS
CITY
STATE
ZIP

Boston Rock, October 1980 [DBA]

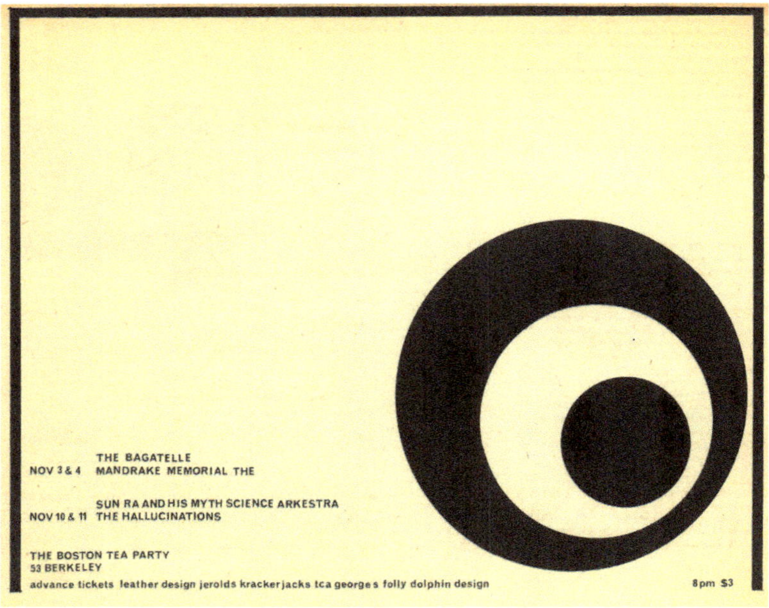
THE BAGATELLE
NOV 3 & 4 MANDRAKE MEMORIAL THE
SUN RA AND HIS MYTH SCIENCE ARKESTRA
NOV 10 & 11 THE HALLUCINATIONS
THE BOSTON TEA PARTY
53 BERKELEY
advance tickets leather design jerolds krackerjacks tca george s folly dolphin design
8pm $3

BRAND X
LOOKS THAT MAKE WAVES
1208 MASS AVE. CAMB
OPEN 11-7 THURS UNTIL 9 864-5919

TOP: ***The Avatar,*** October 27, 1967 [DBA]
BOTTOM: ***Boston Rock,*** June 1980 [DBA]

THE STARK REALITY
4
OCT. 20---5
MY APARTMENT

women
teens
kids
find out what's happening
at the cambridge YWCA
7 temple street
central square
491-6050

TOP: ***Boston After Dark,*** October 22, 1969 [DBA]
BOTTOM: ***Real Paper,*** June 24, 1978 [DBA]

BASIN STREET SOUTH
1844 WASHINGTON ST., BOSTON
MOST COLOSSAL, STUPENDOUS SHOW!
LARRY STEELE'S
FULL REVUE
Starring LOVELACE WATKINS
plus 15 LOVELY SHOWGIRLS
SPECIAL SUN. MAT. 5 P.M.
IN ADDITION MANY GUEST STARS
OPENING DEC. 5 to DEC. 15 REDD FOXX
ALL CHINESE REVUE
REEF
featuring The Stars of "Flower Drum Song" and "World of Suzy Wong"
LARRY LEUNG
COMEDY STAR
FRANCESCA KAE
Singing and Dancing Star
IRENE SUN and MAUREEN TIONGCO
THE RAVENS Featured Every Fri. & Sat. Downstairs
EVERY SUN. TONY BELL'S JAZZ FESTIVAL 3:30 to 7:30
2 DONNELLY SQ., REVERE
RESERVATIONS CALL AT 4-9526
• Reserve for Xmas Parties Now
CANDLELITE Lounge
RES.—CALL SPRING 4-9888
3 DAYS ONLY
Wed.-27th * Fri.-29th * Sat.-30th
EMILY FOSTER
COMEDIENNE
FRANK SMALL
COMEDIAN & SINGER
DIANA
ORIENTAL DANCING STYLIST
RATINO CATINO TRIO for DANCING NITELY

The Devil in Miss Jones
FIRST TIME in ONE THEATRE
3 FANTASTIC HITS
DEEP THROAT
GREEN DOOR
and THE DEVIL IN MISS JONES
Continuous Mon. thru Thur. 5:30-12 midnite
Continuous Friday 5:30-2 A.M.
Continuous Sat. & Sun. 2:30 to midnite
(Proof of age 18 required)
STONEHAM THEATRE
Main St. Stoneham Centre
438-9825

TOP: ***Boston Record American,*** November 25, 1963 [BCA]
BOTTOM: ***Sudbury Fence Viewer,*** June 20, 1974 [BCA]

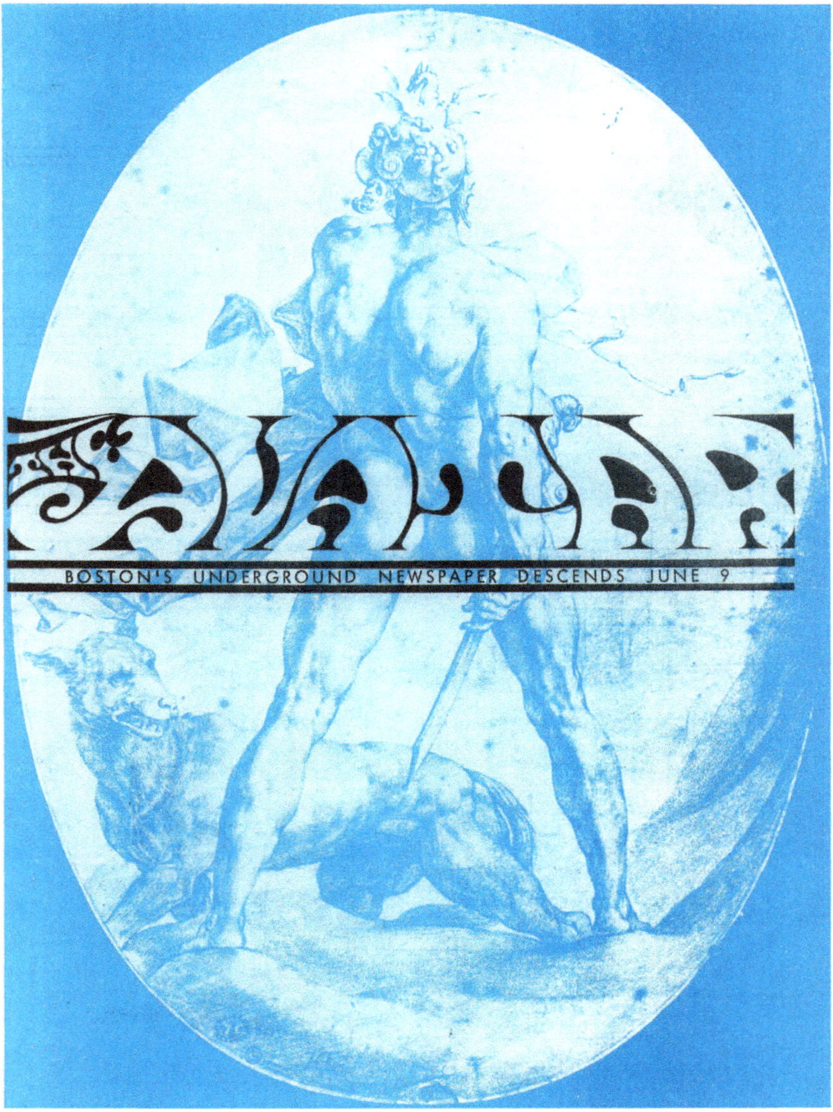
BOSTON'S UNDERGROUND NEWSPAPER DESCENDS JUNE 9

Broadside, May 24, 1967 [BCA]

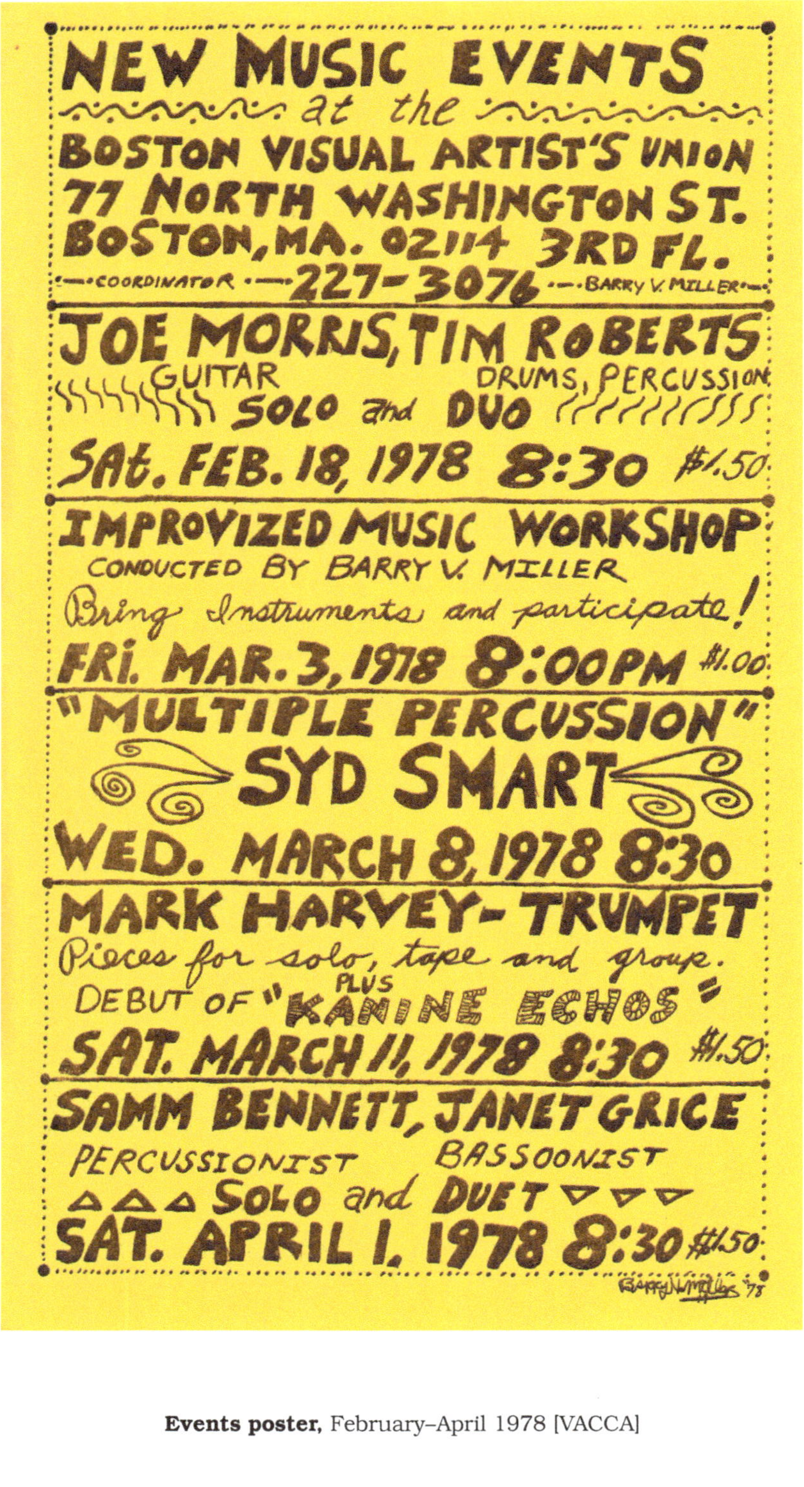
NEW MUSIC EVENTS
at the
BOSTON VISUAL ARTIST'S UNION
77 NORTH WASHINGTON ST.
BOSTON, MA. 02114 3RD FL.
COORDINATOR 227-3076 BARRY V. MILLER
JOE MORRIS, TIM ROBERTS
GUITAR DRUMS, PERCUSSION
SOLO and DUO
SAt. FEB. 18, 1978 8:30 $1.50
IMPROVIZED MUSIC WORKSHOP
CONDUCTED BY BARRY V. MILLER
Bring Instruments and participate!
FRI. MAR. 3, 1978 8:00PM $1.00
"MULTIPLE PERCUSSION"
SYD SMART
WED. MARCH 8, 1978 8:30
MARK HARVEY - TRUMPET
Pieces for solo, tape and group.
PLUS
DEBUT OF "KANINE ECHOS"
SAT. MARCH 11, 1978 8:30 $1.50
SAMM BENNETT, JANET GRICE
PERCUSSIONIST BASSOONIST
SOLO and DUET
SAT. APRIL 1, 1978 8:30 $1.50

Events poster, February–April 1978 [VACCA]

BOBBI BAKER
20 HOLYOKE ST., Harvard Sq., Cambridge
OPEN THURS 'til 9 PM 864-0015
LOOK YOUR BEST BABY...
It's Spring!

LUCIFER PRESENTS
MONDAY THRU NOV. 21
QUEEN OF THE DISCOS
GLORIA GAYNOR
KENMORE SQUARE, BOSTON
NEVER CAN SAY GOODBYE
REACH OUT
HONEY BEE
536-1950

TOP: ***Boston After Dark,*** March 25, 1970 [DBA]
BOTTOM: ***Boston Phoenix,*** November 16, 1976 [BCA]

MELLEN & WHITE
ASSOCIATES
SUITE 2207
131 GREEN STREET
JAMAICA PLAIN
MASSACHUSETTS, USA 02130
1-617-522-2515
DOUGLASS MELLEN
MELLEN AND WHITE ASSOC.
186 HARVARD AVE
ALLSTON, MA USA
02134
(617) 254-9820
(617) 254-9804
DOUGLASS MELLEN
CHARLES W. WHITE III
CARMELITA
MARTIN DOYLE
Shaolin Kenpo Karate
Urban Studio
of Self Defense
131 Green St., Jamaica Plain, MA
Women • Men • Children
Doug Mellen
524-6651
PARTY AT THE REZ
BEER • MUSIC • AMUSEMENTS • POOL TABLES
ALL NIGHT LONG
DONATIONS TO BENEFIT THE HOMELESS
CHUCK WHITE
MARTIN DOYLE
Tel: 1-617-354-5434
Fax: 1-617-547-6960
For Information On
1-800-CLUB-911
1-617-224-CLUB
Call 617-868-8287
Chuck White
Martin Doyle
Tel. (617)354-5434
Fax (617)547-3930
C-LINE #61217
BUSINESS CARD
PUBLISHED BY BOSTON ROCK INC.
1318 Beacon Street
Suite 7
Brookline, MA 02146
(617) 734-7043
U.S. ROCK
BOSTON ROCK
Martin Doyle
Advertising Sales
LEFT NUT
Martin Doyle Productions
Personal Managment
Booking Agent
(617) 782- 6469
Don't you know who I am?
My name is
and someday, I am going to be famous. Therefore, don't even think about charging me to get in here. Thank you. (Subject to change without notice. Not valid for all ages shows. Good for one admission each night)
VIP FREE ADMISSION GREEN ST. STATION
Number Expires Authorized by
DERTÖNZ
(617)
522-8558

Chuck White Business Card Collection, 1980s–1990s [CWA/DBA]

FRISCO EAST
289 WASHINGTON STREET
BRIGHTON, MASS.
– presents –
BLUES
BERRY
JAM
MON., NOV. 23rd thru
SUN., NOV. 29th

Concert flyer, November 1970 [LOCO]

IT'S SPRINGTIME!
...The Decoders
at The Club...
823 Main St., Camb
near Central Sq + MIT
...THUR, APR 22. 10PM
with "Decorum" + "Synapse."
• Also appearing at the Mudd Club, N.Y. City, Fri + Sat, Apr 23 + 24 •

Concert flyer (artwork by Eric Pfeiffer), April 1981 [GERSHON]

ORSON WELLES CINEMA
1001 Mass. Avenue, Cambridge (between Harvard & Central Sq.), 868-3600.
HELD OVER
DON'T MISS IT!
JIMMY CLIFF in
THE HARDER THEY COME
"THE HARDER THEY COME" Soundtrack
is available on MANGO RECORDS (SMAS 7400)
Distributed by Shelter Records through
Capitol Records
MANGO

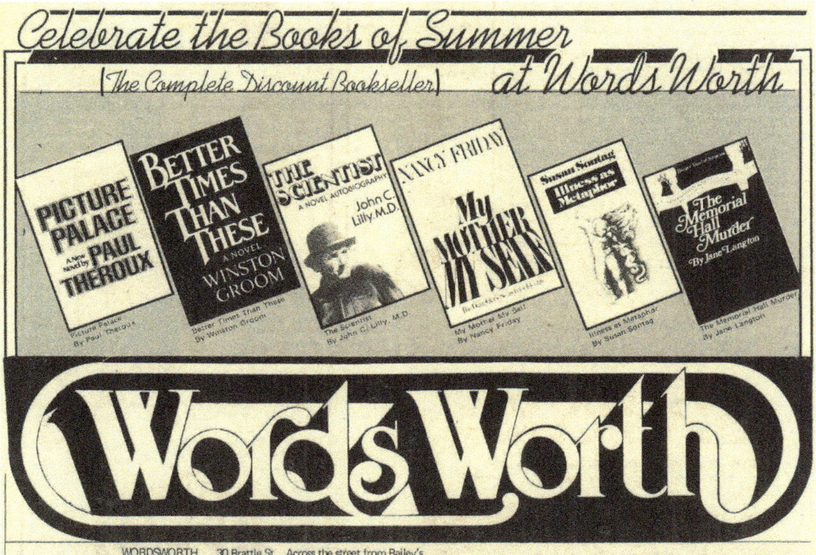
Celebrate the Books of Summer
(The Complete Discount Bookseller) at Words Worth
PICTURE PALACE
A New novel by PAUL THEROUX
BETTER TIMES THAN THESE
A NOVEL
WINSTON GROOM
THE SCIENTIST
A NOVEL AUTOBIOGRAPHY
John C. Lilly, M.D.
NANCY FRIDAY
My Mother My Self
Susan Sontag
Illness as Metaphor
The Memorial Hall Murder
By Jane Langton
Picture Palace
By Paul Theroux
Better Times Than These
By Winston Groom
The Scientist
By John C. Lilly, M.D.
My Mother My Self
By Nancy Friday
Illness as Metaphor
By Susan Sontag
The Memorial Hall Murder
By Jane Langton
Words Worth
WORDSWORTH 30 Brattle St. Across the street from Bailey's

TOP: ***Real Paper,*** May 16, 1973 [DBA]
BOTTOM: ***Real Paper,*** June 24, 1978 [DBA]

THE KIDS ARE WILD ABOUT IT!
"KIQUOTE, KRISPY AND KOKIE'S MOBILE MAGIC, MUSIC SHOW"
A FANTASTIC WAY TO PROMOTE SALES AND STORE OPENINGS
AVAILABLE FOR HOSPITALS AND PRIVATE PARTIES.
PHONE 261-1888 OR WRITE MINOT, 94 FOSTER ST. CAMB. 02138
AN OFF-BEAT PROMOTION CLIENT

WANTED:
IMAGINATIVE
CHILDREN
for fun and fantasy, with swimming. Open House June 20, 12 - 5, register or just visit.
499 Dutton Road Sudbury,
443-6520 or 443-6049

OPEN DAILY 1 PM
Shaheen's
FUN-O-RAMA PARK
of Salisbury Beach
KIDDIES DAY
Every Wed. 1-8
big discounts
DATE NITE
Every Thur.
7 pm - Closing
He Pays-She Rides Free!
FREE ADMISSION
Over 40 Kinds
of Family Fun!
Games ★ Thrill Rides
Exotic Foods ★ Snacks

LEFT: ***Boston Phoenix,*** January 12, 1972 [BCA]
UPPER RIGHT: ***Sudbury Fence Viewer,*** June 20, 1974 [BCA]
BOTTOM RIGHT: ***Sudbury Fence Viewer,*** June 20, 1974 [BCA]

Bob Lee's
Islander
ENJOY THE WORLD'S FINEST FOOD PREPARED BY "TRUE ISLAND CHEFS".
Where Dining Is Relaxing...
FOR LUNCHEONS AND DINNERS
OPEN FROM 11 A.M. to 3 A.M.
No Cover*
No Minimum
At any time
"BOB LEE, MR. POLYNESIA OF THE U.S.A." INVITES EVERYONE TO VISIT HIS
NEW!!
POLYNESIAN AND TAHITIAN HEAVEN
Be thrilled by the true coral and tropical luxury brought to you as only BOB LEE can, directly from the islands.
NOW! The AKU AKU Room . . .
POLYNESIAN MUSICIANS . . .
FREE LESSONS ON THE HAWAIIAN HULA
. . . LEARN IT — TRY IT — YOU'LL LOVE IT!
BE THRILLED BY DINING ON A POLYNESIAN CATAMARAN.
EXCITING EXOTIC DRINKS OF THE ISLANDS
Bob Lee Suggests . . .
"PAGO PAGO" For Excitement
"MAI TAI" For Enchantment
Bob Lee's
20 TYLER STREET, BOSTON
TAKE OUT ORDERS • Liberty 2-3997

Boston Bruins program, 1967–1968 season [BCA]

An Open Letter
From Peter Wolf and the J. Geils Band
Re: The Strike to Save WBCN-FM

THE J.GEILS BAND
T & A Research and Development
405 Park Avenue
New York City, 10022

February 24, 1979

Mr. Michael Wiener
Hemisphere Broadcasting Corporation
5005 Prudential Tower
Boston, Massachusetts 02199

Dear Sir:

As the representative and spokesperson for the J. Geils Band, this letter is to inform you that we support the strike of the WBCN staff members. Furthermore, we insist that any and all WBCN station endorsements made by members of our band be immediately removed from the airwaves until negotiations are completed. It should also be stated that we will not participate in any promotional activities on behalf of the station until that time. Personally, as a former WBCN disc jockey, and now as a listener, it saddens me that such estrangement between management and staff has occurred at a time when I feel the station was sounding better than ever.

With hope for the future,

—Peter Wolf

Peter Wolf

P.S. The only scabs I dig are the ones on my elbow.

Real Paper, March 3, 1979 [DBA]

DON LAW PRESENTS
J.GEILS BAND
THURSDAY DECEMBER 28 ORPHEUM THEATER
TICKETS: ORPHEUM BOX OFFICE, MINUTEMAN, SOUNDSCOPE, OUT OF TOWN, TICKETRON
Because of the great demand the J. Geils Band has agreed to play a second show at 10pm

Real Paper, December 20, 1972 [BCA]

EARTH SONG
BY MARTHA & PAUL BOESING
A NEW PLAY
WITH MUSIC
DIRECTED BY PAUL BOESING
November 14 - Saturday
Charles St. Meeting House
70 Charles St. - Boston
8:30 pm $2.50 suggested donation
AN AMERICAN FRIENDS SERVICE COMMITTEE PRODUCTION
PLEASE POST

Event Flyer, November 1970 [Courtesy of the Lynn Lazar Archives]

I Shop
SPAG'S!

RTE. 9 SHREWSBURY, MA
SPAG'S
MasterCard
VISA
AND OLD FASHIONED CASH
YOU
SAVE
MONEY

Bumper stickers, 1980s–1990s [BCA]

TRICK-JOHN presents APRIL 12 and 13
New York's Street Rock and Roll Band
HARLOTS
42
with Special Guest Star "The Queen of Camp"
MR. SYLVIA SYDNEY
the CRICKET
at The CRICKET 360 Pleasant St., Ashland 881-9847
Tickets - $3.00 - 2 shows nitely 8:30 pm and 10:30 pm
Available at all Ticketron outlets, Soundscope and the Cricket

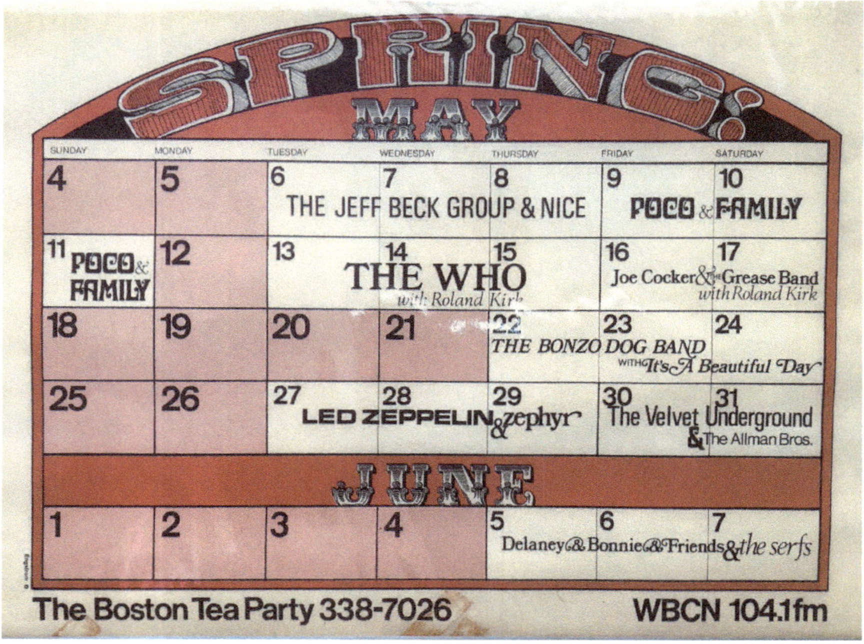
SPRING
MAY
SUNDAY MONDAY TUESDAY WEDNESDAY THURSDAY FRIDAY SATURDAY
4 5 6 7 8 9 10
THE JEFF BECK GROUP & NICE
POCO & FAMILY
11 POCO & FAMILY
12 13 14 15 16 17
THE WHO
with Roland Kirk
Joe Cocker & the Grease Band
with Roland Kirk
18 19 20 21 22 23 24
THE BONZO DOG BAND
WITH It's A Beautiful Day
25 26 27 28 29 30 31
LED ZEPPELIN & zephyr
The Velvet Underground
& The Allman Bros.
JUNE
1 2 3 4 5 6 7
Delaney & Bonnie & Friends & the serfs
The Boston Tea Party 338-7026
WBCN 104.1fm

TOP: ***Free Paper (Real Paper),*** April 10, 1974 [DBA]
BOTTOM: **Calendar flyer,** May – June 1969 [DBA]

ROBIN LANE
& THE
CHARTBUSTERS!

Promotional poster, 1979 [DBA]

LANES & GAMES
Bowling ★ Billiards ★ Videos and more
• TEN PIN & CANDLEPIN
• PUBLIC & LEAGUE BOWLING
• VIDEO GAMES
• RESTAURANT & LOUNGE
• PRIVATE PARTIES
• CORPORATE FUNCTIONS
• BIRTHDAY PARTIES
• 3 BIG SCREEN TV'S
AIR CONDITIONED FOR YOUR COMFORT
OPEN 7 DAYS
PLENTY OF FREE PARKING
Located On Rte 2 On The CAMBRIDGE/ARLINGTON LINE 1/4 Mile West of Alewife T Station
876-5533

The Boston Lobsters...
Serve It Up
Starting May 9th
During the 22 game season see Pilic, Court, Emerson, King, Connors, Newcombe, Casals and more in Men's Singles, Women's Singles and Mixed Doubles Matches.
Choice Seats Are At A Premium
Don't Miss Out
The Boston Lobsters
SEASON TICKETS - CALL 783-2111

TOP: **Yellow Pages ad,** NYNEX 1992–1993 edition [BCA]
BOTTOM: ***Boston Herald American,*** April 9, 1974 [BCA]

CALLING ALL LOVERS, JUNE BRIDES AND COUPLES
AND EVERYONE'S LOOKING . . .
FOR . . .
A DOUBLE COCKTAIL SIP
SUNDAY, JUNE 12, 1988
FROM 4:00 P.M. - 8:00 P.M.
AT
BIFF'S LOUNGE
(IN THE LOWER DECK)
OF THE MASONIC TEMPLE
17 WASHINGTON ST., DORCHESTER, MA.
MUSIC FOR THE HEART
BY . . .
BOBBY TAYLOR
MAKE A NIGHT OF IT WITH YOUR FRIENDS
PLUS LIVE MUSIC AFTER 8:30 P.M.
THAT'S RIGHT . . .
NO GUEST CARD FOR THIS EVENT
DONATION AT THE DOOR $7.00

Event flyer, June 1988 [courtesy of DJ Bobby Taylor]

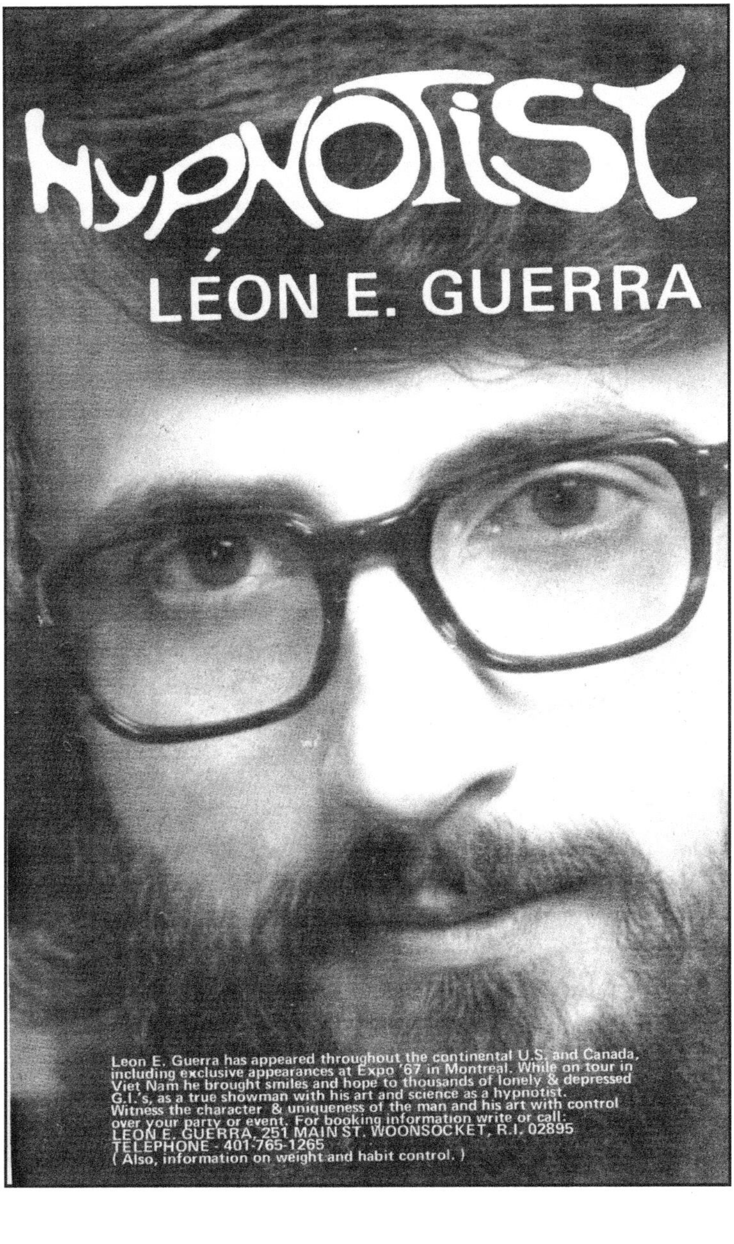
HYPNOTIST
LÉON E. GUERRA
Leon E. Guerra has appeared throughout the continental U.S. and Canada, including exclusive appearances at Expo '67 in Montreal. While on tour in Viet Nam he brought smiles and hope to thousands of lonely & depressed G.I.'s, as a true showman with his art and science as a hypnotist.
Witness the character & uniqueness of the man and his art with control over your party or event. For booking information write or call:
LEON E. GUERRA, 251 MAIN ST. WOONSOCKET, R.I. 02895
TELEPHONE - 401-765-1265
(Also, information on weight and habit control.)

Nightfall, February 1976 [DBA]

ZAP!
Shirts for the Young-at-Heart!!
Mr. Natural, Keep On Trucking
and Fritz the Cat.
Longsleeve S/M/L
Blue, green, yellow, pink, white $5-$6
BeauCoop
at the Coop
Harvard Sq., MIT Student Center, Medical Coop

Boston Phoenix, March 16, 1971 [DBA]

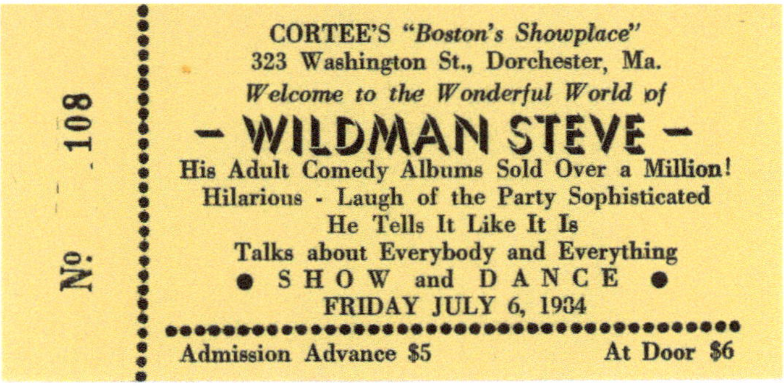
CORTEE'S *"Boston's Showplace"*
323 Washington St., Dorchester, Ma.
Welcome to the Wonderful World of
– WILDMAN STEVE –
His Adult Comedy Albums Sold Over a Million!
Hilarious - Laugh of the Party Sophisticated
He Tells It Like It Is
Talks about Everybody and Everything
• SHOW and DANCE •
FRIDAY JULY 6, 1934
Admission Advance $5 At Door $6
№ 108

VOTE
STEVE·NELSON
CAMBRIDGE
CITY
COUNCIL

TOP: **Concert ticket,** July 1984 [BCA]

BOTTOM: **Campaign poster** (by Stanley Mouse), Fall 1969 [CHC]

Best Wishes
to the
Stanley Cup
Champion
BRUINS
from the "Fussy Folks"
at First National
First
National
Stores
Finast

Boston Record American, April 9, 1971 [BCA]

PEABODY PEABODY
FREE PARKING 8000 CARS
Cinema I
at NORTHSHORE Peabody
TWIN INDOOR THEATRE
JACK LEMMON
SHIRLEY MacLAINE
THIS PICTURE IS FOR ADULTS ONLY
IRMA LA DOUCE
Feature: 1:50-4:30-7:05-9:45 • TECHNICOLOR
AT 1:00-2:45 ONLY! 'SANTA CLAUS' IN COLOR
CINEMA II MAT. EVE.
STARTS TONITE at 7:00-9:25 "ROOM AT THE TOP" WINNER OF 2 ACADEMY AWARDS!
BRAINTREE BRAINTREE
SOUTH SHORE
FREE ELLECTRIC HEATERS SO. SIDE
PLAZA TWIN
BOTH SHOWS START 7 P.M.
"LAWRENCE OF ARABIA" "SUMMER PLACE"
"20,000 LEAGUES UNDER THE SEA" "TO CATCH A THIEF"
CANTON CANTON
$1.50 PER CAR BLUE HILLS DRIVE-IN RTE. 138 828-2122
3—BIG FEATURES—3. Adults Only!
"L-SHAPED ROOM" Leslie Caron-Tom Bell 8:30 P.M.
"IN THE FRENCH STYLE" Jean Seberg-S. Baker
"WEEKEND WITH LULU" 7 P.M. (Sex Comedy)
DANVERS DANVERS
ROUTE 114 Drive-In OFF Rte. 1
THE MIRISCH COMPANY AND EDWARD L. ALPERSON PRESENT
JACK LEMMON SHIRLEY MacLAINE
IN BILLY WILDER'S IRMA LA DOUCE
TECHNICOLOR® PANAVISION®
THIS PICTURE IS FOR ADULTS ONLY
MALDEN MALDEN
STRAND Only—Sun. 'SANTA CLAUS' Full Length Color Feature 1 & 3 p.m.
AMPLE PARKING AT BOTH THEATRES
CONT. 1-11 DAILY
GRANADA DA2-7654 STRAND
CONT. 1-11 SAT.-SUN.-HOL. EVES. 7:45
1:10 - 3:50 - 6:30 - 9:05
JACK LEMMON COLOR IRMA LA DOUCE IS FOR ADULTS ONLY SHIRLEY MacLAINE
LAURENCE HARVEY LEE REMICK NOW RUNNING MAN
JEAN SEBERG STUART BAKER IN THE FRENCH STYLE
MEDFORD MEDFORD
EARLY SHOW TODAY OPEN 5:30 — CONT. FROM 6 P.M.
MYSTIC VALLEY PARKWAY EX 5 3400
MEADOW TWIN GLEN
ELECTRIC HEATERS
BEST 'DAME' SHOW IN TOWN!
1. JAYNE MANSFIELD—"IT TAKES A THIEF"
2. JANE RUSSELL—"LAS VEGAS STORY"
3. DIANA DORS—"THE UNHOLY WIFE"
4. MAMIE VAN DOREN—"UNTAMED YOUTH"
BOLD FEARLESS "PRIVATE PROPERTY"
JULIE LONDON "INFIDELITY" FRANK VITALE
BRAINTREE QUINTREE 'ART' DRIVE-IN HEATERS
JEAN SEBERG "IN THE FRENCH STYLE"
LAURENCE HARVEY "THE RUNNING MAN" LEE REMICK
DORCHESTER WINCHESTER
Phone 436-2100 PA 9-2500
E.M.LOEW'S DORCHESTER 1534 DORCHESTER AVE.
Now at Both Theaters
E.M.LOEW'S WINCHESTER 661 MAIN STREET
POPULAR PRICES
MOST HONORED PICTURE OF THE YEAR! WINNER OF 7 ACADEMY AWARDS!
"LAWRENCE OF ARABIA"
MON. THRU SAT. MAT. 1:45 EVE 8:15 | SUN. at 1:00-4:30-8:10 p. m.
BURLINGTON BURLINGTON
E.M.LOEW'S ROUTE 128 DRIVE IN
PAUL NEWMAN-JOANNE WOODWARD FROM THE TERRACE 8:30
NATALIE WOOD-WARREN BEATTY SPLENDOR IN THE GRASS 7:00
JUNCTION ROUTES 3 and 128—BURLINGTON .... EXIT 41S
Such Goings On
Nature's Playmates
FOR MATURE ADULTS ONLY
and PLEASURE GIRL
STATE
E.M. LOEW'S CENTER Now
YOU SAW HER IN PLAYBOY MAGAZINE NOW SEE ALL OF HER!!
JAYNE MANSFIELD
"PROMISES! PROMISES!"
Plus SECOND FEATURE "STRONGROOM"
The man's absolute sincerity and devotion to his work shines through the con-
a new film
by Jean-Luc Godard "Breathless"
"BRILLIANT"
Time
my life to live
a meditation on the nature of existence
Winner, special jury award, Venice 1962
PARK SQ. CINEMA
opp. Statler, 542-2220
1:30, 2:55, 4:37 6:19 8:01, 9:43
plus "Alexandre Calder's Circus"
E.M. LOEW'S WEST END CINEMA
"A MUST SEE FILM" PEGGY DOYLE, RECORD AMERICAN
The Conjugal Bed
MARINA VLADY 'Best Actress' Cannes Festival
PARKING REAR OF HOTEL MADISON
PILGRIM
ADULTS ONLY!
'WORLD of FLESH'
Plus: "MARILYN" M.M. on the Screen Again
MAYFLOWER
JACK LEMMON • SHIRLEY MacLAINE
Technicolor — Panavision
"IRMA LA DOUCE"

Boston Advertiser, November 24, 1963 [DBA]

MEET ONE OF YOUR CHILDREN'S NEW TEACHERS.
He's Dr. Hugh Morgan Hill, and every day as "Brother Blue," he'll tell stories to your pre-schoolers that will help them learn through "living experiences." Joan Lester is "The Teacher," and Dr. Louise Bates Ames, Co-director of the Gesell Institute for Child Development, explains how pre-schoolers learn. You and your children should watch together every weekday. You'll both learn a lot.
Playmates Schoolmates
WEEKDAYS AT 9AM.
TV4

Boston Phoenix, January 20, 1976 [DBA]

CHOKING MOTORISTS, DON'T YOU THINK THE JOKER LAUGHS AT YOU?

CURB YOUR CAR!

WHY? CARS KILL. CAUSE 3/4 OF BOSTON'S AIR POLLUTION.
DESTROY THOUSANDS OF HOMES FOR NEW HIGHWAYS.
TURN FRIENDLY PEOPLE INTO A MOB OF COMPETING MACHINES.

BUT I NEED MY CAR!

THAT'S WHAT THE ADS TELL YOU; YOU NEED YOUR CAR FOR STATUS, FRIENDS, SEX OR FOR THE GREAT ESCAPE. BUT THIS REALLY MEANS MORE PROFITS FOR GM, PRUDENTIAL, ESSO AND FIRESTONE. MAYBE IT'S THEIR CAR AND THEIR NEED.

BUT I REALLY DO NEED MY CAR TO GET AROUND!

THAT'S BECAUSE THEY'VE MESSED UP OUR COMMUNITIES SO MUCH THERE'S NO OTHER WAY TO TRAVEL. MAZES OF EXPRESSWAYS, TANGLES OF CONCRETE RAMPS AND PARKING GARAGES. YOU CAN'T EVEN WALK ANYMORE. AND PUBLIC TRANSIT IS LOUSY; OVERCROWDED BUSES, JAMMED UGLY SUBWAYS.

HOW COULD IT BE DIFFERENT?

STOP GIVING PROFITS TO THE HIGHWAYMEN. STOP SPRAWLING DEVELOPMENT THAT NECESSITATES CARS AND SPLITS UP OUR LIVES. CREAT MASS TRANSIT, FAST FRIENDLY AND FREE. BUILD CITIES FOR WALKING AND HUMAN CONTACT. PROMOT SHARING AND COOPERATION RATHER THAN THE GREAT ESCAPE.

WHAT CAN I DO NOW?

SHARE YOUR CAR. PICK UP HITCHHIKERS. OPEN UP YOUR BACK SEAT.
FORM CAR POOLS OR CAR COOPERATIVES.
BETTER YET, LEAVE YOUR CAR. HITCH WALK. BICYCLE.
MAKE FRIENDS NOT SMOG!
DON'T BUY NEW CARS.
RECLAIM THE STREETS. MAKE GARDENS FROM PARKING LOTS.
JOIN WITH YOUR NEIGHBORS TO STOP NEW HIGHWAYS AND GARAGES.
GET TOGETHER WITH ALL THE STRANDED SOULS, ALL THE CHOKING COMMUNITIES, AND LET THE JOKER KNOW THAT:

WE AIN'T GONNA WORK ON GM'S FARM NO MORE!

Hitchhiking Day is April 20. It is the beginning of an overall attack on the present automobile and public transportation systems, organized by an ad hoc group called "Free Wheel." The hitchhiking campaign will provide "Free Wheel" stickers for cars whose drivers pick up hitchhikers and buttons with the symbol will be sold. A slide show, short films, leaflets and other media information are also in the works.

Hitchhiking is only one aspect of the campaign against present transportation. A "Free Bus" to take people to various parts of the city and to serve as a traveling communication center is planned; and on "Toll Day" people will get out in the streets to demand fines from drivers who are alone in their cars.

***Old Mole* newspaper,** April 17, 1970 [DBA]

IT'S ONLY ROCK & ROLL
with host WBCN's LARRY "CHACHI" LOPRETE
March 30 Rods & Cones and Good Question
April 6 Mass and special guests
April 13 The Fools and Forever 19
April 20 Tribe and The Lemmings Boy's Camp
18+
WEDNESDAYS AT chameleon
Live television taping for Warner Cable 13 !
830 LYNNWAY • LYNN • 581-5555

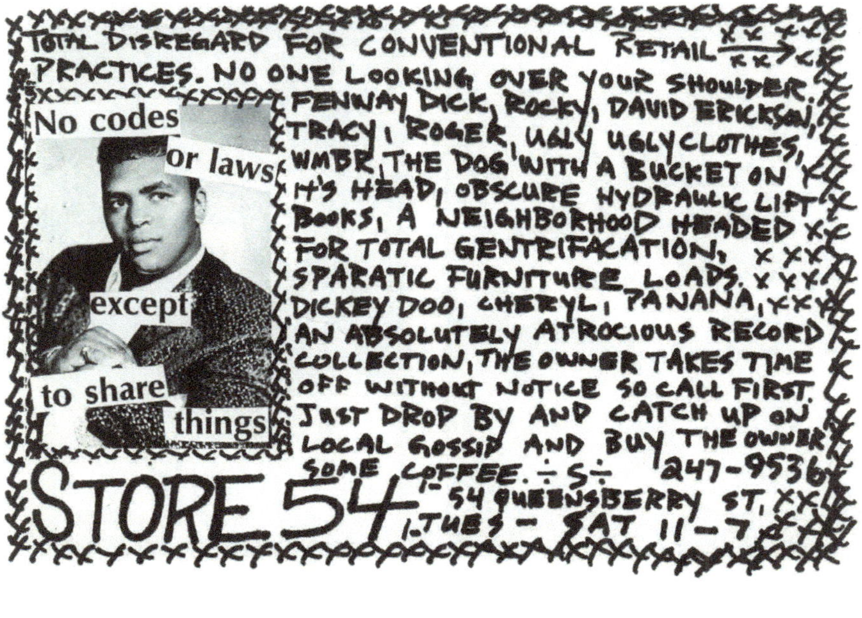
TOTAL DISREGARD FOR CONVENTIONAL RETAIL PRACTICES. NO ONE LOOKING OVER YOUR SHOULDER.
No codes
or laws
except
to share
things
FENWAY DICK, ROCKY, DAVID ERICKSON, TRACY, ROGER, UGLY UGLY CLOTHES, WMBR, THE DOG WITH A BUCKET ON IT'S HEAD, OBSCURE HYDRAULIC LIFT BOOKS, A NEIGHBORHOOD HEADED FOR TOTAL GENTRIFACATION, SPARATIC FURNITURE LOADS, DICKEY DOO, CHERYL, PANANA, AN ABSOLUTELY ATROCIOUS RECORD COLLECTION, THE OWNER TAKES TIME OFF WITHOUT NOTICE SO CALL FIRST. JUST DROP BY AND CATCH UP ON LOCAL GOSSIP AND BUY THE OWNER SOME COFFEE.
247-9536
STORE 54
54 QUEENSBERRY ST.
TUES - SAT 11-7

TOP: ***Boston Rockwire* magazine,** 1988 [DBA]
BOTTOM: ***The Noise,*** August 1985 [DBA]

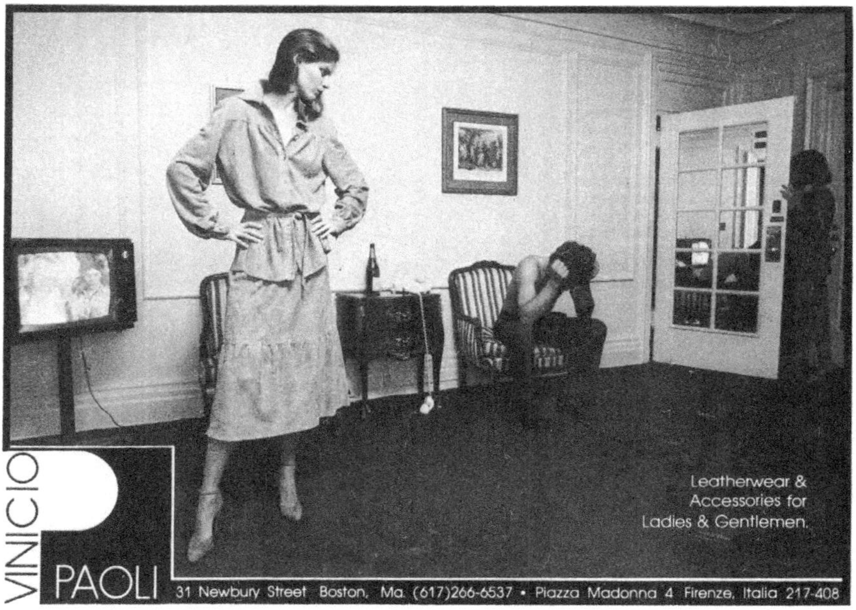
Leatherwear &
Accessories for
Ladies & Gentlemen.
VINICIO
PAOLI
31 Newbury Street Boston, Ma. (617)266-6537 • Piazza Madonna 4 Firenze, Italia 217-408

DANCE
with a different frequency
101.7 FM
WFNX
101.7

TOP: ***Boston Magazine,*** December 1977 [DBA]
BOTTOM: ***The Noise,*** September 1984 [DBA]

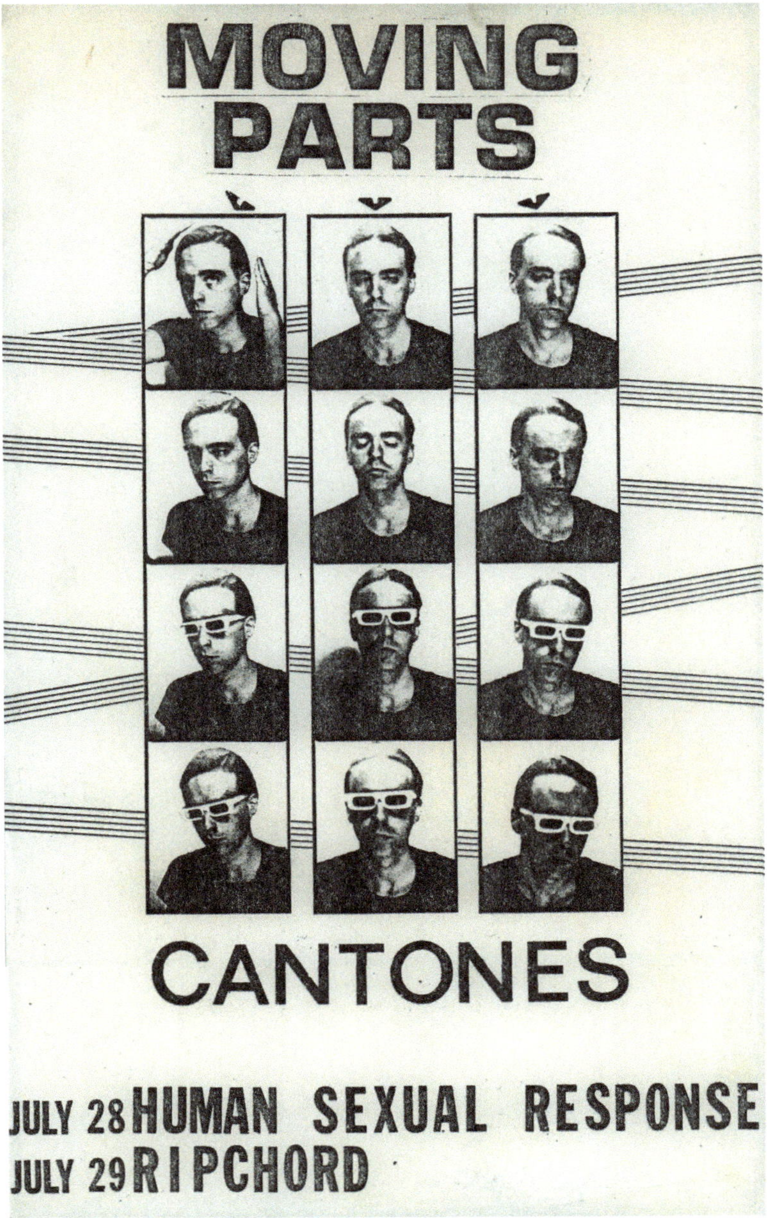
MOVING
PARTS
CANTONES
JULY 28 HUMAN SEXUAL RESPONSE
JULY 29 RIPCHORD

Concert poster (designed by Erik Lindgren; model: Clint Conley), July 1978 [ELA]

MR. BUTCH
The King of Kenmore Sq.
T-SHIRTS
Large and X-Large only
$10 ppd. to: T Max
74 Jamaica St.
Jamaica Plain, MA 02130

TAKE YOUR EARS TO THE
HI FI WIZARD!
Harvard Square
Kenmore Square
Prudential
Allston
Framingham
Braintree
Providence, R.I.
New Haven, Conn.
Atlantis Sound

TOP: ***The Noise,*** October 1988 [DBA]
BOTTOM: ***Boston Phoenix,*** October 8, 1974 [BCA]

at Michael's Pub

Mon. .... **Fringe**
Tues. .... **David Jackson & Friends**
Wed. .... **Jackie Byard and The Apollo Stompers**
Thurs.-Sat. .... **Sorcery**
Sun. .... **Open Jam**

The finest jazz that Boston has to offer, seven nights a week
52A Gainsboro St. Boston
247-7262

SHOWCASE

Saturday & Sunday, Nov. 12, 13
Joan Johnson Jazz Quartet
Monday, Nov. 14
Andrea McLane with The Cambridgeport Jazz Ensemble
Tuesday & Wednesday, Nov. 15 & 16
Napua Davoy Jazz Quartet
Thursday & Friday, Nov. 17 & 18
Steve Veikley Jazz Quartet
Saturday, Nov. 19
Joan Johnson Jazz Quartet

RYLES

CAFE • BAR • 876-9330
INMAN SQUARE, CAMBRIDGE

Downstairs At the Hofbrau

1314 Comm. Ave., Boston
232-8748
Boston's Newest singles & couples
Bar, Lounge & Gameroom

a Concerts North presentation
Thurs.-Sat., Nov. 17-19
THE ESTES BOYS

Fri. & Sat., Nov. 25 & 26
CLEAN LIVING

Thurs.-Sat., Dec. 1-3
THE ESTES BOYS

Fri.-Sat. 8:30-12:30 Res. Accepted

Cantone's
Rock & Roll

Tues., Nov. 15
NEIGHBORHOODS
with Careful Mike

Wed., Nov. 16
MARSHALLS

Thurs. & Fri., Nov. 17 & 18
MARSHALLS and SEA KING

Sat., Nov. 19
A Party With
AFRICAN CORE and BABY'S ARM

Happy Birthday Miss Lynn

69 Broad St., Boston
338-7677

BERKLEY DISCO & STAN'S KITCHEN

173 Mass. Ave., Boston
NOW INTRODUCING
JUKE BOX DISCO MUSIC
EAT, DRINK, & BE MERRY!

Boston Phoenix, November 15, 1977 [DBA]

MON. thru SAT.
9:30–5:30
OPEN FRI. til 9 P.M.
Gorins
YOU'RE IMPORTANT TO US!
SAVINGS ON MEN'S SHIRTS
Lively Styles for Today's Men At Sensational Prices!
1. Permanent Press Dress Shirts 2.99 reg. 3.98
Smooth, cool and flattering permanent press long-sleeved dress shirts with 4" long pointed collar and two-button cuffs. Today's fashion look in solids, stripes, checks and plaids. Sizes 14 1/2 to 17.
2. Crewneck and T-Neck Knits 2.44 reg. 2.98
A "get-away-from-it" choice of crewneck cotton blend knit shirts in solid colors and contemporary stripes; also, T-neck all cotton (no additives!) one inch rib. In snappy colors of blue, navy, gold, red, wine. Both in S, M, L, XL.
3. Flannel Sport Shirts 2.99 reg. 3.98
The power of plaid in a carefree blend of 80% sanforized cotton and 20% polyester flannel sport shirts. Permanent press long-sleeved in a choice of plaids. Buy now and save for the coming fall.
BacktoCollege
HERE'S A GUIDE FOR GETTING A GUY TOGETHER FOR FALL
VERSATILE TOPS FOR FALL
U-Neck Sleeveless sweaters
3.99 reg. $5
Mixing and matching with 75% acrylic and 25% polyester ribbed U-neck sleeveless sweaters in a fall array of colors — navy, burgundy, brown, ivory. In sizes S, M, L, XL.
Warm, Great Looking 100% Wool
Shetland sweaters
8.99 reg. 10.98
FOR THE ACTIVE LIFE
warm-up jackets
6.99 reg. 8.98
Just right for teeing off on the course or leisure fall walking — our 100% nylon taffeta kasha warm-up jackets. Two welt pockets, 6-snap front enclosure, drawstring bottom, and elasticized cuffs. Colors of navy, burgundy, green. Sizes S, M, L, XL.
SPORTSMEN'S FAVORITE
pile lined C.P.O. shirts
15.99 reg. 19.98
Rugged warmth plus great looks in free form styling C.P.O. pile lined shirts. Pile lapels and button down front, in an assortment of bold handsome plaids. Sizes S, M, L, XL.
DOUBLE DUTY
denim jeans
3.99 REG. 5.50 & 5.98
Great fitting — great looking — 10 oz. navy blue denim jeans with fashion flares. Four patch pockets with zipper and button fly closing. Waist sizes 29 to 38.
bow ties and neckties
1.59 2 for $3 reg. $2
They're fashion — they're fun — they're "in" for fall — super bows and regular ties in solids, polka dots, plaids and prints. Come see what a bow tie can do for you!
USE YOUR GORIN, BANKAMERICARD OR MASTER CHARGE CARD
GORIN'S
253 ELM ST.
DAVIS SQ.

Somerville Journal, August 16, 1973 [BCA]

ann
taylor
IMPORTED AND DOMESTIC SPORTSWEAR
391 Boylston Street, BOSTON
44 Brattle Street, HARVARD SQUARE
BRAINTREE-BURLINGTON-NATICK
PEABODY-NANTUCKET

On Sunday evening
at 9p.m., WMEX will present
The Year One
Starting with the words of John F. Kennedy, this is the story of that Journey that gave birth to a new world.
Apollo 11, Man on the Moon
Sunday 9 P.M.
WMEX
The Human Thing • 1510

LEFT: ***Panorama* magazine,** July 17, 1972 [BCA]
RIGHT: ***Boston Globe,*** July 15, 1969 [BCA]

★ ROCK AGAINST RACISM PROUDLY PRESENTS ★
Open Arts Festival
SUNDAY SEPT 13 1981 NOON–6 PM
AT JAMAICA POND OPEN DOOR THEATER
Located off Jamaica Way across from Moraine St. Take Arborway bus from Copley Sq. to Moraine St.
Masters of Ceremony:
Jose Masso, Mackie McLeod, Dinah Vaprin
One People
Orquesta Tropica
Cimarron
African Arts Folkloric Group
Just Visiting
The Jarius Ensemble
Circle of Friends
and other Boston Artists and Performers
Brother Blue, Ted Thomas, Brenda Walcott (scenes from Dreams)
FOOD • ARTISTS • CRAFTS • HEALING ARTS BOOTH • CHILDREN'S ENTERTAINMENT
This project is funded in part by the Massachusetts Council on the Arts and Humanities, a State agency
rain site: The Group School, 345 Franklin St., Central Sq. Cambridge

Event flyer, September 1981 [REEBEE]

Brigham's Ice Cream
& Sandwich Shoppe
of Chinatown
11 Tyler Street • 338-9280
First privately owned Brigham's
ADVERTISEMENTS
BOSTON 131

THE
BICYCLE
PEDDLER
SELLS: RALEIGH
TRIUMPH
PHILLIPS
JEUNET
MAGNEET
ROGER RIVIERE
RENTS: NEW 3 SPEEDS
FIXES: SAME DAY SERVICE
PARTS & ACCESSORIES
832 COMMONWEALTH AVE.
(NEAR B.U. BRIDGE)
DAILY 10-6
CLOSED THURSDAYS 731-3550
OPEN SUNDAYS

TOP: ***Boston Magazine,*** January 1980 [DBA]
BOTTOM: ***Boston Phoenix,*** April 5, 1972 [BCA]

THE BACKSTREET BAR
Paoletti '79
P-TOWN
Disco • Cruise Lounge
Corner of Bradford & Carver Streets in the historic Gifford House Hotel

Hit Parade of Boston, August 1979 [DBA]

ZIRCON
298 Beacon St. on the Cambridge-Somerville Line 354-9242
See our ad in the Real Paper for further details
Sun., Nov. 13 Grey Larson
Wed., Nov. 16 Short Straw

Ahmed's Discothèque
96 WINTHROP ST., HARVARD SQ., 547-9382

WESTERN FRONT
Live Jazz and DISCO every weekend
343 Western Ave., Camb 492-7772

3 APPLE STREET BOSTON
LuLu's Presents
LULU WHITE
THE LASTIE BROTHERS and CRICKETT FLEMING
A Very Hot 6-pc. New Orleans Rhythm Dance Band
Every Tues.-Sat., 9:30-2:00 a.m.
SUNDAY BRUNCH 1:00-4:00 p.m.
Appearing Sunday Evening, Nov. 13
THE WAYNE NAUS-GREG HOPKINS BIG BAND
Creole Buffet 423-3652
Free Parking

SPEAKEASY
Sun., Mon., Tues., Nov. 13,14,15
GUITAR JOHNNY and the RHYTHM ROCKERS
Wed. & Thurs., Nov. 16 & 17
Chicago's Premier Blues Guitarist
SHUBIE SUMLIN with THE RHYTHM ROCKERS
Fri. & Sat., Nov. 18 & 19
NONIES BLUES

MATT TALBOTS
In The Hotel Diplomat
Berkeley and Chandler Streets, Boston 338-9089
Open 10 AM to 2 AM Lots of Free Parking
Sun. JANE CRAIG
Mon. TALENT NIGHT $30 Cash Prize
Tues. JANE CRAIG
Wed. LIVE MUSIC
Thurs. THE HOUNDOG BLUES BAND
Fri. & Sat. PROFESSOR HARP AND HIS BLUES BAND

WE'RE OPEN
JACQUES
—DISCO—
"Whatever You Want. . . We've Got It!!"
77 Broadway Boston
338-7502

The RED BARN
Rte. 9 Westboro
366-1382
Wed., Thurs., Sat., Sun., Nov. 16, 17, 19, 20
FATE
Wed. Night
Quarter Night
25¢ Drinks
Fri., Nov. 18 ONLY
CIRCUS

CASEY'S TOO
Nantasket Beach, Hull
15 miles south of Boston
925-9850
Wed.-Sat.
SOUTHERN COMFORT
Wed. nite Drink & Drown
Most Drinks & Beers 50¢
Next Week
KASHMIR
Coming
DEAD END KIDS
Casey's Winter Schedule
Happy Hour 8-9:30 every nite
Most Drinks & Beers 50¢
CASEY'S ONE
Wed. Nite Bingo Nite
No Charge
Over $600 worth of prizes
every Wed. nite.

Boston Phoenix, November 15, 1977 [DBA]

Boston's Own
"BOSTON"
BOSTON
including:
More Than A Feeling/Peace Of Mind
Foreplay/Long Time/Rock & Roll Band
Smokin'/Hitch A Ride
A WHOLE NEW
EXPERIENCE
Available
Wherever Records
Are Sold

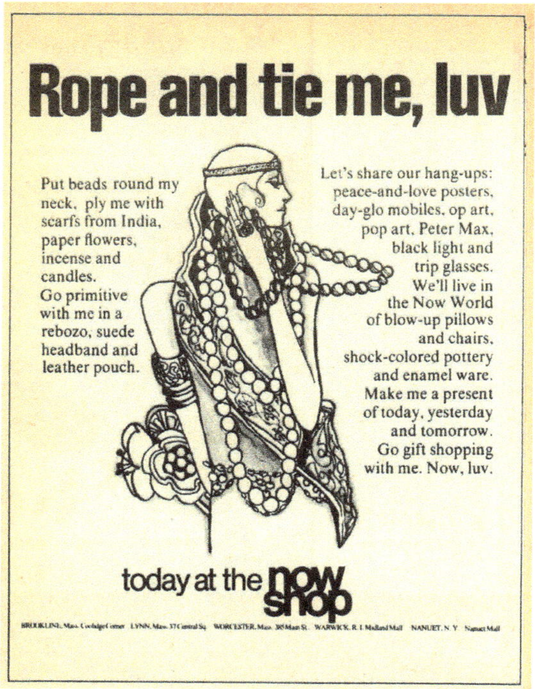
Rope and tie me, luv
Put beads round my neck, ply me with scarfs from India, paper flowers, incense and candles. Go primitive with me in a rebozo, suede headband and leather pouch.
Let's share our hang-ups: peace-and-love posters, day-glo mobiles, op art, pop art, Peter Max, black light and trip glasses. We'll live in the Now World of blow-up pillows and chairs, shock-colored pottery and enamel ware. Make me a present of today, yesterday and tomorrow. Go gift shopping with me. Now, luv.
today at the now shop

TOP: ***Boston Phoenix,*** September 21, 1976 [DBA]
BOTTOM: ***Boston After Dark,*** December 3, 1969 [DBA]

WELLFLEET PUB
FRISCO
CARTER
WILLIE LOCO
TONY INCOGNITO
THE COOK
THE RADIO HEARTS
MAY 16,17,18TH
THURS. FRI. SAT.
THE Pub is on the Docks

Concert flyer, May 1974 [LOCO]

Fran's
LYNN MASS
FRAN'S PLACE
Nov. 1
HALLOWEEN COSTUME PARTY
$150 IN CASH PRIZES
Nov. 8 50's NIGHT
Nov. 15
MR. GAY LYNN CONTEST
Nov. 22
ROSIE & THE HARLETTES
AIDS Benefit Show
Nov. 29
NIGHT OF 100 STARS
AIDS Benefit
776 WASHINGTON ."ON THE LYNNWAY" • LYNN, MASS.

72 WATT
STA 65 B AM/FMRECEIVER
Better reception! Great Value! FET front end and IC I.F. circuitry for more FM stations and an AM section designed to cut through station clutter. Flip-Lever front panel switches and multi-speaker selection switch, ganged bass and treble controls, hi-filter and loudness switch. All silicon amplifier provides continuous power through the entire tonal range. Luxurious brushed aluminum panel plus a FREE walnut cabinet valued at $24.95.
$189.95
SAVE $100
ON COMPLETE SYSTEM
REALISTIC STA-65B AM/FM Stereo Receiver
REALISTIC Lab-12 Automatic Changer with Custom Base and Shure Cartridge
2 REALISTIC Optimus-1 Speaker Systems
Reg. Separate parts Price $399.30
$299.80
The "best buy system" of the new sound explosion. Stop in the Shack and let your ears decide ...
JOIN THE SOUND EXPLOSION
RADIO SHACK
730 COMM. AVE., BROOKLINE
659 BOYLSTON ST., BOSTON
FRESH POND SHOPPING CTR., CAMB.

TOP: ***Guide To The Gay Northeast* magazine,** November 1987 [BCA]
BOTTOM: ***Boston After Dark,*** March 11, 1970 [DBA]

THE ARK
15 LANSDOWNE ST. BOSTON
THE ARK
INTERPERSONAL CONCERT SERIES—ONLY 3.00
GOOD, CLEAN FUN
WITH THE
MC5
and
CLOUD
INTERPERSONAL CONCERT SERIES—ONLY 3.00
THE ARK
MON., TUES. & WED.—JUNE 16, 17, 18
THE ARK
TICKETS AVAILABLE AT (BOSTON) FREAQUE BOUTIQUE, MANHOLE LTD.
(CAMBRIDGE) HEADQUARTERS EAST, KRACKERJACKS. FOR FURTHER INFORMATION PHONE 536-0915.

Concert flyer, June 1969 [DBA]

You too can learn to pick up girls!
As well as pianos, crickets, guitars, pots, pans, earthquakes, and MORE With a
FRAP
pick-up
available at:
THE BOSTON SCHOOL OF ELECTRONIC MUSIC
326 Dartmouth Street, Boston. 261-1634
AS WELL AS: ARP synthesizers, Lamb mixers, custom equipment, and courses on how to use them!
GIRLS: Frap's don't pick up boys too well - But then, who would want to? Try it on your guitar instead.

***Driving Wheel* magazine,** December 15, 1973 [BCA]

GREEN STREET STATION

FRI OCT 14 RUN WESTY RUN
NIXON'S HEAD
THE MERCHANTS

SAT OCT 15 CARMAIG de FOREST BAND (W/GORDON GANO, DENISE FRAZIER, CRAIG NEAL + DOUG WEASALMAN) XANNA DON'T
NOBODY HOME

SUN OCT 16 NOISE 7th ANNIVERSARY
GALAXIE 500
DANNY MYDLACK
WILLIE ALEXANDER + JERI ROSSI

THURS OCT 20 DENIROS
DRUMMING ON GLASS
special guests

FRI OCT 21 SLAUGHTER SHACK
special guests

SAT OCT 22 UNIVERSAL CONGRESS OF
LOVING SIX
special guests

SUN OCT 23 OATS FOR PEACE BENEFIT
SUBSKIN CABLES
BULKHEAD
HEYDAY
BACK KNIFE SPOT

THURS OCT 27 we'll be at the Somerville Theatre to see SONIC YOUTH

FRI OCT 28 TITANICS
LAZY COWGIRLS
VOODOO DOLLS

SAT OCT 29 A SCANNER DARKLY
UT + special guests

SUN OCT 30 URGE OVERKILL
special Guests

131 GREEN ST.
JAMAICA PLAIN 522-0792

Helldorado Productions present "Live at the Middle East"

TUES 10-18 GILBERT MAKES
MONTY ROCK
"TOM JONES" featuring Springa
THE OLD CURMUDGEONS
SMOKIN' DAZE from Lexington, KY.

SUN 10-23 Benefit for WZBC
NOMAN'S BAND
featuring Roger Miller
DAVID PRESCOTT
AND OTHERS

TUES 10-25 ALL AGES
BEAT HAPPENING
GIRL TROUBLE
ED's REDEEMING QUALITIES
FAB MOTION

SUN 10-30 URGE OVERKILL
ON TOUCH + GO
SPICK DOG
MUDHONEY
BACK KNIFE SPOT

the earth have your blood... You are indeed totally unique and wholly in all! the great wedding hall is filled, and all are wearing the wedding garment... let the heavens welcome your spirit... but let

J. CAG'S BIG BLACK BOOK
WEDNESDAYS 530-730PM
MIDDLE EAST RESTAURANT
472 MASSACHUSETTS AVENUE
CENTRAL SQUARE CAMBRIDGE

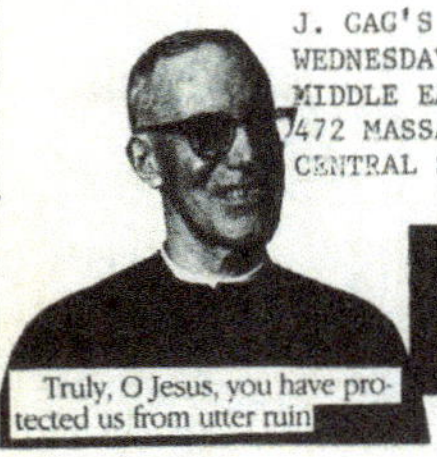
Truly, O Jesus, you have protected us from utter ruin

Every Wednesday
OPEN MIKE

T.T. THE BEAR'S LIVE ROCK

FRI OCT 14 Record release party for LAST STAND w/ BULLET LAVOLTA
CHAOTIC PAST

SAT OCT 15 CUCUMBERS/MEN + VOLTS
XANNA DON'T

TUES OCT 18 BOY/GIRL • BRIDGE
THE HARD TOPS • BLEEDING HEARTS

WED OCT 19 TERRI BRIGHT • FAB MOTION
WHITE FIRE • MASTERS of the OBVIOUS

THURS OCT 20 BIG TRAIN • ED'S REDEEMING QUALITIES • STOP CALLING ME FRANK

FRI OCT 21 TRIBE • THE NATIVES
• DRAMA CLUB

SAT OCT 22 ZULUS • GLASS EYE
THINGS THAT AREN'T FOOD

TUES OCT 25 SWINGING TEENS • THE TIME BEINGS
SPELLMAN BLOCK • VITAL IMAGE

WED OCT 26 SEPTEMBER REIGN • DON'T TRY THIS AT HOME
PARADE • STICK PEOPLE

THURS OCT 27 ABSOLUTE • TAX COLLECTORS • TALKING TO ANIMALS

FRI OCT 28 DREAMS SO REAL
GAME THEORY • THE MARIARVANS

SAT OCT 29 LYRES • THE CATHEADS
THE VINDICATORS

THURS NOV 3 KNOTTS + CROSSES
GARY SHANE

FRI NOV 4 GUTBANK HOBOKEN NIGHT
RITUAL TENSION

SAT NOV 5 THE CONNELLS
WILD SEEDS • AGENT 13
(FROM AUSTIN, TX)

FRI NOV 11 THE NEATS
AMAZING MUD SHARKS

SAT NOV 12 GANG GREEN
LAST STAND

COMING:
DUMPTRUCK
BARRENCE WHITFIELD & THE SAVAGES

KITCHEN CLOSED DURING RENOVATIONS

TUES + WED NIGHTS FEATURE NEW BANDS!

10 BROOKLINE ST., CAMBRIDGE
CENTRAL SQ. T 492-0082

THE Rat
BOSTON ROCK & ROLL
528 COMM. AVE.
BOSTON, MASS. 02215
(617) 536-9438

THE BALCONY HAS MALE SENSITIVITY NIGHT
featuring CIRCLE OF STRENGTH

FRI 10/14 RICK BERLIN THE MOVIE
RUNAWAY DAN • FUN HOUSE

SAT 10/15 TITANICS
THE HIGHWAYMEN • IMMORTALS

THURS 10/20 HELLDORADO NIGHT
SLOTH • PORN ORCHARD

FRI 10/21 SALEM 66 • CAVEDOGS
GALAXIE 500 • BITCH MAGNET

SAT 10/22 STRAW DOGS
FROM NY HARI KARI ALL GIRL HEAVY METAL • LEFT NUT

FRI 10/28 TENTATIVE THE FLESHTONES

SAT 10/29 4th ANNUAL BENTMEN w/CXEMA
HALLOWEEN EXTRAVAGANZA

SUN 10/30 REPTILICUS • JOHNNY & THE JUMPER CABLES
FAB MOTION • JUDGEMENTAL

THURS 11/3 KRUSE RECORDS > ALL
X-DESENDENTS
FROM CA CHEMICAL PEOPLE • GRIN

FRI 11/4 UNATTACHED • BONEYARD

SAT 11/5 THE RAIN • JONESES • THRILL HAMMER

THURS 11/10 TENTATIVE BILLY RUANE'S BIRTHDAY BASH!

FRI 11/11 ZULUS • THE BRISTOLS

The Noise, October 1988 [DBA]

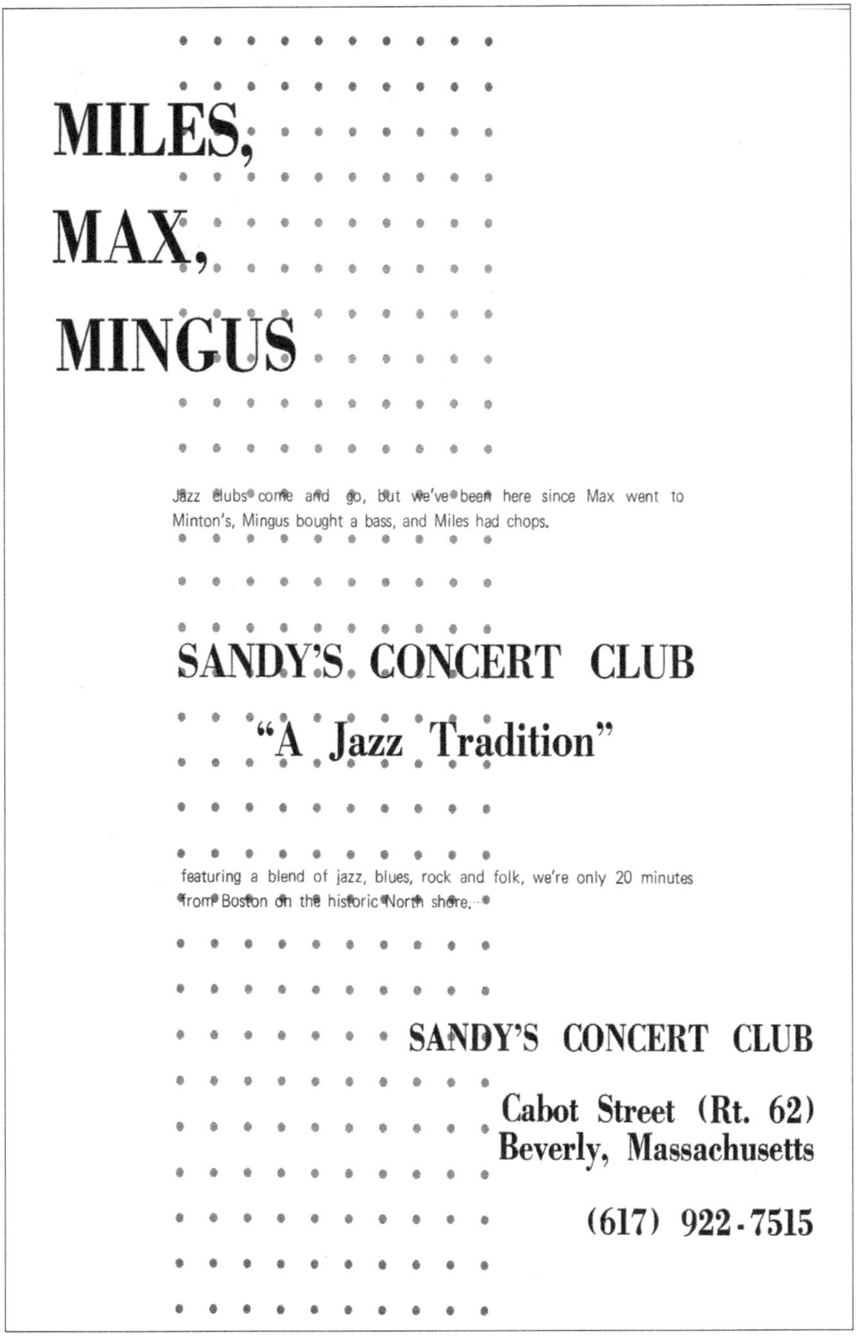
MILES,
MAX,
MINGUS
Jazz clubs come and go, but we've been here since Max went to Minton's, Mingus bought a bass, and Miles had chops.
SANDY'S CONCERT CLUB
"A Jazz Tradition"
featuring a blend of jazz, blues, rock and folk, we're only 20 minutes from Boston on the historic North shore.
SANDY'S CONCERT CLUB
Cabot Street (Rt. 62)
Beverly, Massachusetts
(617) 922-7515

***Jazz New England* magazine,** October 1974 [VACCA]

REFLECTIONS
Contemporary Hair Design / Men-Women-Children
John Nichols
Cosmetics
Complexion Care
544 Boston Post Road, Weston
Five Minutes From Mass Pike and Route 128
893-9313
894-9313

Boston Magazine, September 1977 [DBA]

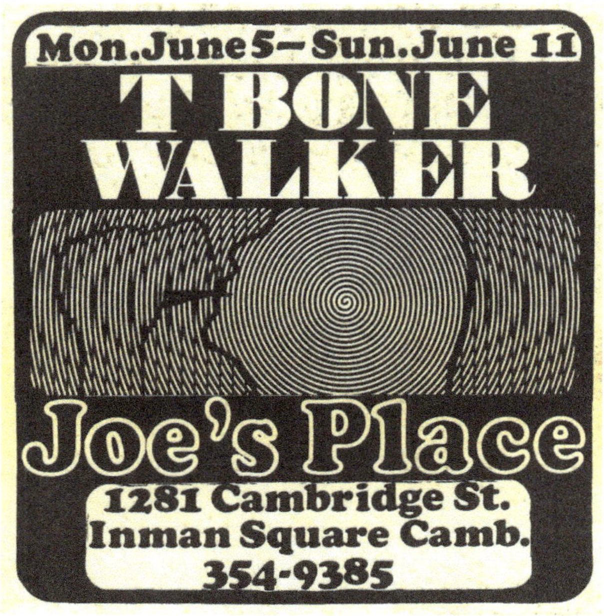
Mon. June 5—Sun. June 11
T BONE
WALKER
Joe's Place
1281 Cambridge St.
Inman Square Camb.
354-9385

BIRDSONGS
OF
THE
MESOZOIC
8:30 P.M.
FRI. OCT. 7
AT THE
B.F.V.F.
1126 Boylston St.
BOSTON

TOP: ***Boston Phoenix,*** August 2, 1972 [BCA]

BOTTOM: **Concert flyer** (design by Roger Miller), October 1983 [ELA]

Thursdays 8:30 p.m. Channel 2
SAY BROTHER

Television show flyer, 1968 [from the book *Black Power TV* by Devorah Heitner]

Sound Productions
Music Arrangements
Cassette Label
Distribution & Licensing
CAMARADERIE MUSIC
P.O. Box 403 - Kenmore Station
Boston, Mass. 02215
Curt Naihersey ("Mr. Curt")
(617)-524-5113
Song Publishing (B.M.I.)
Band Consultations
Jim Clements
(617) 641-2288
Curt Naihersey
(617) 524-5113
the EXIs
an electro-acoustic ensemble
("The Boho - Beat")
Cameraderie Music Co.
P.O. Box 403 - Kenmore Station
Boston, MA 02215
CHARLES T. GRAVES
Manager
Harvard Sq.
NEWBURY COMICS INC.
"a wicked good time"
332 Newbury St. Boston 236-4930
36 JFK St. H. Sq. Cambridge 491-1098
341 Cochituate Rd. Framingham 620-0735
new alliance
audio productions
don foote alvan long andrew murdock
547 3099 825 9575 267 1656
254-2603
HARVARD SQUARE
36 JFK St.
491-0337
BOSTON
332 Newbury St.
236-4930
NEWBURY COMICS, INC.
P.O. Box 2692, Cambridge, MA 02238
KATHEI LOGUE
Advertising
491-1098
MIT
Student Center
225-2872
FRAMINGHAM
Rt. 30 Mall
(508) 620-0735
BURLINGTON
Vinebrook Plaza
270-9860
PICTURE PARADISE
Framed Prints
Advertising, Mirrors & Lamps
1800's-1960's
Mardi Gras-New Orleans Poster Art
Rock and Roll Collectables
Picture Framing
Decorating for Homes & Businesses
Prop Rentals
109 Brighton Ave.
Allston, MA 02134
ED SAVAGE
(617) 783-4072
C-LINE #61217
BUSINESS CARD
PETER GATES
Manager
247-3007
NEWBURY COMICS INC.
New Music and Fashion
332 Newbury St. Boston 236-4930
36 JFK St. H. Sq. Cambridge 491-0337
East Coast Coffee
Harry Moulla,
Vice President
160 Harvard Ave.
Allston, MA 02134
(617) 789-5983
Beeper: 465-7784
PERFORMING ARTIST
WRITER MEMBER ASCAP
RICHARD NOLAN
"UNIQUE NEW MUSIC"
1840 COMMONWEALTH AVENUE
BOSTON, MA 02135
(617)-731-5784
MBM
"WHERE THE INDUSTRY COMES TO YOU"
MUSIC BUSINESS MONTHLY
CAREER WORKSHOPS
RECORD PRODUCER
JOE VIGLIONE
(617) 935-5386
P.O. BOX 2392
WOBURN, MA 01888

Chuck White Business Card Collection, 1980s–1990s [CWA/DBA]

THE RaT

BOSTON ROCK & ROLL

528 COMM. AVE.
BOSTON, MASS 02215
(617) 247-7713

Mon. & Tues., July 25 & 26
Werewolves and Sea King

Wed., July 27
Baby's Arm and East King

Thurs. & Fri., July 28-29
Thunder-train and The Dead Boys

Sat. & Sun., July 30 & 31
DMZ and The Dead Boys

Coming Next Week:
The Electric Chairs
Direct from England

LIVE RAT LP DOUBLE ROCK
$8.99 + 75¢ handling = **$9.74** • Rat Recording "A" • 528 Commonwealth Ave., Boston, Mass.

PAULA FONTAINE'S
(formerly Palm Gardens)

SPEAKEASY
(upstairs)
Floor Show every Thurs.-Sun.
July 28 thru 31
RICK RICARDO
Singing Impressionist
ASMIS BELLY DANCER
Paula Fontaine, M.C.
Rt. 114 Peabody, Mass. 531-2024

BACK STAGE
(downstairs)
The No. Shore's Newest Singles and Couples Lounge
Every Sun. GONG SHOW
Every Mon. THE GRADUATES
Tues.-Sun. "Surprise"
Dancing nightly 8 p.m. til closing.
Open 11 a.m.-1 a.m. (2 p.m. Sat.)

Mon., July 25
MAD JOHN
Tues., July 26
JOY RIDE EXPRESS
Wed., July 27
BACK ST. AFFAIR
Thurs., July 28
BONGO MOON
Fri.-Sun., July 29, 30, 31
BIG SCREAMIN' McGREW

THE OXFORD ALE HOUSE

DUNSTER'S PUB
BIG T.V.
BIG DRINKS

36 CHURCH STREET—HARVARD SQ./DIRECTLY BEHIND THE HARVARD COOP

ROCK & ROLL
FLEA MARKET
FROM ELVIS TO ZEPPELIN
FEATURING
RECORDS, POSTERS, T-SHIRTS, AND
MANY OTHER COLLECTORS ITEMS
plus
rare movies shown by wbcn's 'little walter'- 5to6pm
featuring
chuck berry, frankie lymon & teenagers, elvis presley,
bill haley & his comets, beatles, johnny burnette trio, etc
SUNDAY JULY 31 · 12NOON · 6PM
PRINCE PALACE · MELROSE, MASS
free parking · air conditioned · food & drinks available
on train route from north station · wyoming ave exit
advance tickets $1.00 at the door $1.50 call:246-0704
SPECIAL ADDED ATTRACTION
ROCK & ROLL DANCE 7-TO-12 PM
with
DUKE & THE DRIVERS
advance Tickets $3:50

Boston Phoenix, July 26, 1977 [DBA]

Ken's Steaks make you famous...
Mark Hanna equally famous host of Ken's Steak House.
Russ Francis famous tight end of the New England Patriots.
or famous people eat at Ken's Steak House.
Route Nine, Framingham, Mass.
875-4455 or 235-5414

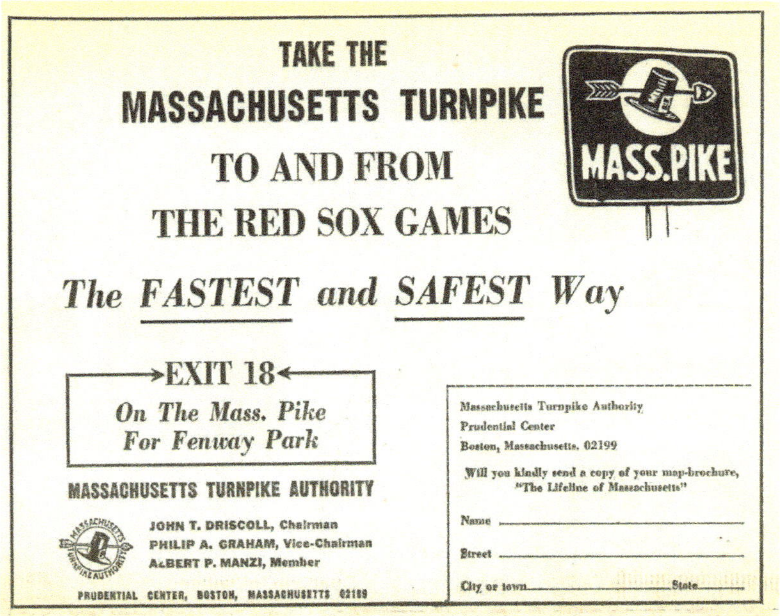
TAKE THE
MASSACHUSETTS TURNPIKE
TO AND FROM
THE RED SOX GAMES
MASS.PIKE
The FASTEST and SAFEST Way
EXIT 18
On The Mass. Pike
For Fenway Park
MASSACHUSETTS TURNPIKE AUTHORITY
JOHN T. DRISCOLL, Chairman
PHILIP A. GRAHAM, Vice-Chairman
ALBERT P. MANZI, Member
PRUDENTIAL CENTER, BOSTON, MASSACHUSETTS 02199
Massachusetts Turnpike Authority
Prudential Center
Boston, Massachusetts. 02199
Will you kindly send a copy of your map-brochure, "The Lifeline of Massachusetts"
Name
Street
City or town
State

TOP: ***Boston Magazine,*** January 1980 [DBA]

BOTTOM: ***Boston Record American,*** April 15, 1969 [BCA]

the real kids
RED STAR RECORDING ARTIST
AND INTRODUCING
SYLVAIN SYLVAIN'S NEW BAND
the CRIMINAL$
FROM N.Y.C.
rock and roll!
and the
real kids return to
the RAT...
KENMORE SQ.
NOV. 10-13
CRIMINALS - FRI + SAT MECHANICS - THURS + S

Concert poster, November 1977 [LOCO]

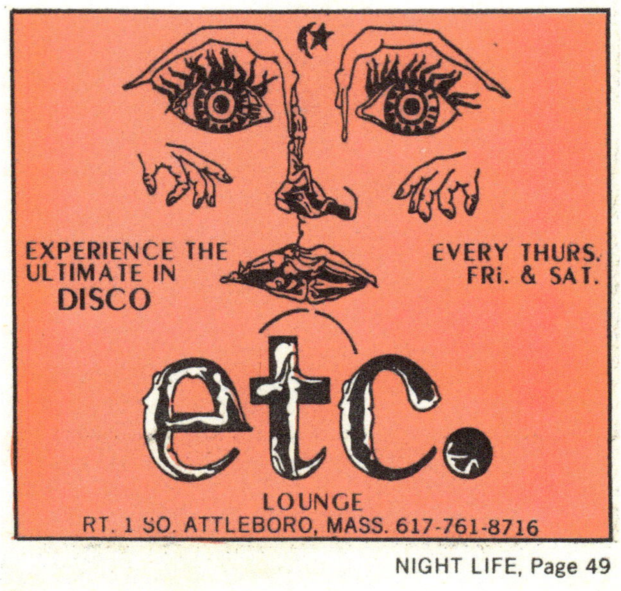
EXPERIENCE THE
ULTIMATE IN
DISCO
EVERY THURS.
FRi. & SAT.
etc.
LOUNGE
RT. 1 SO. ATTLEBORO, MASS. 617-761-8716
NIGHT LIFE, Page 49

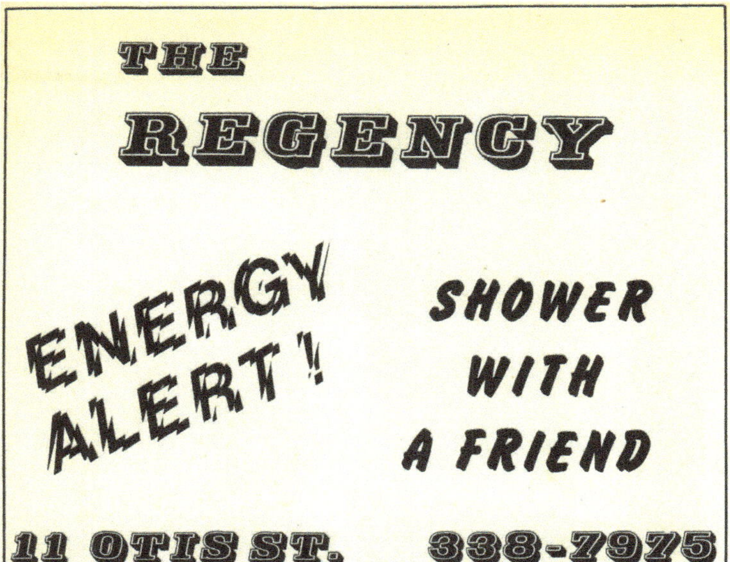
THE
REGENCY
ENERGY
ALERT!
SHOWER
WITH
A FRIEND
11 OTIS ST.
338-7975

TOP: ***Night Life* magazine,** October/November 1978 [DBA]
BOTTOM: ***Hit Parade of Boston,*** August 1979 [DBA]

JEFF McGINNIS - CHRIS MELIA - TOM MOSCETTO - DAVE GORDON
guitar vocals drums bass
GET YOUR
«PASSION» tm
ROCKING!
for booking info
contact ...
"MICKEY D. PRODUCTIONS"
(617) 683-5830

***Boston Rock In* magazine**, July 1987 [DBA]

Everybody!
Come on strong!!
NO DEPOSIT
NO RETURN
COME ON STRONG is a groovy new soft drink! No deposit-no return bottles! Wild, exciting flavors . . . bitter-sweet (chinoto), juicy orange, black raspberry, creme soda, cola, ginger ale, grape, guanabama, tamarindo!
Available at JACK & MARION'S, KING BAGEL, Brookline; TOWER OF PIZZA, Allston-Cambridge; M. Gordon Drug Store, Clipper Ship, Coffee Shop, Jack's Allston Deli, Friendly Spa, Model Cafe, Allston; Luigi's Restaurant, Burden's Drug, Boston; Eaton's, Teddy's Sub, A & B Beverage, United National Super Mkt., Dons Bottled Beverage, Brighton; Beach City Auto, Allen's Sales, Revere; Blue Hills Baths, Mattapan; The Foto Mart, Nashua, New Hampshire; Cafe Italia, Johnston, Rhode Island; Wolfe's Inc., Newport, Rhode Island.
Bottled under authority of Come On Strong Enterprises, 99 Chauncy Street, Boston by Come On Strong Bottling Co., 125 Orleans Street, East Boston - LO 7-5111.

New England Teen Scene, October 1967 [ELA]

BOSTON'S FAMOUS
WATERFRONT RESTAURANT
Kevin's Wharf
Famous Seafood Specialties
Steaks & Chops
426-8165
DAILY EXCEPT SUN.
FROM 11:30 A.M.
SAT. FROM 3:00 P.M.
254 SUMMER ST.

An Interesting
place to visit
in Boston for
Magic, Tricks,
Jokes, Puzzles,
and Souvenirs
at
4A PARK SQUARE
and
32 BROMFIELD ST.
426-9640
Jack's Trick & Joke Shop

If all you know about crêpes
is suzette, you're in for
51 other delicious treats!
La crêpe
Authentic French Crêpes
from 60¢ to $3.15
731 BOYLSTON STREET
(ACROSS FROM LORD & TAYLOR)
OPEN UNTIL AFTER MIDNITE
267-1534
IMPORTED FRENCH BEER AND WINE

Club
CasaBlanca
Omar
Lunch · Supper · Drinks
40 Brattle Street
Cambridge, MA 02138
· (617) 876-0999

LEFT: ***Panorama,*** July 17, 1972 [BCA]
RIGHT: ***Real Paper,*** June 24, 1978 [DBA]

PAUL'S MALL
AEROSMITH
Opens Wed. thru Sun.
TRACY NELSON & Mother Earth
"Poor Man's Paradise" on Columbia
–Coming April 2-8–
BILLY PAUL
JAZZ WORKSHOP
NOW THRU SUN.
HERBIE HANCOCK SEXTET
feat on Columbia Records
SUN. MAT. 4 - 7
–Coming March 26-April 1–
HORACE SILVER
–April 2 - 8–
GROVER WASHINGTON, Jr
733 Boylston St., Boston, 267-1300

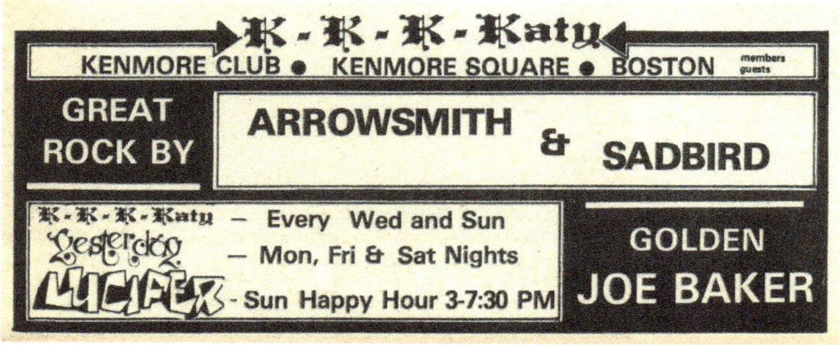
K - K - K - Katy
KENMORE CLUB • KENMORE SQUARE • BOSTON
members guests
GREAT ROCK BY
ARROWSMITH & SADBIRD
K - K - K - Katy – Every Wed and Sun
Yesterday – Mon, Fri & Sat Nights
LUCIFER - Sun Happy Hour 3-7:30 PM
GOLDEN
JOE BAKER

SCARBOROUGH FAIR
PRESENTS
AEROSMITH
APRIL 26-29
w/ ING
302 REVERE BEACH BLVD.
284-9876
CLIP THIS AD FOR A BEER!

TOP: ***Boston Phoenix,*** March 20, 1973 [DBA]
MIDDLE: ***Real Paper,*** April 4, 1973 [BCA]
BOTTOM: ***Real Paper,*** April 25, 1973 [BCA]

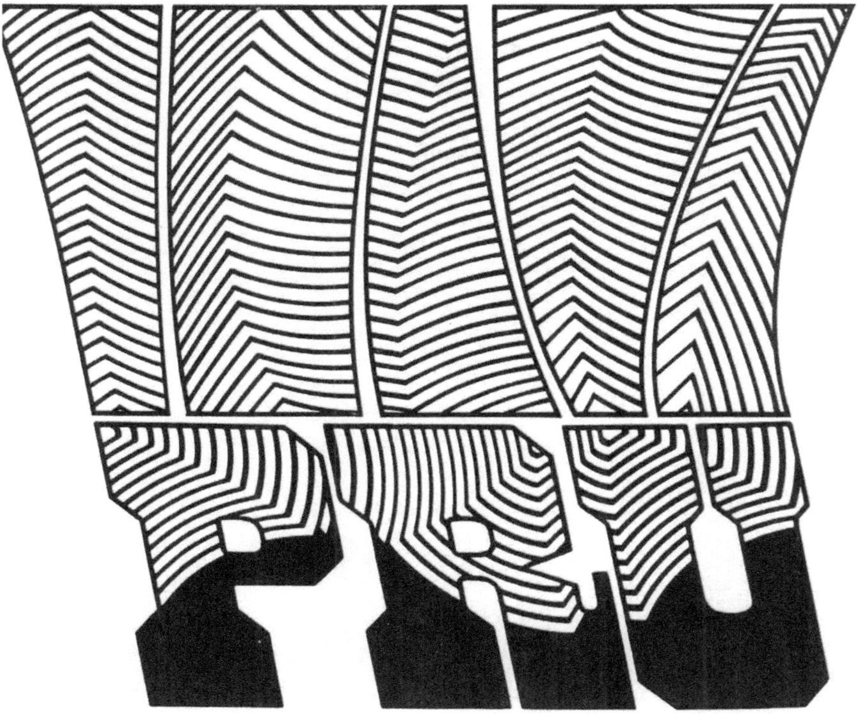

Mod, pop, straight,
square, Carnaby and Nehru
anythings and *everythings* in
39 of Boston's swingingest
stores. Pru means shoes, hats,
coats, travel, theaters,
conventions, hotels, records,
tapes, books . . . you name it,
Pru has it. Pru means
leaping 52 stories in a
single bound. Catching
a view of Boston's wide-
wide-wild. Or Skywalking it.
Getting the telescopes
to zero in on your dormitory
windows. It's all here at
The Pru . . . the swinging new
section of Old Boston
that grew up and got smart.

Prudential Shopping Plaza
Prudential Center, Boston

***Harvard Lampoon* magazine,** April 1970 [DBA]

OPENS
MON., NOV. 16
THE PARLIAMENTS
& FUNKADELICS
NOV. 23
THE
O'JAYS
NOV. 30
B. B.
KING
Rudy Guarino's
SUGAR SHACK
110 BOYLSTON ST., BOSTON
TEL. 426-0086
COMING JAN. 14-19
IN CONCERT
Xmas Gift Tickets Available
IN PERSON
The Living Legend
James Brown
the world's number one
entertainer with his entire
all star Revue.

BOSTON UNIVERSITY
SOCIAL COUNCIL
PRESENTS
the last poets
the parliament
the unifics
SAT. OCT.17 8:00P.M.
one show only
all tickets $2.50
for information call 353-3651
limited number of tickets still available
at B.U. box office
775 comm. ave.
2nd floor

TOP: ***Boston Herald Traveler,*** November 15, 1970 [DBA]

BOTTOM: ***Free Paper (Cambridge Phoenix),*** October 14, 1970 [DBA]

PSYCHOALPHADISCOBETABIOAQUADOLOOP
Motor Booty Affair
starring
PARLIAMENT
also
featuring
FUNKADELIC
Special Added Attraction
FUNK OR WALK
BRIDES OF FUNKENSTEIN
Presented by Frank J. Russo
FIRST BOSTON APPEARANCE SATURDAY,
MARCH 3, 8 P.M.
ALL SEATS GENERAL ADMISSION
$8.00 IN ADVANCE $9.00 DAY OF SHOW INCLUDES PARKING
NORTH SHORE COLISEUM. DANVERS. MASS.
FROM BOSTON TAKE ROUTE 1 NORTH TO 114 EAST JUST 14 MINUTES FROM DOWNTOWN BOSTON
TICKETS AVAILABLE NOW AT ALL TICKETRON LOCATIONS,
HUB TICKETS, OUT-OF-TOWN CAMBRIDGE,
AND AT THE COLISEUM BOX OFFICE
WE GOTTA RAISE ATLANTIS TO THE TOP!

Real Paper, March 3, 1979 [DBA]

We have a great catalog of redecorating ideas for you.
Telephones, of course.
Telephones with unique "personalities"— to express your family's lifestyle, to accent your home's decor, to say good things about you all year long!
You'll find an unexpected variety of colors and styles, all shown in our new full-color, 16-page catalog that also includes prices and a wealth of phone-service information.
New England Telephone
To get your own catalog, just call
1-800-241-9800
or fill out the coupon and mail it. It's easy to get a wide choice of the best at Bell.
New England Telephone Catalog
P.O. Box 5555
Dept. NW
Mt. Vernon, NY 10550
Please send me my copy of Telephones: The Forgotten Home Improvement.
Name
Street
City
State
Zip
Telephone
(Area Code)

Boston Magazine, September 1977 [DBA]

You can find the books you want at Phillips
BOOKS
Phillips
At Harvard Square
JAY MOTORS
Inc.
71 BROADWAY
CAMBRIDGE, MASSACHUSETTS
Complete Foreign Car
SALES & SERVICE
FOLKLORE
FOLK MUSIC
FOLK DANCE
CANTABRIGIA BOOK SHOP
18 Palmer St., Harvard Square
BOSTON'S LARGEST SELECTION
OF FINE QUALITY FURNITURE
popular contemporary
foam pieces at huge savings
citymart
518 Washington Street, Boston
Daily 9:30-6 — Mon. & Wed. til 9:30 P.M.

Collegiate Guide to Greater Boston (Harvard Crimson), 1963 [VACCA]

May Day Celebration
Thursday, May 5
CPCS 1st floor lounge ~
11:30 ~ 1:00 & 5:00 ~ 6:30
Celebrate International Workers' Day
with a free speech fiesta!
Music · Speakers · Refreshments · Balloons
Come express yourself on a "free speech grafitti wall"
Free speech
Free speech
Free speech
Free--
--speech
Celebrating and defending free speech!
Sponsored by the CPCS Socialist Collective

Event flyer (designed by Marie Kennedy), May 1988 [REEBEE]

"No Surfin' in Dorchester Bay"
No Surfin in Dorchester Bay
by The Gremies
Modern Method Records
268 Newbury St.
Boston, MA 02116 (617) 247-7590
Now available at: NEWBURY COMICS, NE MUSIC CITY, STRAWBERRIES, POPCORN, ROCKIT RECORDS, DISCOUNT RECORDS.
A SPECIAL LIMITED EDITION VERSION OF THIS SINGLE IS AVAILABLE ONLY AT SELECTED STORES IN DORCHESTER.

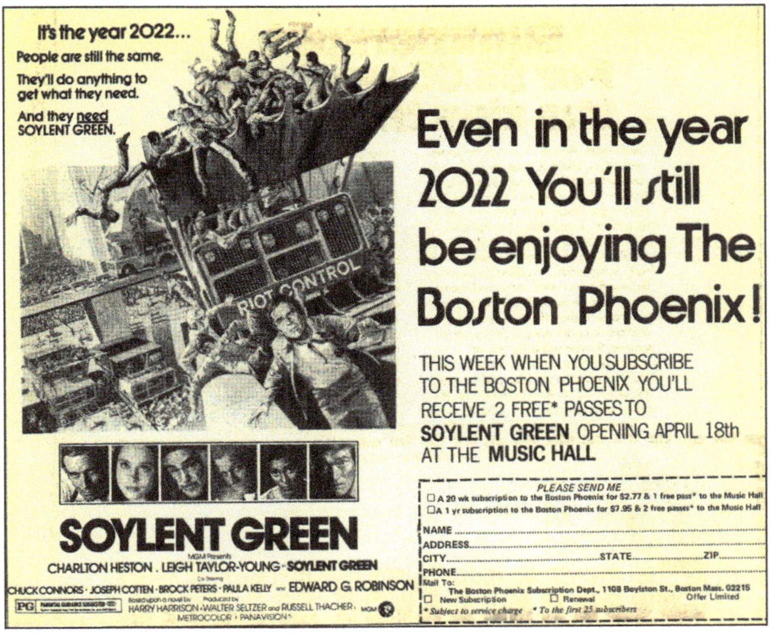
It's the year 2022...
People are still the same.
They'll do anything to get what they need.
And they need SOYLENT GREEN.
RIOT CONTROL
SOYLENT GREEN
MGM Presents
CHARLTON HESTON . LEIGH TAYLOR-YOUNG · SOYLENT GREEN
CHUCK CONNORS · JOSEPH COTTEN · BROCK PETERS · PAULA KELLY and EDWARD G. ROBINSON
PG
Based upon a novel by HARRY HARRISON · Produced by WALTER SELTZER and RUSSELL THACHER · MGM
METROCOLOR · PANAVISION
Even in the year 2022 You'll still be enjoying The Boston Phoenix!
THIS WEEK WHEN YOU SUBSCRIBE TO THE BOSTON PHOENIX YOU'LL RECEIVE 2 FREE* PASSES TO SOYLENT GREEN OPENING APRIL 18th AT THE MUSIC HALL
PLEASE SEND ME
☐ A 20 wk subscription to the Boston Phoenix for $2.77 & 1 free pass* to the Music Hall
☐ A 1 yr subscription to the Boston Phoenix for $7.95 & 2 free passes* to the Music Hall
NAME
ADDRESS
CITY STATE ZIP
PHONE
Mail To:
The Boston Phoenix Subscription Dept., 1108 Boylston St., Boston Mass. 02215
☐ New Subscription ☐ Renewal
Offer Limited
* Subject to service charge * To the first 25 subscribers

TOP: ***Boston Rock,*** October 1980 [DBA]
BOTTOM: ***Boston Phoenix,*** April 17, 1973 [BCA]

BERKLEY STREET
a club whose mainspring is music
a home for the blues
OPENING Fri., March 20th-7:57 p.m.
BUDDY GUY
and
BIG MAMA THORNTON
53 BERKELEY STREET, BOSTON
tickets at:
TRUC - HEADQUARTERS EAST - SEBASTIANS

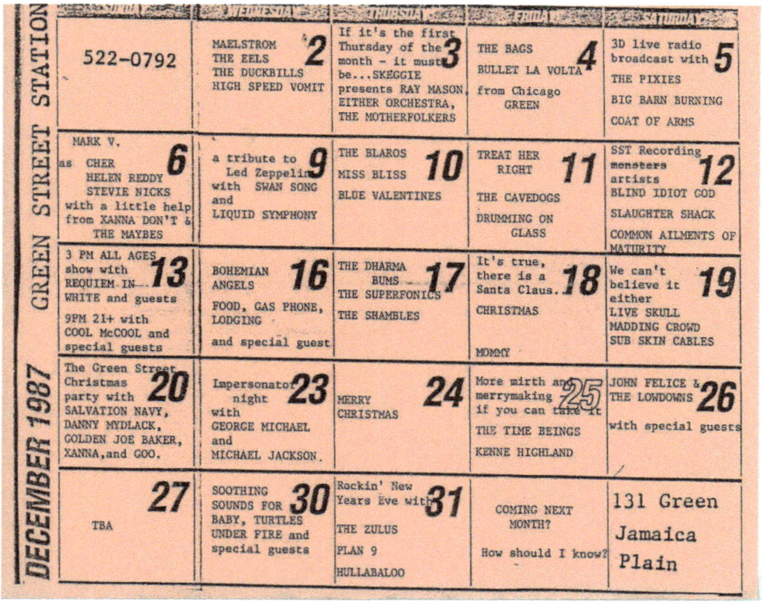
DECEMBER 1987 GREEN STREET STATION
522-0792
2 MAELSTROM THE EELS THE DUCKBILLS HIGH SPEED VOMIT
3 If it's the first Thursday of the month - it must be...SKEGGIE presents RAY MASON, EITHER ORCHESTRA, THE MOTHERFOLKERS
4 THE BAGS BULLET LA VOLTA from Chicago GREEN
5 3D live radio broadcast with THE PIXIES BIG BARN BURNING COAT OF ARMS
6 MARK V. as CHER HELEN REDDY STEVIE NICKS with a little help from XANNA DON'T & THE MAYBES
9 a tribute to Led Zeppelin with SWAN SONG and LIQUID SYMPHONY
10 THE BLAROS MISS BLISS BLUE VALENTINES
11 TREAT HER RIGHT THE CAVEDOGS DRUMMING ON GLASS
12 SST Recording monsters artists BLIND IDIOT GOD SLAUGHTER SHACK COMMON AILMENTS OF MATURITY
13 3 PM ALL AGES show with REQUIEM IN WHITE and guests 9PM 21+ with COOL McCOOL and special guests
16 BOHEMIAN ANGELS FOOD, GAS PHONE, LODGING and special guest
17 THE DHARMA BUMS THE SUPERFONICS THE SHAMBLES
18 It's true, there is a Santa Claus. CHRISTMAS MOMMY
19 We can't believe it either LIVE SKULL MADDING CROWD SUB SKIN CABLES
20 The Green Street Christmas party with SALVATION NAVY, DANNY MYDLACK, GOLDEN JOE BAKER, XANNA, and GOO.
23 Impersonator night with GEORGE MICHAEL and MICHAEL JACKSON.
24 MERRY CHRISTMAS
25 More mirth and merrymaking if you can take it THE TIME BEINGS KENNE HIGHLAND
26 JOHN FELICE & THE LOWDOWNS with special guests
27 TBA
30 SOOTHING SOUNDS FOR BABY, TURTLES UNDER FIRE and special guests
31 Rockin' New Years Eve with THE ZULUS PLAN 9 HULLABALOO
COMING NEXT MONTH? How should I know?
131 Green Jamaica Plain

TOP: ***Boston After Dark,*** March 18, 1970 [DBA]
BOTTOM: **Calendar flyer,** December 1987 [GERSHON]

dave wilson
presents
MISSISSIPPI
JOHN HURT
FIRST BOSTON ENGAGEMENT
FEBRUARY 10-15
CAFE YANA
8·30 nightly
50 BROOKLINE AVE.. 1 BLOCK FROM KENMORE SQ.

Concert flyer, February 1964 [DBA, originally from John Campoli]

FENWAY PARK
SHER-WOOD
Wilson
SLALOM
prince

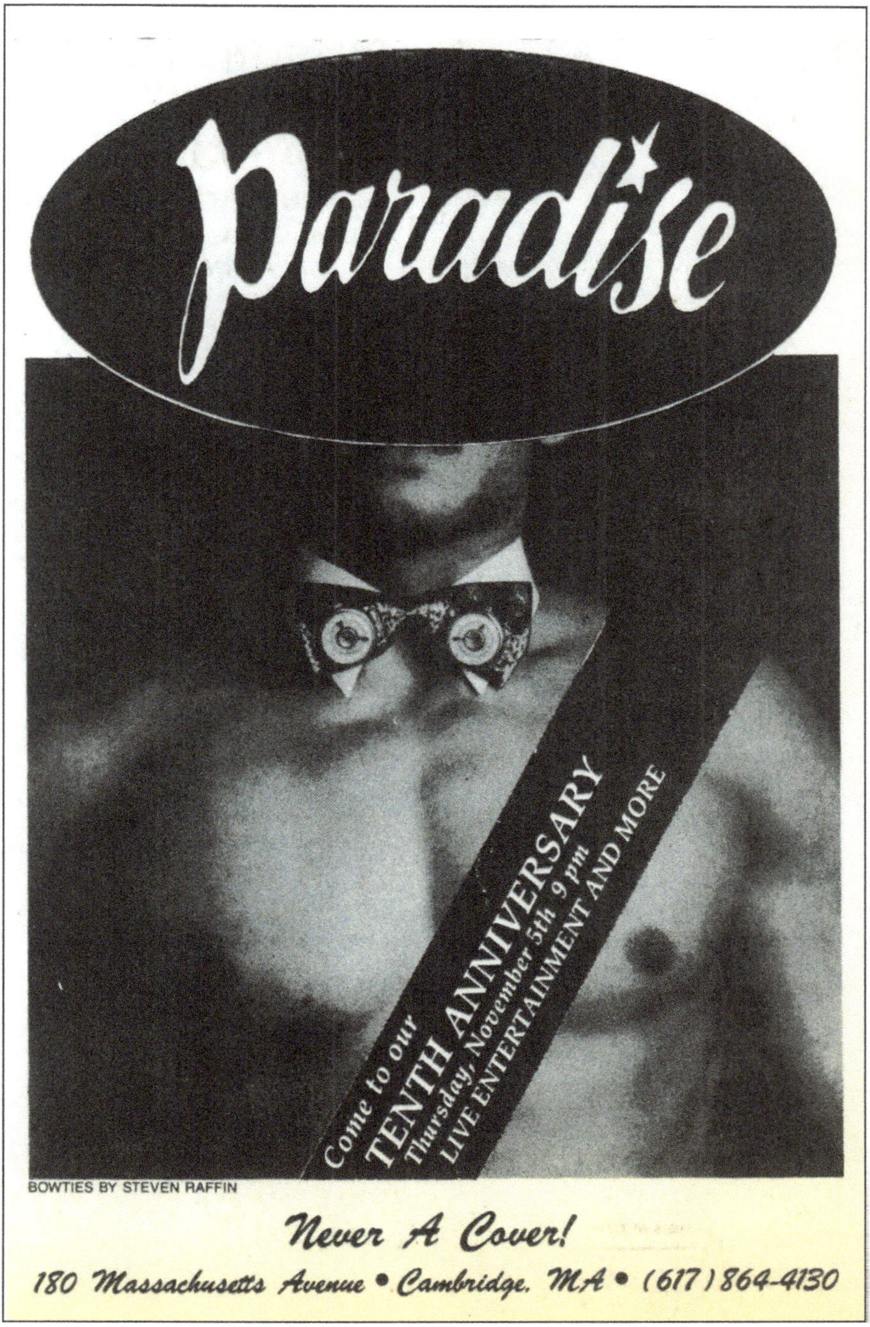
Paradise
Come to our
TENTH ANNIVERSARY
Thursday, November 5th 9 pm
LIVE ENTERTAINMENT AND MORE
BOWTIES BY STEVEN RAFFIN
Never A Cover!
180 Massachusetts Avenue • Cambridge, MA • (617) 864-4130

FACING PAGE: **Red Sox program,** 1987 [BCA]
THIS PAGE: ***Guide To The Gay Northeast,*** November 1987 [BCA]

Cambridge Schools turn kids into
THE UNGRATEFUL DEAD
CHARLES PIERCE
Cambridge School Committee
Paid for the committee to elect Charles Pierce
1

Now Jo-Jo's Room
Presents
Minors Sunday
This Sun. See-Hear-Dance to
The Turning Point
Minors Sunday begins June 4th
open 2-6 pm
admission $1.50
Dance Concert 3pm & 5pm
Show Concert 4 pm
Short order foods prepared in Jo-Jo's kitchen. Soft drinks served
Located at 107 Revere Beach Boulevard across from bandstand
Hosted by Joseph J. Cacciatore

TOP: ***Boston Phoenix***, October 26, 1971 [BCA]
BOTTOM: ***Boston Phoenix,*** August 2, 1972 [BCA]

64
New England
SCOUTING FOR
LOCAL TALENT
TEEN SCENE
The magazine for YOU!
Switch on to . . . New England TEEN SCENE
6 talent-packed issues only $2.10
SUBSCRIBE NOW!
who knows . . .
YOU may be our next feature!
Write to:
6 issues - only $2.10
New England
TEEN SCENE
P. O. Box 67
Boston, Mass. 02112
Name
Age
Address
City
State
Zip Code

New England Teen Scene, March/April 1967 [ELA]

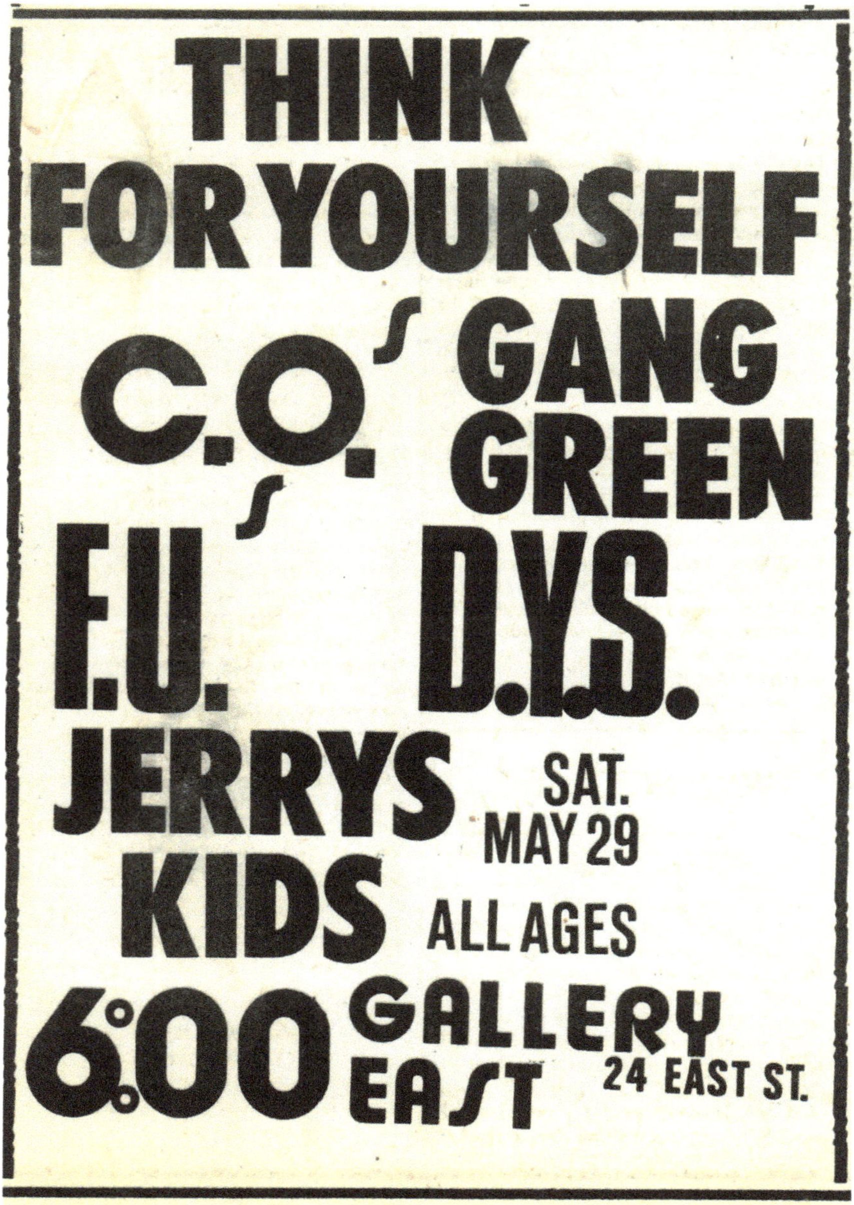
THINK
FOR YOURSELF
C.O.'s
GANG GREEN
F.U.'s
D.Y.S.
JERRYS KIDS
SAT. MAY 29
ALL AGES
6:00
GALLERY EAST
24 EAST ST.

Boston Rock, May 1982 [BCA]

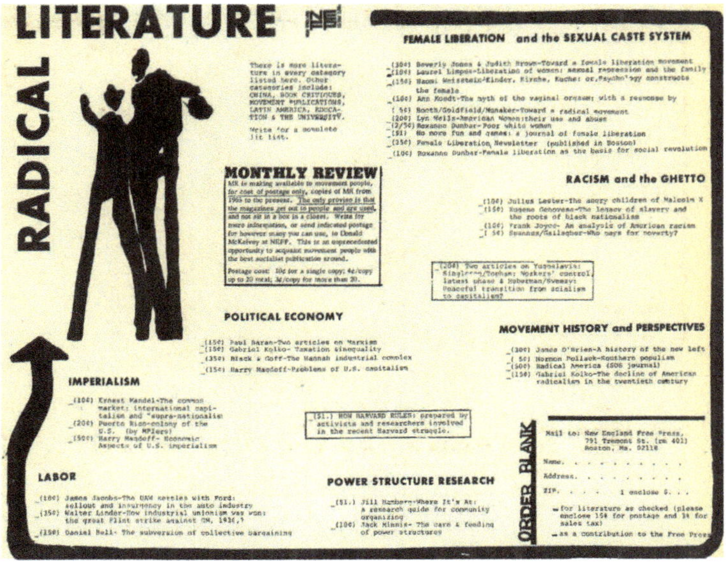
RADICAL LITERATURE
FEMALE LIBERATION and the SEXUAL CASTE SYSTEM
(30¢) Beverly Jones & Judith Brown-Toward a female liberation movement
(10¢) Laurel Limpus-Liberation of women: sexual repression and the family
(15¢) Naomi Weisstein-Kinder, Kirche, Kuche: or, Psychology constructs the female
(10¢) Ann Koedt-The myth of the vaginal orgasm; with a response by
(5¢) Booth/Goldfield/Munaker-Toward a radical movement
(20¢) Lyn Wells-American Women: their use and abuse
(2/5¢) Roxanne Dunbar-Poor white women
($1) No more fun and games: a journal of female liberation
(25¢) Female Liberation Newsletter (published in Boston)
(10¢) Roxanne Dunbar-Female liberation as the basis for social revolution
There is more literature in every category listed here. Other categories include: CHINA, BOOK CRITIQUES, MOVEMENT PUBLICATIONS, LATIN AMERICA, EDUCATION & THE UNIVERSITY.
Write for a complete lit list.
MONTHLY REVIEW
MR is making available to movement people, for cost of postage only, copies of MR from 1965 to the present. The only proviso is that the magazines get out to people and are used, and not sit in a box in a closet. Write for more information, or send indicated postage for however many you can use, to Donald McKelvey at NEFP. This is an unprecedented opportunity to acquaint movement people with the best socialist publication around.
Postage cost: 10¢ for a single copy; 4¢/copy up to 20 total; 3¢/copy for more than 20.
RACISM and the GHETTO
(10¢) Julius Lester-The angry children of Malcolm X
(15¢) Eugene Genovese-The legacy of slavery and the roots of black nationalism
(10¢) Frank Joyce- An analysis of American racism
(5¢) Seannas/Gallagher-Who pays for poverty?
(20¢) Two articles on Yugoslavia: Singleton/Topham: Workers' control, latest phase & Huberman/Sweezy: Peaceful transition from socialism to capitalism?
POLITICAL ECONOMY
(15¢) Paul Baran-Two articles on Marxism
(15¢) Gabriel Kolko- Taxation &inequality
(35¢) Black & Goff-The Hannah industrial complex
(15¢) Harry Magdoff-Problems of U.S. capitalism
MOVEMENT HISTORY and PERSPECTIVES
(30¢) James O'Brien-A history of the new left
(5¢) Norman Pollack-Southern populism
(50¢) Radical America (SDS journal)
(15¢) Gabriel Kolko-The decline of American radicalism in the twentieth century
IMPERIALISM
(10¢) Ernest Mandel-The common market: international capitalism and "supra-nationalism"
(20¢) Puerto Rico-colony of the U.S. (by MPIers)
(50¢) Harry Magdoff- Economic Aspects of U.S. imperialism
($1.) HOW HARVARD RULES: prepared by activists and researchers involved in the recent Harvard struggle.
LABOR
(10¢) James Jacobs-The UAW settles with Ford: sellout and insurgency in the auto industry
(35¢) Walter Linder-How industrial unionism was won: the great Flint strike against GM, 1936,7
(15¢) Daniel Bell- The subversion of collective bargaining
POWER STRUCTURE RESEARCH
($1.) Jill Hamberg-Where It's At: A research guide for community organizing
(10¢) Jack Minnis- The care & feeding of power structures
ORDER BLANK
Mail to: New England Free Press, 791 Tremont St. (rm 401) Boston, Ma. 02118
Name. . . . .
Address. . . . .
ZIP. . . . I enclose $. . .
for literature as checked (please enclose 15¢ for postage and 3% for sales tax)
as a contribution to the Free Press

Filene's Automatic Bargain BASEMENT
SATURDAY AT 9:30 A.M. — CLOSEOUTS OR IRREGULARS — MANY PERMANENT PRESS
BOYS' NEW OFF-PRICE SUMMER CAMP PLAY CLOTHES
$2 to $6.99
• POLO SHIRTS
• SWIM TRUNKS
• DUNGAREES
• JEANS
• PANTS
• SHORTS
• PAJAMAS
• JACKETS
SIZES 8 to 20 or SMALL, MEDIUM, LARGE.
SOME SLIMS OR HUSKIES IN THE COLLECTION.
OUR AUTOMATIC PLAN —First prices must be at least 10% LOWER than competition. We lose through automatic reductions of 25% after 12 selling days, 50% after 18 selling days, 75% after 24 selling days. Goods unsold after 30 selling days given away to charitable institutions.

TOP: ***Old Mole,*** June 20, 1969 [DBA]

BOTTOM: ***Boston Record American,*** May 13, 1972 [BCA]

Only Boston area appearance this season
our own
TOM RUSH
IN CONCERT
Saturday, January 15th 8:30 P.M.
Tickets: $2.50, $3.50, $4.00
TICKETS AVAILABLE AT:
Club 47, Harvard Square, Cambridge
Jordan Hall, Box Office, Boston
and Ticket Agencies
BY MAIL ORDER TO:
Jordan Hall
30 Gainsboro Street
Boston, Massachusetts
JORDAN HALL
BOSTON

Club 47 calendar flyer, December 1965 [VALDEZ]

A-8313
B-8312
C-8314
sweater stitch knits make the day! Coloray® Rayon by Rawson Square
13.00
Always ready to go, these knit dresses have a great daytime look. The fabric is all Coloray® Rayon, to stay in shape and resist wrinkles. Sizes 10-20, 14½-22½.
A-8313) "A" line skimmer with zip back. Blue or green.
B-8312) Coat skimmer. Patch pockets. Fudge or blue.
C-8314) Zip front skimmer. Green or fudge.
JORDAN MARSH
DAYTIME DRESSES—FOURTH FLOOR—MAIN STORE
Available in our Boston Store. A representative selection also available in our Branch Stores in Framingham, Malden, Peabody, Braintree, Burlington, Bedford, N.H., So. Portland, Me., and Warwick, R.I.
20—PICTORIAL LIVING COLOROTO MAGAZINE, October 11, 1970
Please add 60c handling charge for delivery outside our normal delivery area.
JORDAN MARSH COMPANY
Box 191, Boston, Mass. 02101
MAIL THIS COUPON TODAY or phone any number listed below, any hour, day or night. In Metropolitan Boston Area, call 221-3131.
SUBURBANITES: Call (Peabody) 531-9000; (Lynn) 5[illegible]9-5000; (Brockton) 583-8640; (Lawrence) 687-7156; (Worcester) 7[illegible]6-6247; (Rockland) 878-7831; (Haverhill) 374-7425; (Framingham) 879-0100; (New Bedford) Enterprise 7250; (Concord) 369-3728 (Lowell) 458-6866.
In New Hampshire Call:
(Manchester) 669-4200; (Nashua) 889-6116; (Concord) 2[illegible]4-7769; (Peterborough) 924-3357; (Exeter) 772-4755.
In Warwick, R.I. Area Call: 738-9400
In So. Portland, Me. Area Call: 775-5431
Please send Rawson Square dresses @ 13.00
SA-190-10 11-70
Quan. | Style # | Size | Color | 2nd Color | Price
Name
Street
City State Zip #
CHARGE TO MY ACCOUNT NO.
OR I ENCLOSE A CHECK ☐ OR MONEY ORDER ☐
SEND CHARGE ACCOUNT APPLICATION ☐
Add State Sales Tax Where Applicable

Boston Sunday Advertiser, October 11, 1970 [BCA]

GALA! ★★★★★★ GALA! ★★★★★★ GALA!
Emperors & Woodchoppers Present A
New Year's Eve Cabaret
HYNES AUDITORIUM
(PRUDENTIAL CENTER)
MON. DEC. 31
FEATURING THE
DYNAMIC SOUNDS OF
AURA
(Formerly RYTHM)
RCA Recording Artists
And The Electrifying Funk Of
HAWKEYE
DISCO PROVIDED BY
UNLIMITED SOUNDS
GUESTS M.C.'s FROM MAGIC 109 (W.I.L.D.)
THE SEVENTH SON AND BUTTERBALL JR.
9 p.m. 3 a.m. — Reserve Tables Available — $15.00 Admission
TICKETS ON SALE AT ALL NUBIAN NOTION STORES, HORTON BROTHERS 427-8751, BROTHER LORD'S MUSIC 436-9207,
COLONIAL LOUNGE 427-9130 OR CALL JACQUI 442-9500, ABE 298-9472, RICHIE 296-5659

Concert poster, December 1978 [DBA]

ROCK
WCVB5TV
BOSTON METROMEDIA
METRO
A WORLD OF DIFFERENCE
104 FM
WBCN
AGAINST
RACISM

"A World Of Difference" event poster, July 26, 1985 [DBA]

JAMES BROWN
JAMES BROWN
JAMES BROWN
JAMES BROWN
JAMES BROWN
JAMES BROWN
The LIVING LEGEND
at the SUGAR SHACK
JANUARY 14 - 19
For more information call
the SUGAR SHACK
426-0068
TICKET PRICES
Thurs - Sun $6.00
Mon & Tues $5.00

01258
SEC ROW SEAT
GEN. ADM.
JULY 30. 1980
HARVARD SQUARE TALENT CORP. Presents
JAMES BROWN
& HIS REVUE
THE BRADFORD HOTEL
JULY
30
1980
BOSTON, MA
WEDNESDAY
8:00 P.M.
THIS TICKET GOOD FOR 8:00 PM SHOW ONLY
$10.00
ADVANCE
GEN. ADM.
01258
JAMES BROWN
ADVANCE
$10.00
JULY 30–8 PM

TOP: **Concert poster,** January 1971 [Found online]
BOTTOM: **Concert ticket,** July 1980 [BCA]

THE
MODERN
LOVERS!
FRIDAY & SATURDAY
JANUARY 12&13 9PM
stone phoenix coffeehouse
1120 BOYLSTON ST. BOSTON
523-9168

Concert flyer, January 1973 [LOCO]

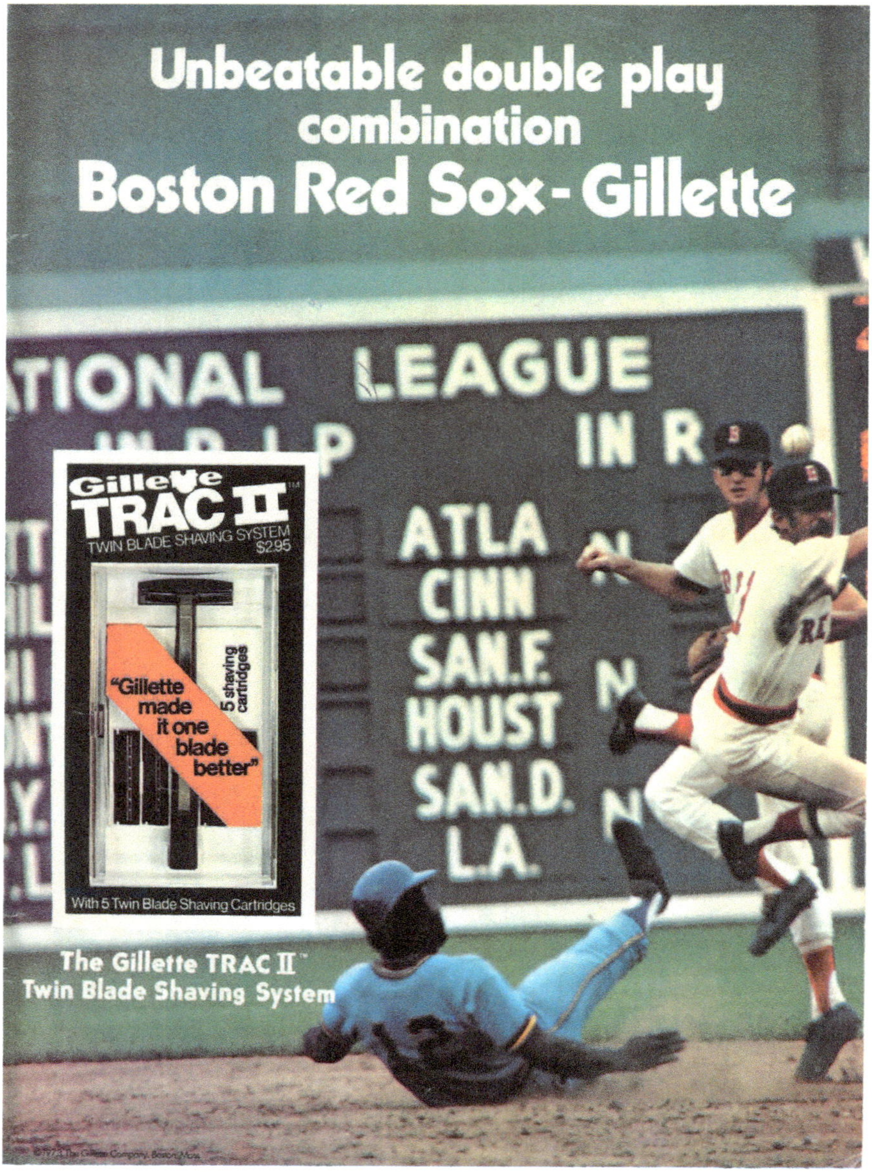
Unbeatable double play combination
Boston Red Sox - Gillette
NATIONAL LEAGUE
IN R
ATLA
CINN
SAN.F.
HOUST
SAN.D.
L.A.
Gillette
TRAC II
TWIN BLADE SHAVING SYSTEM
$2.95
"Gillette made it one blade better"
5 shaving cartridges
With 5 Twin Blade Shaving Cartridges
The Gillette TRAC II Twin Blade Shaving System

Red Sox Scorebook, 1973 season [BCA]

YOUR
SEAT
ON THE
50 YARD LINE
CBS
WEEI-590
Boston
PATRIOTS
BOSTON COLL
BRENDA FLAVIN,
A Carol Nashe Model
WITH BOB GALLAGHER AND FRED CUSICK
COMPLETE 1962 FOOTBALL SCHEDULES
BOSTON PATRIOTS • BOSTON COLLEGE
WEEI-590
CBS / RADIO, BOSTON
BOSTON COLLEGE • Sponsored by PHILLIPS "66" DEALERS
BOSTON PATRIOTS • Sponsored by ZAYRE DEPARTMENT STORES, LINCOLN-MERCURY DEALERS OF NEW ENGLAND

Boston College football program, October 27, 1962 [BCA]

LE PAPILLON
Boston's International Nightclub
The Fashion. The Touch. The Sensation. An Explosion of Color and Sound.
Wednesday — Saturday, Valet garage parking available
In The Back Bay Hilton, 40 Dalton St., Boston, 236-1100

EAROS WRKO 68

TOP: ***Boston Magazine*** (design by Caryn Hirsch), August 1987 [DBA]
BOTTOM: ***Boston After Dark,*** May 2, 1972 [DBA]

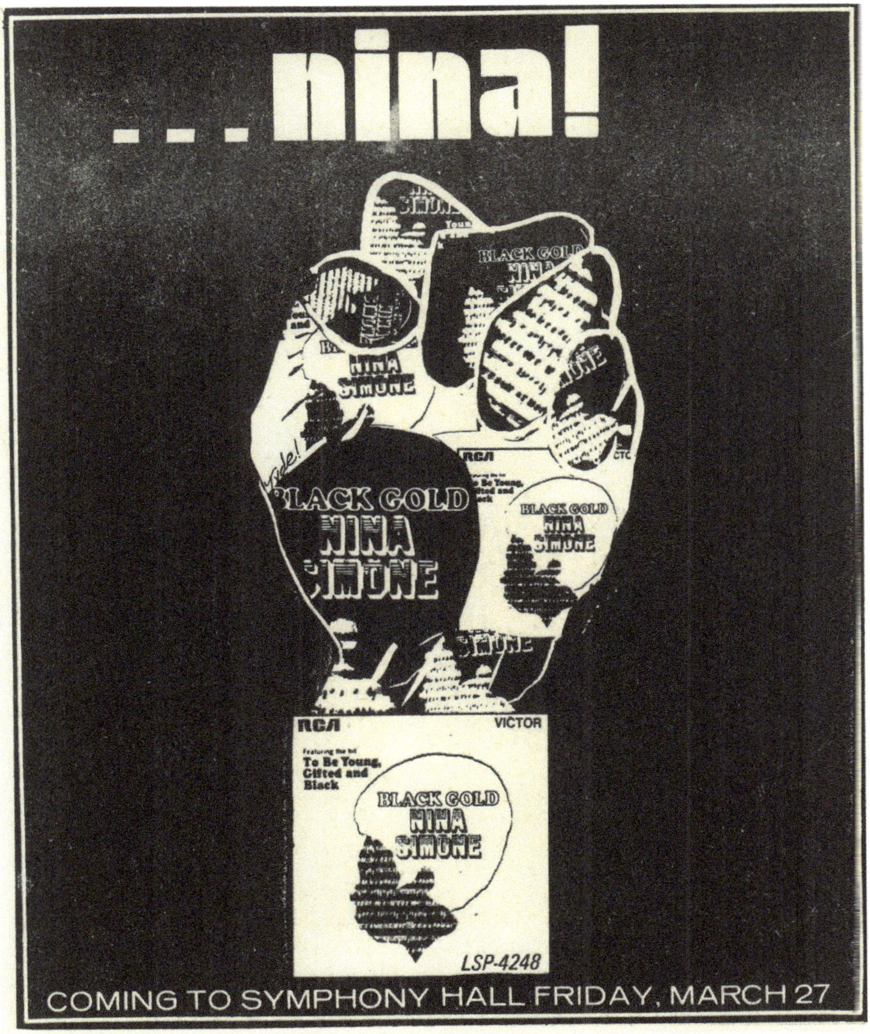
. . . nina!
BLACK GOLD
NINA
SIMONE
RCA
VICTOR
Featuring the hit
To Be Young, Gifted and Black
BLACK GOLD
NINA
SIMONE
LSP-4248
COMING TO SYMPHONY HALL FRIDAY, MARCH 27

Boston After Dark, March 18, 1970 [DBA]

Boston Beatmakers
RACHEL J. TANZER
Writer/Producer
Six Arbor Court
Peabody, MA 01960
Phone (617) 531-4931
Boston Beatmakers, Inc.
FAST TRACK
RECORDS
89 Massachusetts Avenue
Suite 193
Boston, Massachusetts 02115
mickey o'halloran
(617) 254-9820
THE PROJECT
"Boston Rock 'N' Roll Encyclopedia"
Please send Bio's Resumes, Vinyl
1954 - Present!
89 Mass. Ave., Suite 193
Boston, MA 02115
c/o Mickey Ohalloran
JOYCE LINEHAN
creative artist management
p. o. b o x 12
brookline,mass. 02146
(617) 436·7209
JOYCE LINEHAN
creative promotion
artist management
p. o. box 435
kenmore station
boston,mass. 02215
617 · 436 · 7209
MANAGEMENT
BOOKING
PROMOTION
PUBLICITY
MAVERICK
P.O. BOX 435 • KENMORE STATION
BOSTON, MA 02215 • (617) 437-0684
MANAGEMENT
BOOKING
PROMOTION
PUBLICITY
MAVERICK
Tom Johnston
P.O. BOX 435 • KENMORE STATION
BOSTON, MA 02215 • (617) 437-0684
BIG MOUTH ENTERTAINMENT
JANE GULICK
443 ALBANY ST. • BOSTON, MA • 02118-2506
PH: 617-695-9104 • FAX: 617-338-1466
EVIL, INC.
JANE GULICK
89 BEACON ST. • SOMERVILLE, MA • 02143 • 617-661-7040
C-LINE #61217
BUSINESS CARD

Chuck White Business Card Collection, 1980s–1990s [CWA/DBA]

COME HERE
ZION
INITATION
#1 REGGAE BAND
AT
WESTERN FRONT
343 WESTERN AVE. CAMBRIDGE
FRI., & SAT., SEPTEMBER 11 & 12
YUH RIGHT! ZION A DE LION!
DON'T MISS DIS REGGAE TREAT
KOME WITH LOVE!
INFO:- 427-3813 ... 492-7772

Concert flyer, September 1981
[***Take Us Home*** liner notes book, Cultures of Soul Records]

a 45 called
KEROUAC
by Willie Alexander
BUY EM AT: the RECORD GARAGE 12A ELLIOT Harvard SQ
the RECORD GARAGE 12A ELLIOT st HARVARD SQ.
by Willie Alexander
A.G. PHOTO PRODUCED BY STEPHAN LOVELACE + JACK GRIFFIN for LOCO 75
B/W
MASS AVE
WILLIE ALEXANDER %GARAGERECORDS BOX308
NEWTONVILLE, MASS 02160

Single release flyer, Summer 1975 [LOCO]

IT'S A BUSINESS DOING PLEASURE WITH YOU
526 Leathers
526 Tremont Street, Boston
Hours: Tuesday thru Friday—4:30 to 9:00 pm
Saturday—Noon to 8:00 pm
451-0194

TAPES
THE SUPERSTARS SWING ON COMPACT, LIVELY TAPES & 8-TRACK CASSETTES
1.67 ea.
Original Mfg's. list 6.98
• The Association
• Ike & Tina Turner
• Rod McKuen
• Dean Martin
• Vogues
• Everly Bros.
• First Editions
• Crazy Horse
• Frank Sinatra
• John B. Sebastian
• Young Bloods
• Trini Lopez
• Mason Williams
• Peter, Paul & Mary
• The Kinks
• Paul Stookey
• Bill Cosby
• Sammy Davis
• Mothers of Invention
• Don Ho
• Tom Paxton
• Beach Boys
• Tim Buckley
• plus many, many more with great sounds . . . from the soothing to sunshine superstars!
Some artists not available on both tape & cassette.
J.M. FIELDS
451 FELLSWAY WELLINGTON CIRCLE MEDFORD
STORE HOURS: DAILY 10 A.M. TO 10 P.M.
• BANKAMERICARD
• MASTER CHARGE
• J.M. FIELDS CREDIT CARD

TOP: ***Hit Parade of Boston,*** April 1980 [DBA]
BOTTOM: ***Somerville Journal,*** January 25, 1973 [BCA]

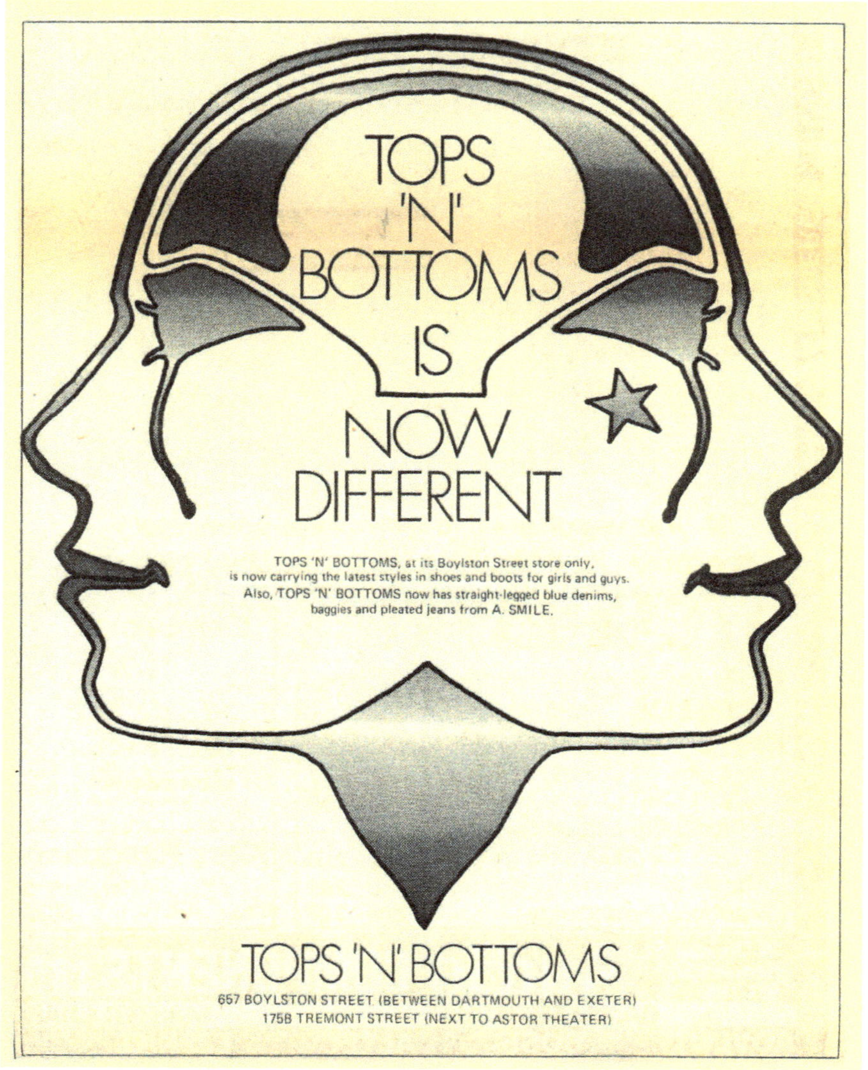
TOPS 'N' BOTTOMS IS NOW DIFFERENT
TOPS 'N' BOTTOMS, at its Boylston Street store only, is now carrying the latest styles in shoes and boots for girls and guys. Also, TOPS 'N' BOTTOMS now has straight-legged blue denims, baggies and pleated jeans from A. SMILE.
TOPS 'N' BOTTOMS
657 BOYLSTON STREET (BETWEEN DARTMOUTH AND EXETER)
175B TREMONT STREET (NEXT TO ASTOR THEATER)

Boston Phoenix, January 26, 1972 [BCA]

Boston Daughters of Bilitis

Invites the Women of Boston

To Its Birthday Party!

We are five years old!
9:00 pm at The Saints
Come help us celebrate:
dancing, refreshments
and homemade birthday cake

Sunday, Dec. 8, 1974

WHITCH
WHITCH
WHITCH
WHITCH
WHITCH
WHITCHWHITCH

THE All Women's Rock Band

WENDY
KAREN
MERRY
KAREN

For Booking Information
Call ELAINE 289-8363

WHITCH

MEDICAL PROBLEMS?

Come to...

GAY HEALTH NIGHT

at Fenway Community
Health Center
16 Haviland St.
Boston, Mass.
Phone: 267-7573

Every Wednesday
6:30-9:30 pm
for Medical help (inc. VD)
for Gay women & men
Co-sponsored by H.C.H.S.
266-5477

Focus: A Journal For Gay Women, December 1974 [THP]

"YOUR MOTHER'S ON THE ROOF"
The Television Show
Hosted by Cha-Chi Loprete and John O'Neill
Featuring the Best Bands in Boston
"Hiding in Public"
"Happy Campers"
"Motor City Kings"
"The Premiers"
"The Down Staircase"
"G.G. Turner"
Produced by Linda Eppich at Cablevision in Norwood
Check local listings for exact channels & times
CABLEVISION

Me&Lee
Lee
Flight Jacket
and Slacks
Step into adventure with the Lee Flight Jacket. Angular pockets and classic colors are matched in the Lee Flight Slack. Both are 50% polyester, 50% Cotton Twill and Lee Prest. An experience in comfort and style.
Lee Flight Jacket – sizes: 36 – 44 $37.50
Lee Flight Slack – sizes: S, M, L, XL waist 29 – 38 $16.
Headquarters for LEE jeans, jackets and western shirts.
NOBBY'S
APPAREL FOR MEN
151 HARVARD AVE. ALLSTON
267 HARVARD ST. BROOKLINE

TOP: ***The Beat,*** December 21, 1989 [DBA]
BOTTOM: ***Real Paper,*** September 18, 1974 [BCA]

2nd ANNUAL
NIGHTFALL MAGAZINE
DISCO AWARDS PRESENTATION
M.C. JOHN LUONGO
publisher NIGHTFALL MAGAZINE
GUEST HOST:
Sonny Joe White—WILD
Ron Robin — WVBF
Best Foreign record (Sunshine Love)
Performances will be by some of the top artists
(schedule and names announced in Feb. NF.)
Top Celeberaties will present awards for:
Best Male Artist
Best Female Artist
Best Instrumental Artist
Best New Group
Best LP
Best 45
Best Label
For advance reservations
call 723-3768 (Arnie)
389-9300 (Fred)
Tickets $5.00 in advance) $7.00 at the door
First come 1st serve—1,500 max.
Proceddings will be held at the
Grand Ballroom of the Sheraton Boston Hotel Prudential Center
Boston Ma February 13, 1976 (Sunday)

Nightfall, January 1977 [DBA]

Paul's Mall
NOW THRU SUN.
First U.S. appearance . . .
THE WAILERS
Explosive Jamaican "Reggae" Sound "Catch a Fire" on Island Records
plus extra special guests
Fri. thru Sun. (July 13-15)
PROCTOR & BERGMAN
formerly with Firesign Theatre "TV or not TV" on Columbia Records July 16-22 MASON PROFFIT
733 Boylston St. — 267-1300
Jazz Workshop
NOW THRU SUN.
the electrifying
EDDIE HARRIS
"Excursions" on Atlantic
SUN. MAT. 4-7
Coming July 16-22
GARY BURTON

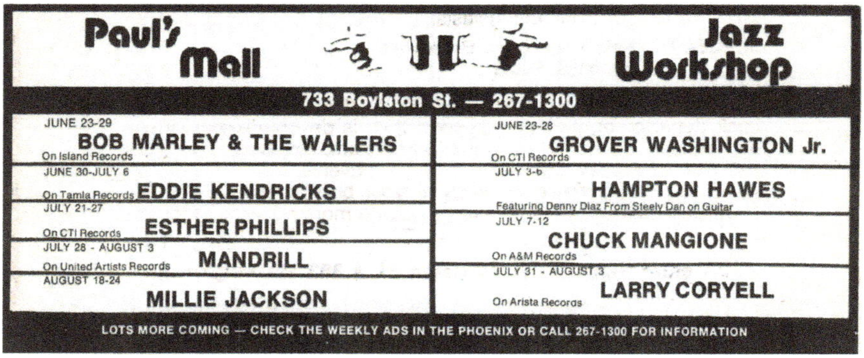
Paul's Mall
Jazz Workshop
733 Boylston St. — 267-1300
JUNE 23-29
BOB MARLEY & THE WAILERS
On Island Records
JUNE 30-JULY 6
On Tamla Records EDDIE KENDRICKS
JULY 21-27
On CTI Records ESTHER PHILLIPS
JULY 28 - AUGUST 3
On United Artists Records MANDRILL
AUGUST 18-24
MILLIE JACKSON
JUNE 23-28
GROVER WASHINGTON Jr.
On CTI Records
JULY 3-6
HAMPTON HAWES
Featuring Denny Diaz From Steely Dan on Guitar
JULY 7-12
CHUCK MANGIONE
On A&M Records
JULY 31 - AUGUST 3
On Arista Records LARRY CORYELL
LOTS MORE COMING — CHECK THE WEEKLY ADS IN THE PHOENIX OR CALL 267-1300 FOR INFORMATION

TOP: ***Real Paper,*** July 11, 1973 [DBA]
BOTTOM: ***Boston Phoenix,*** June 24, 1975 [DBA]

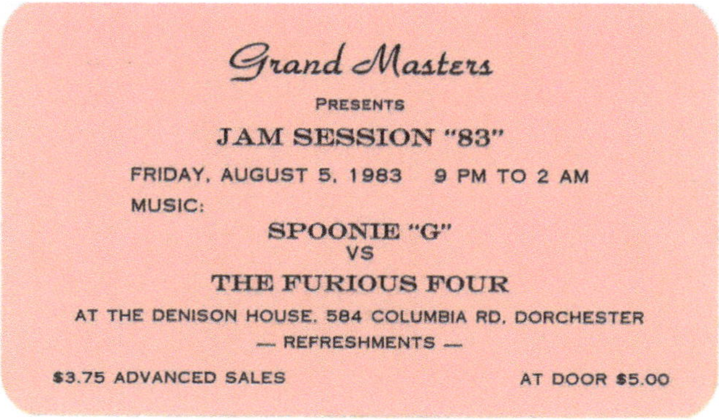
Grand Masters
PRESENTS
JAM SESSION "83"
FRIDAY, AUGUST 5, 1983 9 PM TO 2 AM
MUSIC:
SPOONIE "G"
VS
THE FURIOUS FOUR
AT THE DENISON HOUSE, 584 COLUMBIA RD, DORCHESTER
— REFRESHMENTS —
$3.75 ADVANCED SALES
AT DOOR $5.00

INSPECTA WILLIE
• PRESENTS •
RAGAMUFFIN HIP HOP '89
DIRECT FROM N.Y.C.
ELEKTRA RECORDING ARTIST
SHINEHEAD
CHAIN GANG-RAP
HELLO Y'ALL
AUDIOPHILE
* ALONG WITH BOSTON'S OWN
T.I.C. AND THE CHOICE dancers *
PETER RIGHTEOUS
MUSIC BY:
WALLACE T. FROM wrbb
EVERTONE HI-POWER
SATURDAY
JAN-21-1989
•WINDSOR CRICKET CLUB•
321 TALBOT AV.
dorchester
admission : $ 15

TOP: **Concert ticket,** August 1983 [BCA, acquired from In Your Ear Records]
BOTTOM: **Concert poster** (by Rob Stull), January 1989 [Rob Stull & MHHA]

The Composé
for Fall 1977
(The inimitable Composé look, originally introduced by Mr. Sid, has been redefined for the fall season.)
Ermenegildo Zegna, Italy's foremost designer, has created expressly for Mr. Sid the Composé look for fall 1977.
It is for the gentleman who appreciates and can afford the very finest in men's clothing.
The Zegna look in Composé, suitings or sportcoats is quite possibly the most distinctive clothing you will ever own.
Unmistakably,
mr. Sid
NEWTON CENTRE

Boston Magazine, September 1977 [DBA]

BAPTIST

BOSTON

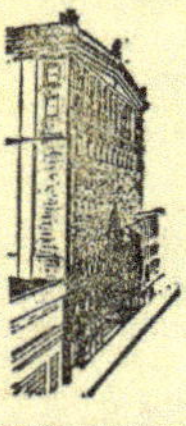

Tremont Temple

Boston's Downtown Baptist Church
next to Parker House
Dr. A. Paterson Lee, Pastor
On the air every Sunday at 11:00 a.m., WRYT, 950 KC.
9:30 a.m. Family Bible School
HEAR
DR. DANIEL WEISS
10:45 a.m. Morning Worship
6:45 p.m. Evening Service
Air-Conditioned auditorium
Programa En Espanol—Domingo, 12:15 p.m. Culto de predicacion

RUGGLES ST. BAPTIST CHURCH

Ruggles St., Boston

SUNDAY, JULY 27th
10:30 A.M.
"THE TIME IS NOW"
Dr. Donald Ewing
Preaching
6:30 P.M.
MR. BLAIR RICHARDSON
Former Middleweight Boxing Champion of Canada and British Empire

RADIO: Sunday Morning Worship WEZE (1260) 8:30 A.M. to 9:00 A.M.

PARKING: Large off-the-street parking lot at the rear of the church under the supervision of Boston Police Dept.

First Baptist Church of Boston

Founded 1665
Commonwealth Ave. at Clarendon St.
REV. CHARLES W. GRIFFIN
11:00 A.M. Sermon
"GOD'S BEST REMEMBERED WORD"
Wednesday 6:00 P.M.
Summer Supper Program

NEWTON

First Baptist Church In Newton

corner Beacon and Centre Streets
Newton Centre
10:00 A.M. *Morning* Worship and Church School
(Infant Care)
DR. CHARLES L. SEASHOLES
Interim Minister
"EXPOSING GOOD"

CHRISTIAN SCIENCE

Christian Science Services

10:45 A.M. SUNDAY
10:45 A.M. SUNDAY SCHOOL
WEDNESDAY 7:30 P.M.
Free parking, Westland and Massachusetts Avenues
Child Care Facilities Available

The First Church of Christ, Scientist
Boston
Falmouth and Norway Streets

CONGREGATIONALIST

BOSTON

Park Street Church

Home of "America" on Boston Common
1809—1969
Dr. Paul E. Toms, Minister

10:30 A.M. & 7:30 P.M.
Dr. C. Ralston Smith
Washington, D.C.
A Cordial Welcome to All

SUNDAY BROADCASTS
WHDH 7:35 A.M.
WCOP 10:30 A.M.
WCOP-FM 7:30 P.M.
WEZE 10:45 A.M.-7:30 P.M.
THURSDAY TELECAST
WHDH-TV (Ch. 5) 6:45 P.M.

300th ANNIVERSARY YEAR

Old South Church

COPLEY SQUARE
Dr. Frederick M. Meek, Minister
11 A.M. MORNING WORSHIP
Sermon by
Rev. Louis C. Toppan
"RESPONSIBLE WORSHIP"
Nursery Care Provided for Children during the Service

Covenant Congregational Church

455 ARBORWAY, BOSTON
Richard J. Swanson, Minister
10:00 A.M.
Morning Worship Service
"THE LIFTING POWER OF PURPOSE"
Dial-A-Message 524-3133

PRESBYTERIAN

THE UNITED PRESBYTERIAN CHURCH

Park and Vernon Streets, Newton
10:00 A.M. DR. JAMES FORRESTER
7:00 P.M. "ARE YOU A 97 LB. WEAKLING?"
Nurseries provided at all services
Burton S. Smith, Pastor
Norman Curtis, Minister of Music
Leonore Curtis, Soloist

NOTICE

PHILOSOPHICAL THEOLOGICAL

Discussion Group Forming! If interested in this or other Philosophical-Theological activities, write Philosophical-Theological Society, P.O. Box 1371, Boston 02104.

NON-SECTARIAN

BOSTON UNIVERSITY MARSH CHAPEL

Worship Service 11 A.M.
SERMON:
"CHRISTIANS HAVE NO MONOPOLY OF LOVE."
DR. JOSEPH FLETCHER
Prof. of Christian Social Ethics of the Episcopal Theological School of Cambridge

Boston Herald Traveler, July 25, 1969 [BCA]

HUBBA
HUBBA
スのリ
DRESSING LIKE THERE'S NO TOMORROW. 960 MASS AVE, CAMBRIDGE. MON-SAT 11-6. Tel 492-9082.
PERFORMANCE AT MAN RAY, THURS OCT 24, WITH DIVINE, BOYS SAY GO, FETISH FASHIONS FROM HUBBA-HUBBA WITH RUBBER AND LEATHER FROM PURE SEX, LONDON

The Noise, November 1985 [DBA]

MINUTEMEN
SORRY
SUNDAY • APRIL 21
$5/6 • DOORS 4:00
ALL AGES
CHANNEL

Concert flyer, April 1985 [Courtesy of Peter Prescott]

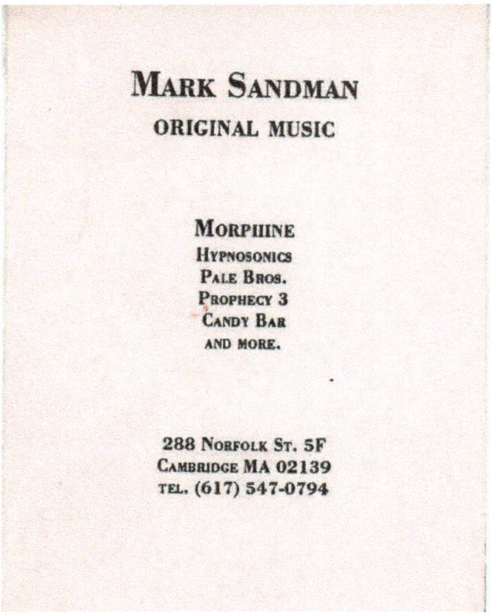
MARK SANDMAN
ORIGINAL MUSIC
MORPHINE
HYPNOSONICS
PALE BROS.
PROPHECY 3
CANDY BAR
AND MORE.
288 NORFOLK ST. 5F
CAMBRIDGE MA 02139
TEL. (617) 547-0794

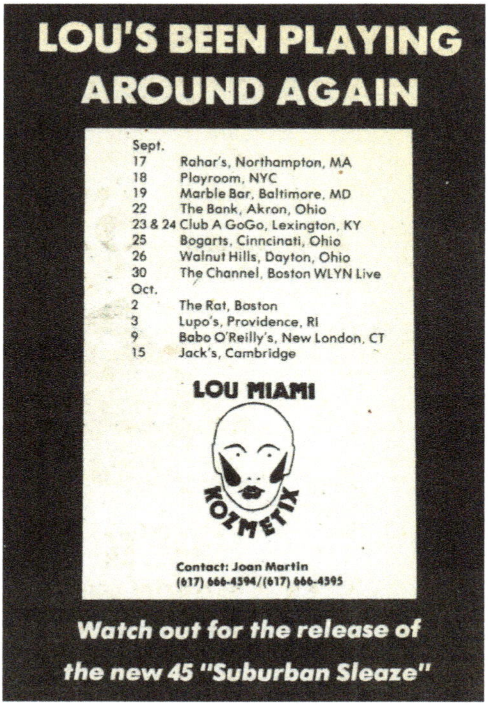
LOU'S BEEN PLAYING AROUND AGAIN
Sept.
17 Rahar's, Northampton, MA
18 Playroom, NYC
19 Marble Bar, Baltimore, MD
22 The Bank, Akron, Ohio
23 & 24 Club A GoGo, Lexington, KY
25 Bogarts, Cinncinati, Ohio
26 Walnut Hills, Dayton, Ohio
30 The Channel, Boston WLYN Live
Oct.
2 The Rat, Boston
3 Lupo's, Providence, RI
9 Babo O'Reilly's, New London, CT
15 Jack's, Cambridge
LOU MIAMI
KOZMETIX
Contact: Joan Martin
(617) 666-4594/(617) 666-4595
Watch out for the release of the new 45 "Suburban Sleaze"

TOP: **Calling card,** early to mid-1990s [RIVARD]
BOTTOM: ***Boston Rock,*** October 1981 [DBA]

A CHILLING SATANIC OVERVIBE
X-MEMBERS
OF
KILSLUG
AND FROM
DINOSAUR JR.
J. MASCIS
J MASCIS APPEARS ON DRUMS COURTESY OF BLANCO Y NEGRO / WEA RECORDS

DENNIS BROWN
LLOYD PARKS & WE THE PEOPLE
ZION INITATION
Special Guest
PRINCE MOHAMMED
M.C. ELROY R.C. SMITH
Saturday July 25 9 pm
BRADFORD BALLROOM
275 TREMONT ST BOSTON
TICKETS Advance $8.00
Day of Show $9.00
AVAILABLE AT: STRAWBERRIES — MUSIC CITY, Kenmore Sq. — SCORPIO RECORDS, Dorchester — OUT OF TOWN — MOUKASSA RECORDS — BRADFORD HOTEL — NEWBURY COMICS — MONTEGO BAY IMPORTS

TOP: **Promotional sticker,** 1991 [DBA]
BOTTOM: ***Boston Phoenix,*** July 21, 1981 [DBA]

wcrb 102.5 fm
24-hour Classical Music

Boston Magazine, December 1980 [DBA]

November 19-20-21
Fri. & Sat. 10am-9pm
Sun. 10am-6pm
Information & free directory at
Salamandra Glass
143 Market St. Portsmouth, N.H.
leather jewelry stained glass
furniture weaving blown glass
embroidery porcelain stoneware
Boston Black Repertory Company
presents the world premiere musical
THERE'S A STRUGGLE GOING ON!
Three weeks of laughing, singing, dancing & crying
Nov. 12 thru Dec. 5 at St. Alphonse Hall
1545 Tremont St. Bost. 427-9292
Tickets: Wed., Thurs., Sun. 8pm $5.50; Fri. & Sat. 8pm $6.50; Sun. Mat. 2pm $4.50
Boston University
School for the Arts
Norman Dello Joio, Dean
855 Commonwealth Ave.,
Boston 02215/353-3345
November 17, 18, 19, 20 — 8:00 P.M.
Jean Genet
THE BALCONY
William Young, Director
Boston University Theatre
264 Huntington Avenue
(across from Symphony Hall)
Tickets: $4, $3, $2
Students, Senior Citizens $2
Box Office: 353-3392
Information: 353-3345
School of Theatre Arts
Mouzon Law, Director
claude kipnis
mime theatre
"Bravos, laughter and people filled the house all evening." —The New York Times
Performing at BRANDEIS UNIVERSITY'S
SPINGOLD THEATER
November 17 - 21
CALL 894-4343 FOR INFORMATION
LIVE, IN CONCERT
BARRY MANILOW
FEATURING:
Lady Flash
SAT. NOV. 20 • 8P.M.
SUN. NOV. 21 • 8 P.M.
MUSIC HALL THEATRE
BOX OFFICE NOW OPEN
PRICES $8.00, $7.00, $6.00

Boston Phoenix, November 16, 1976 [BCA]

FEEL LIKE A NEW PEACE OUTFIT?
PATCH WORK KNIT BY
Leeds
BOSTON, MASS.
280 Boylston St

NARRAGANSETT BREWING COMPANY
Proudly Presents
LED ZEPPELIN
With the MC-5 and Extra ✪ Attraction
JOHNNY WINTER
SATURDAY OCTOBER 25 8:00 P.M.
BOSTON GARDEN, North Sta. Bos. 02114
Tickets-$3.50, $4.50, $5.50
Boston Garden by mail or at box office, with this ad
also Krackerjacks, and Headquarters East,
and on all college campuses.
Produced by Robert Chernov for the Narragansett BREWING COMPANY
Boston Garden, North Station, Boston, Mass. 02114
Enclosed is Check M.O.
TOTALING $ .... FOR
........TICKETS AT $........EACH
NAME
STREET
CITY
STATE .... ZIP ....

LEFT: ***Boston After Dark,*** November 12, 1969 [DBA]
RIGHT: ***Boston After Dark,*** October 22, 1969 [DBA]

TOP OF THE WORLD PRODUCTIONS
present
Cabaret Dance & Show
featuring . . . RUDY RAY MOORE
LITTLE SCOTTY ★ KIM TAYLOR
Saturday, JANUARY 26, 1980 — 9:00 p.m. until
CARVER AUDITORIUM
80 Talbot Avenue — Dorchester, Mass.
Packages allowed — Set-ups available
Advance Ticket: $9.00
№ 154

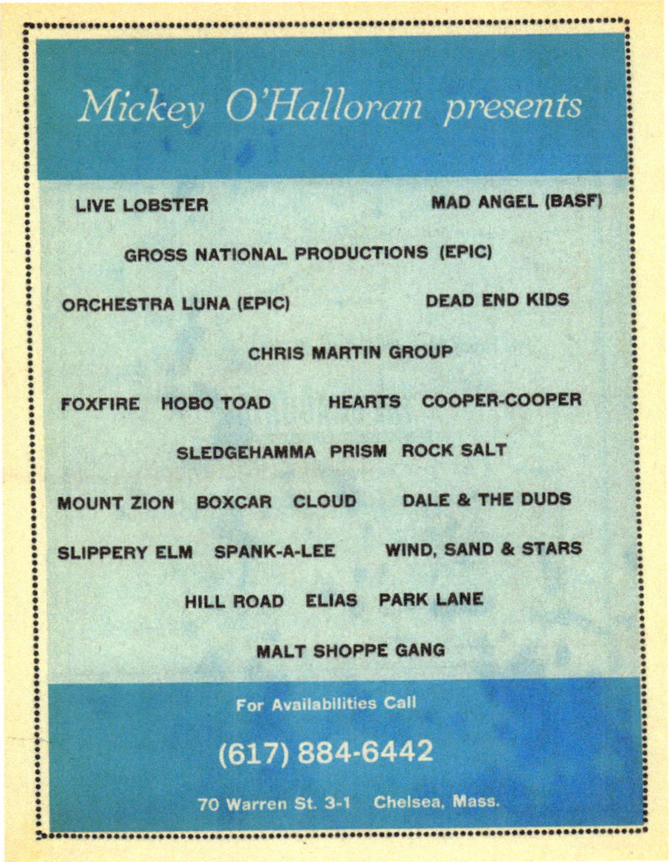
Mickey O'Halloran presents
LIVE LOBSTER
MAD ANGEL (BASF)
GROSS NATIONAL PRODUCTIONS (EPIC)
ORCHESTRA LUNA (EPIC)
DEAD END KIDS
CHRIS MARTIN GROUP
FOXFIRE HOBO TOAD HEARTS COOPER-COOPER
SLEDGEHAMMA PRISM ROCK SALT
MOUNT ZION BOXCAR CLOUD DALE & THE DUDS
SLIPPERY ELM SPANK-A-LEE WIND, SAND & STARS
HILL ROAD ELIAS PARK LANE
MALT SHOPPE GANG
For Availabilities Call
(617) 884-6442
70 Warren St. 3-1 Chelsea, Mass.

TOP: **Concert ticket,** January 1980 [BCA]
BOTTOM: ***Night Time*** magazine, October 1974 [DBA]

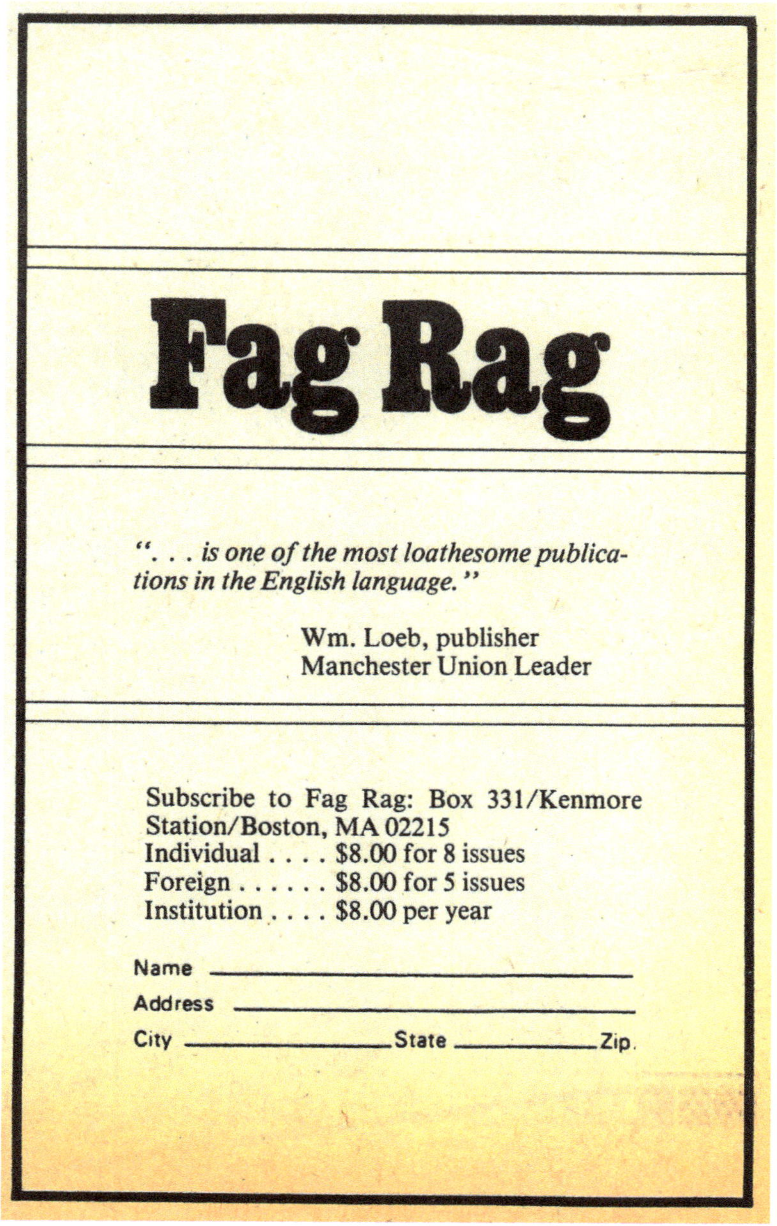
Fag Rag
". . . is one of the most loathesome publications in the English language."
Wm. Loeb, publisher
Manchester Union Leader
Subscribe to Fag Rag: Box 331/Kenmore Station/Boston, MA 02215
Individual . . . . $8.00 for 8 issues
Foreign . . . . . . $8.00 for 5 issues
Institution . . . . $8.00 per year
Name
Address
City
State
Zip.

Hit Parade of Boston, November 1979 [DBA]

MAY is Magic Music Month!
Sunday
Monday
Tuesday
Wednesday
Thursday
Friday
Saturday
1 Love Songs
2 Yesterday
Strawberry Fields
She Loves You
The Long and Winding Road
Best of the Beatles
3 The Piano Man
4 Listen & Win
5 Sunday Morning Jazz
6 Mc & Mac Monday (McCartney & Fleetwood Mac)
7 Taylor-Made Tuesday
8 Wednesday's Women (Women in Pop Music)
9 Thursday's Themes (Movie Magic)
10 The Mamas & The Papas
The Rolling Stones
The Beatles
The Supremes
Supergroups of the 60's & 70's
11 Listen & Win
12 Sunday Morning Jazz
13 My Guy
Stop in the Name of Love
Dancing in the Streets
Heat Wave
Motown Monday
14 Tunes from New England
15 Wednesday's Wonder (Stevie)
16 Hall & Oates
17 British Invasion
18 Listen & Win
19 Sunday Morning Jazz
20 Modern Music Monday
21 All in the Family (Doobies, Pointers, etc.)
22 Woodstock Wednesday
23 Roger
Phil
Linda
Sue
Peggy
Stevie
Rob
Dave
The Name Game
24 Class of '69
25 Class of '59
CLASS REUNION - ALL REQUEST WEEKEND
Class of '68
Class of '73
Listen & Win
26 Class of '64
27 Class of '72
CLASS REUNION - ALL REQUEST WEEKEND
Sunday Morning Jazz
Class of '70
28 Originals & Remakes
29 Surfin' Safari
California Girls
Help Me Ronda
Good Vibrations
Wild Wednesday with The Beach Boys
30
31
SUMMER CELEBRATION
wmjx 106.7fm
Magic

Boston Magazine, May 1985 [DBA]

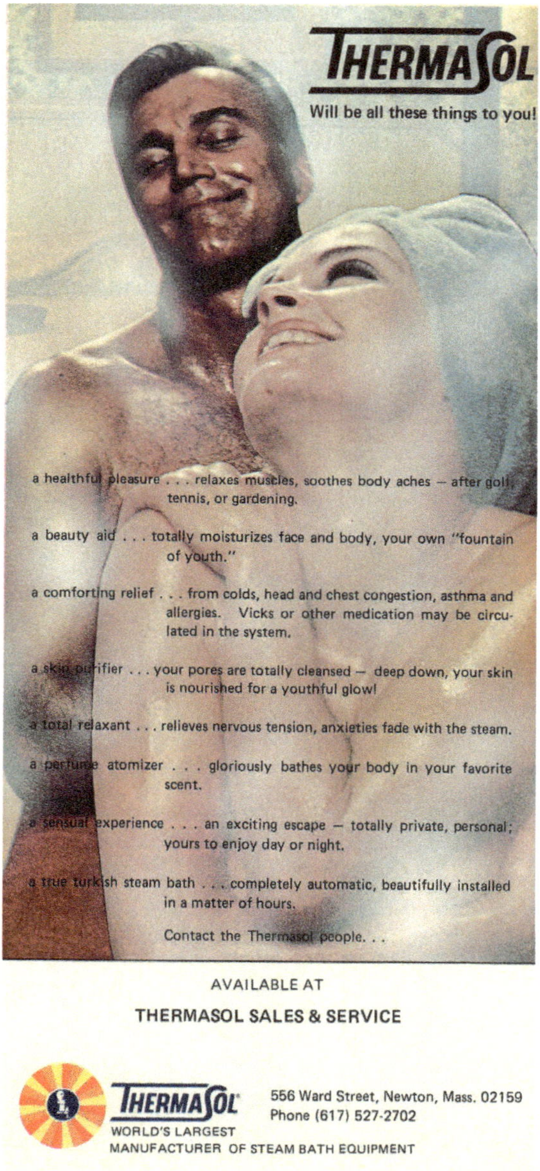
THERMASOL
Will be all these things to you!
a healthful pleasure . . . relaxes muscles, soothes body aches – after golf, tennis, or gardening.
a beauty aid . . . totally moisturizes face and body, your own "fountain of youth."
a comforting relief . . . from colds, head and chest congestion, asthma and allergies. Vicks or other medication may be circulated in the system.
a skin purifier . . . your pores are totally cleansed – deep down, your skin is nourished for a youthful glow!
a total relaxant . . . relieves nervous tension, anxieties fade with the steam.
a perfume atomizer . . . gloriously bathes your body in your favorite scent.
a sensual experience . . . an exciting escape – totally private, personal; yours to enjoy day or night.
a true turkish steam bath . . . completely automatic, beautifully installed in a matter of hours.
Contact the Thermasol people. . .
AVAILABLE AT
THERMASOL SALES & SERVICE
THERMASOL
WORLD'S LARGEST
MANUFACTURER OF STEAM BATH EQUIPMENT
556 Ward Street, Newton, Mass. 02159
Phone (617) 527-2702

Boston Magazine, December 1977 [DBA]

Leather & Lace
Carrying a Full Line of . . .
• Rock T's & Stage Wear
• Leather: Jackets, Vests
SPANDEX
JACKETS DRESSES
PANTS
BANDANAS
BOOT CHAINS
PATCHES
STERLING JEWELRY
ALL THE STAGEWEAR
YOU'LL EVER NEED
1415 Main St. Worcester (508) 755-8188

TAPEX
4 Haviland Street
Boston, MA 02115
Boston call (617) 437-9449
Hollywood call (213) 465-2466
REALTIME DUPLICATION
where
We Match Your Mix!
also
AMPEX Agfa Scotch and all recording accessories
computer controlled quality by
TDOS
TOUCH THE SOLUTION

***Basements and Backstage* magazine,** January 1990 [BCA]

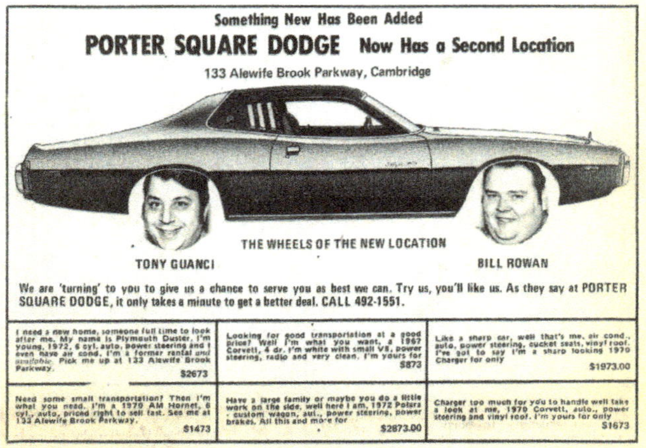
Something New Has Been Added
PORTER SQUARE DODGE Now Has a Second Location
133 Alewife Brook Parkway, Cambridge
THE WHEELS OF THE NEW LOCATION
TONY GUANCI
BILL ROWAN
We are 'turning' to you to give us a chance to serve you as best we can. Try us, you'll like us. As they say at PORTER SQUARE DODGE, it only takes a minute to get a better deal. CALL 492-1551.
I need a new home, someone full time to look after me. My name is Plymouth Duster. I'm young, 1972, 6 cyl. auto, power steering and I even have air cond. I'm a former rental and available. Pick me up at 133 Alewife Brook Parkway. $2673
Looking for good transportation at a good price? Well I'm what you want, a 1967 Corvett, 4 dr. I'm white with small V8, power steering, radio and very clean. I'm yours for $873
Like a sharp car, well that's me, air cond., auto, power steering, cucket seats, vinyl roof. I've got to say I'm a sharp looking 1970 Charger for only $1973.00
Need some small transportation? Then I'm what you need. I'm a 1970 AM Hornet, 6 cyl., auto, priced right to sell fast. See me at 133 Alewife Brook Parkway. $1473
Have a large family or maybe you do a little work on the side, well here I am, 1972 Polara - custom wagon, aut., power steering, power brakes. All this and more for $2873.00
Charger too much for you to handle well take a look at me, 1970 Corvett, auto., power steering and vinyl roof. I'm yours for only $1673

I WILL NOT BE SWAYED BY ANY DEMONSTRATION.
JOIN THE MORATORIUM
IN WASHINGTON!
ROUND TRIP $35.00
including food and drink on bus trip.
These are coach buses with reclining seats. You will be able to sleep on the trip down and back, no hassle for accommodations. Sandwiches, fruit and beverages will be provided.
Buses leave Friday, November 14th from B.U. March Chapel at 12 midnight
for information call 267-4836 days or 267-6073 and 267-5909 evenings.

TOP: ***Somerville Journal,*** April 26, 1973 [BCA]

BOTTOM: ***Boston After Dark,*** November 12, 1969 [DBA]

ULTIMATE DISCO DANCE
FEATURING
BOSTON'S FINEST DISCO D.J.'s
RUSS PRESTO
JIMMY FOURNIER
(JACOB'S LADDER)
ANDREW
DONNY
(ZELDA)
JOHN LUONGO
(RHINOCEROS)
DANAE JACOVIDIS
(STYX)
JOE CARVELLO
(MIRAGE)
JIMMY STEWART
(1270)
HOSTS
RON ROBIN of WBVF
SONNY JOE WHITE of WILD
SPECIAL THANKS TO AUDIO TRANSPORT SYSTEM
FOR TOTAL SOUND ....
SET YOUR SIGHTS ON
SUNDAY, SEPT. 28, 1975
GRAND BALLROOM
STATLER HILTON HOTEL
PARK SQUARE, BOSTON
7:00 P.M. - 2:00 A.M.
tickets on sale at: ALL OF THE ABOVE DISCOS
EVERETT MUSIC
30 Norwood St.
Everett, Mass.
SKIPPY WHITE'S
Mattapan Sq.
Mattapan, Mass.
ADMISSION $3.00

Nightfall, September 1975 [DBA]

OPEN DAILY 9 AM till 11:30 PM
ONLY SHOW of it's KIND ··· ANYWHERE!
LIVE on STAGE
AND ON OUR INTIMATE RUNWAY!
GIRLESK
WORLD'S BIGGEST, HOTTEST NON-STOP ALL GIRL SHOW
SCOOP! On Person
Engagement Extraordinary
STAR of STAGE • SCREEN • TV !
•Authoress of Best Seller "My Face For the World to See"...
LIZ Renay
ONE of the WORLD'S MOST BEAUTIFUL WOMEN in SHOW BUSINESS, & her BAG of TRICKS
Exclusive Engagement See Liz Renay in TOTAL 'nuf said. Adults Only
STAGE 12:30 3:00
SHOWS 7:30 10:00
PILGRIM BURLESK THEATRE
COR. WASH. & BOYLSTON ST., BOSTON, MASS.
TEL. 426-5734 & 426-5735
Plus Super X Films
LADIES, BRING YOUR HUSBANDS

Real Paper, May 29, 1974 [DBA]

In Boston and South Shore Plaza
Chubby Shop
Mix or Match these pretty sportsters freshly styled for Jr.-Teens who wear sizes 9½ to 15½
Cool, wash cottons freshly combining new tapestry print-n-checks in blue and white, and as pretty as can be!
Button Shirt 3.99
Pullover Shirt 4.99
Flared Skirt 7.99
Bermudas 11½-17½ 4.49
Chub Dept. second floor
If you're not on our mailing list, send for our Girls' new Fashion Book, it's FREE!
Lane Bryant
has everything for Chubs!
MAIL AND PHONE ORDERS FILLED PROMPTLY, HU 2-9800
Add 25c for delivery; C.O.D. is 25c more.
30 WEST ST., BOSTON

Boston Herald, May 17, 1963 [BCA]

NIGHTFALL, STRAWBERRIES and WILD present SIZZLIN' SOUL
WILD Air Personalities: Charlene Watts (PD) and Marvin Knight (DJ)
Listen to these great records on SONNY JOE WHITE'S WORLD of DISCO mon.-fri. 12-1 pm on WILD...
Keep listening for details on his STRAWBERRIES in-store remote
AVERAGE WHITE BAND SOUL SEARCHING
HAPPINESS IS BEING WITH THE SPINNERS
MARGIE JOSEPH HEAR THE WORDS, FEEL THE FEELING
LOU DONALDSON A DIFFERENT SCENE
The TRAMMPS
IMPACT
SIZZLIN' SUMMER SOUL
BEN E. KING I HAD A LOVE
MAJOR HARRIS JEALOUSY
THE JIMMY CASTOR BUNCH featuring the Everything Man SUPERSOUND
SPINNERS LIVE!
HERBIE MANN "SURPRISES" featuring CISSY HOUSTON
STANLEY CLARKE JOURNEY TO LOVE
LENNY WHITE VENUSIAN SUMMER
BARRABAS WATCH OUT
Eddie Harris That is Why You're Overweight
ARETHA FRANKLIN SPARKLE
Produced by Eddie Harris/ Vonio Productions Atlantic SD 1683
Produced by Curtis Mayfield Atlantic SD 18176
On Atlantic, Atco, Cotillion and Nemperor Records and Tapes
strawberries I
711 Boylston St., Boston
strawberries II
Harvard Square
ATLANTIC

Nightfall, August 1976 [DBA]

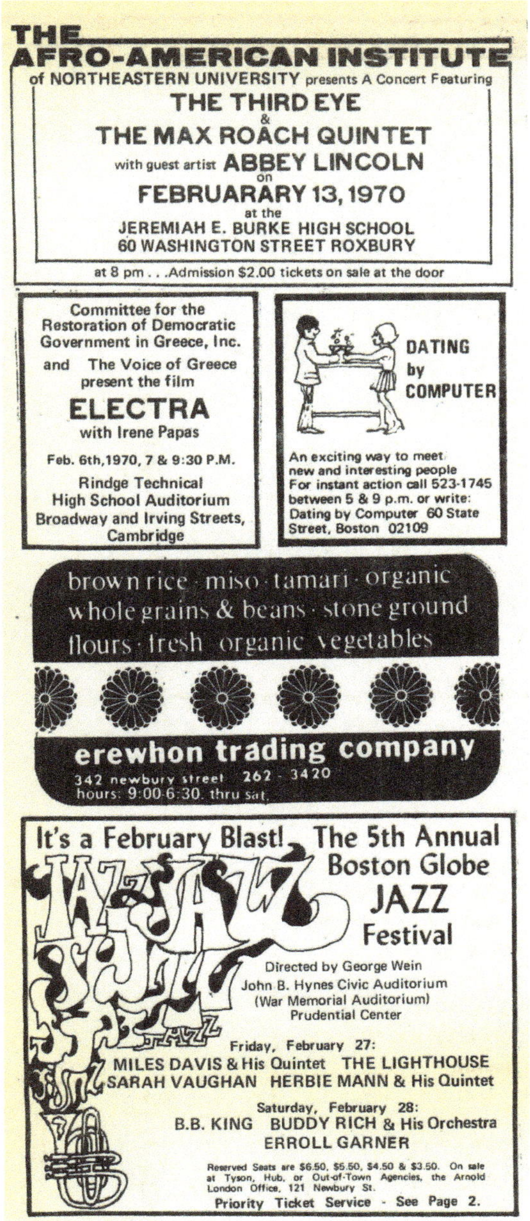

THE AFRO-AMERICAN INSTITUTE
of NORTHEASTERN UNIVERSITY presents A Concert Featuring
THE THIRD EYE
&
THE MAX ROACH QUINTET
with guest artist ABBEY LINCOLN
on
FEBRUARARY 13, 1970
at the
JEREMIAH E. BURKE HIGH SCHOOL
60 WASHINGTON STREET ROXBURY
at 8 pm . . .Admission $2.00 tickets on sale at the door

Committee for the Restoration of Democratic Government in Greece, Inc.
and The Voice of Greece present the film
ELECTRA
with Irene Papas
Feb. 6th, 1970, 7 & 9:30 P.M.
Rindge Technical High School Auditorium
Broadway and Irving Streets, Cambridge

DATING by COMPUTER
An exciting way to meet new and interesting people
For instant action call 523-1745 between 5 & 9 p.m. or write:
Dating by Computer 60 State Street, Boston 02109

brown rice · miso · tamari · organic whole grains & beans · stone ground flours · fresh organic vegetables
erewhon trading company
342 newbury street 262 - 3420
hours: 9:00-6:30. thru sat.

It's a February Blast! The 5th Annual Boston Globe JAZZ Festival
Directed by George Wein
John B. Hynes Civic Auditorium
(War Memorial Auditorium)
Prudential Center
Friday, February 27:
MILES DAVIS & His Quintet THE LIGHTHOUSE
SARAH VAUGHAN HERBIE MANN & His Quintet
Saturday, February 28:
B.B. KING BUDDY RICH & His Orchestra
ERROLL GARNER
Reserved Seats are $6.50, $5.50, $4.50 & $3.50. On sale at Tyson, Hub, or Out-of-Town Agencies, the Arnold London Office, 121 Newbury St.
Priority Ticket Service - See Page 2.

Boston After Dark, February 4, 1970 [DBA]

Cap'n Swing
An Almost Famous Band!
"MAXANNË
is
INTENSE
WBCN

104FM
WBCN
№ 6150
the
CARS
Available on Elektra Records
THE BOSTON
Phoenix

TOP: **Band flyer** (with dedication to WBCN's Maxanne), mid-1970s [DBA]
BOTTOM: **Promotional bumper sticker,** 1978 [DBA]

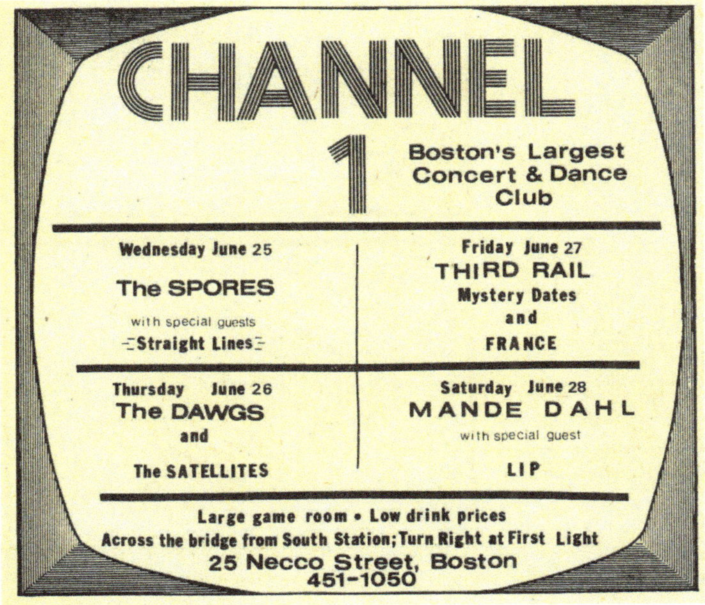
CHANNEL
1
Boston's Largest
Concert & Dance
Club
Wednesday June 25
The SPORES
with special guests
Straight Lines
Friday June 27
THIRD RAIL
Mystery Dates
and
FRANCE
Thursday June 26
The DAWGS
and
The SATELLITES
Saturday June 28
MANDE DAHL
with special guest
LIP
Large game room • Low drink prices
Across the bridge from South Station; Turn Right at First Light
25 Necco Street, Boston
451-1050

THE NEW
BOSTON COMEDY CLUB
All Local Talent
July-August
Featuring:
LENNY CLARKE
DON GAVIN
JACK GALAGHER
STEVE SWEENEY
CHRIS COLLINS
JOAN BORWITZ
MARCI ROSE
Coming In September
EDDIE MURPHY
GEORGE CARLIN
SHIRLEY HEMPHILL
Every Wednesday Open Mike Night (Free Admission)
Every Thursday 2 for 1 Admission plus Drink Special
823 Main Street, Cambridge, MA
For Information Call: 547-2020, 491-7313

TOP: ***Real Paper,*** June 28, 1980 [DBA]
BOTTOM: ***The Calendar*** **magazine** (WCOZ), July 1982 [DBA]

ATTENTION DANCERS!
AUDITION FOR A NEW
MUSIC VIDEO
TELEVISION
DANCE SHOW
AUDITIONS ARE BEING HELD for
BEAUTIFUL BOYS AND GIRLS BETWEEN THE AGES OF 15 and 21
YEARS OLD FOR A NEW MUSIC TELEVISION VIDEO-DANCE SHOW.
THE FIRST OF ITS KIND IN BOSTON AND GUARANTEED TO BE
ROCKIN'!!! SO, IF YOU LOVE TO DANCE and YOU THINK YOU
QUALIFY, CALL: 442-8721.
ATTENTION DANCERS!!!!
The producer is also looking for local bands
singers, and rappers to appear on the show.***

TV show audition flyer (producer: Tony Rose), 1989 [KBA]

advertisement
skunk piss mag.
in A-ssociaton with
Ciddy Limitz productions
"present"
PUNK NITE AT MASS ART
starring
"Umatural Axe"
PHOBIA
and
MISSION TO BURMA
plus
A Mickey Finney slideshow
FRI. night May 11. 8:30 3 dollars
MASS COLLEGE OF ART. LONGWOOD THEATRE no ID REQUIRED
advertisement

Omar
DAVID OMAR WHITE
opaque genius
ART WORK OF ALL SORTS,
NEAT, FAST, AND TO THE POINT
145 COLUMBIA ST., MASS. 02139
617/ 868 9788

TOP: **Event flyer,** May 1979 [FLYNN]
BOTTOM: ***Broadside,*** May 18, 1968 [DBA]

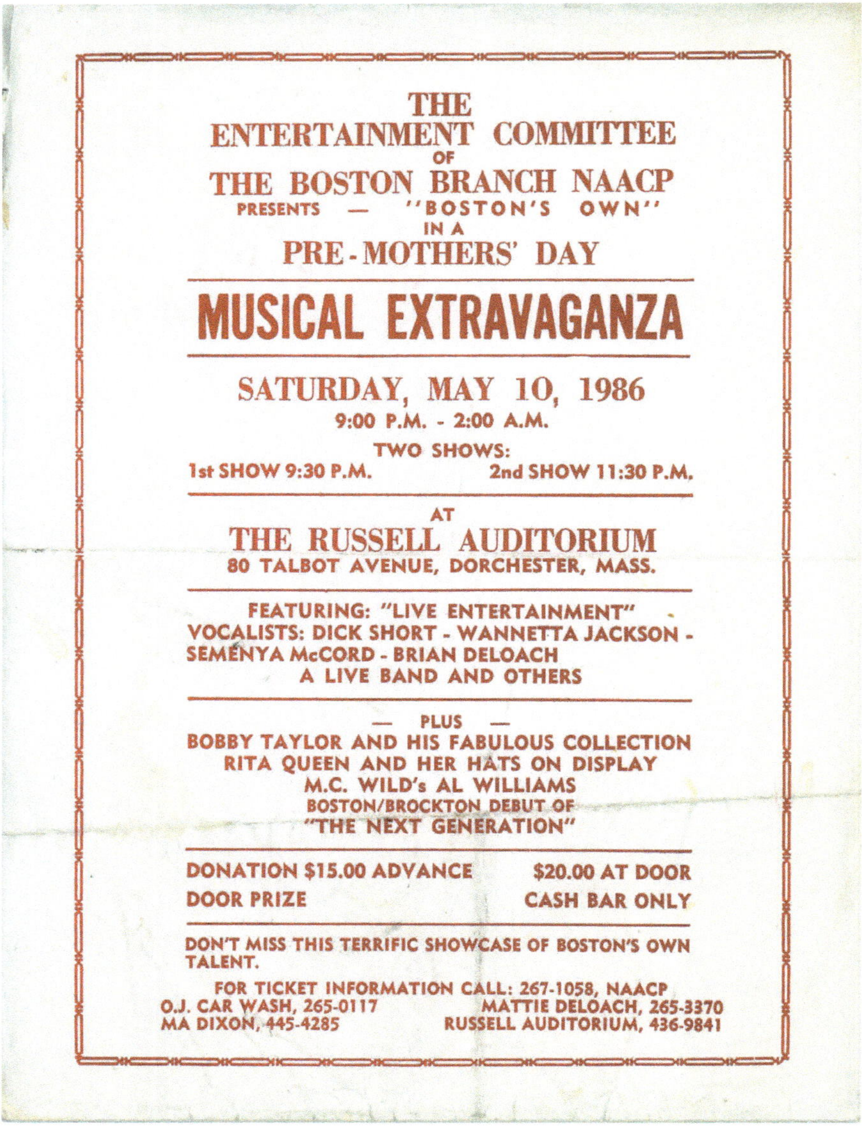

THE
ENTERTAINMENT COMMITTEE
OF
THE BOSTON BRANCH NAACP
PRESENTS — "BOSTON'S OWN"
IN A
PRE-MOTHERS' DAY

MUSICAL EXTRAVAGANZA

SATURDAY, MAY 10, 1986
9:00 P.M. - 2:00 A.M.
TWO SHOWS:
1st SHOW 9:30 P.M. 2nd SHOW 11:30 P.M.

AT
THE RUSSELL AUDITORIUM
80 TALBOT AVENUE, DORCHESTER, MASS.

FEATURING: "LIVE ENTERTAINMENT"
VOCALISTS: DICK SHORT - WANNETTA JACKSON -
SEMENYA McCORD - BRIAN DELOACH
A LIVE BAND AND OTHERS

— PLUS —
BOBBY TAYLOR AND HIS FABULOUS COLLECTION
RITA QUEEN AND HER HATS ON DISPLAY
M.C. WILD's AL WILLIAMS
BOSTON/BROCKTON DEBUT OF
"THE NEXT GENERATION"

DONATION $15.00 ADVANCE $20.00 AT DOOR
DOOR PRIZE CASH BAR ONLY

DON'T MISS THIS TERRIFIC SHOWCASE OF BOSTON'S OWN TALENT.

FOR TICKET INFORMATION CALL: 267-1058, NAACP
O.J. CAR WASH, 265-0117 MATTIE DELOACH, 265-3370
MA DIXON, 445-4285 RUSSELL AUDITORIUM, 436-9841

Event flyer, May 1986 [courtesy of DJ Bobby Taylor]

Bay State BANNER and the
Boston Negro Artists Assoc.
Present...
Sunday in the park
SEPTEMBER 11, 1966

Event flyer, September 1966 [KBA]

Give them help, love, hope...
Love and guidance for forgotten youngsters, counseling for troubled families . . . you have the power to increase voluntary agency innovation. Help meet the challenge of urban living! --- through your Fair Share gift to the Massachustts Bay United Fund.
This space contributed by GILLETTE SAFETY RAZOR COMPANY

Boston Magazine, September 1969 [DBA]

His
and Her
WIGS
Real human hair shaped Beatle style . . . but you can cut and style them to suit yourself. $29.90 at Gilchrist's in Boston.

There was no place for Warren in Boston.
We think there should be.
HELP BUILD A NEW ZOO FOR BOSTON
Join The Boston Zoological Society
Boston Zoological Society
Franklin Park
Dorchester, Mass. 02121
Enclosed is $........................
Please enter my membership
.... Family $ 5.00
.... Sustaining $25.00
.... Supporting $50.00

TOP: ***New England Teen Scene,*** January/February 1967 [ELA]
BOTTOM: ***Boston Magazine,*** December 1968 [DBA]

417.
King Curtis Fashion Affair
Sponsored by Darlene Curtis
"Featuring" "Simply Us" (Fashion Models)
Fashion Show Buffet and Disco
Prince Hall Masonic Temple
Washington Street
Dorchester, Massachusetts 02124
Saturday November 24, 1979
9:00 P.M. — 2:00 A.M.
Bar Service
Admission: $10.00

BRING YOUR HEAD TO CARL
...he's got something to lay on you
CARL
custom made hair fashions
THE MOST DISTINCTIVE
IN HAIR PIECES AT
123 NEWBURY ST.
FOR APPOINTMENT, TELEPHONE
266-6050

TOP: **Event ticket,** November 1979 [BCA]
BOTTOM: ***Boston After Dark,*** September 17, 1969 [DBA]

The best Deli in New York is in Brookline. The B&D.
If you're in the mood for deli, B&D is the deli for you. Sit down and enjoy. Take out and enjoy. B&D caters to every deli craving. From breakfast bagels to a good night knish. With full lunches, dinners and all sorts of noshes and kabobs, soups and salads in between. Plus tasty favorites like a real New York size hot pastrami or corned beef sandwich. What's for dessert? You name it. B&D bakes it fresh for you. Discover the best deli this side of New York, in beautiful downtown Brookline. Call and we'll even deliver
for a mere $5 delivery charge, within a 3 mile radius. Minimum order, $15. Additional charge beyond 3 miles. We'll also cater any affair from office parties to weddings.
You call 232-3727. We deliver.
SUN thru WED 7 AM to 9 PM
THURS thru SAT 7 AM to 10 PM
B&D The DELI
1653 BEACON ST. BROOKLINE

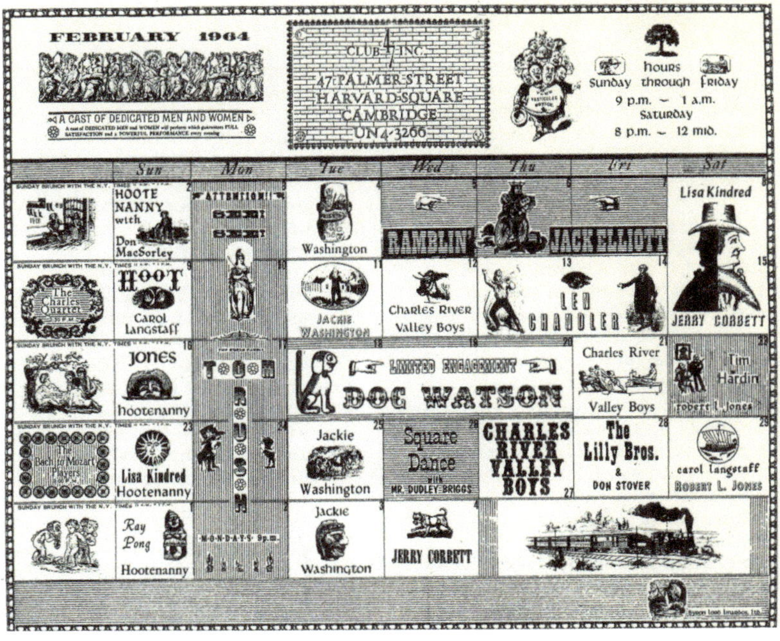
FEBRUARY 1964
A CAST OF DEDICATED MEN AND WOMEN
CLUB 47 INC.
47 PALMER STREET
HARVARD SQUARE
CAMBRIDGE
UN 4-3266
hours
Sunday through Friday
9 p.m. – 1 a.m.
Saturday
8 p.m. – 12 mid.
Sun
Mon
Tue
Wed
Thu
Fri
Sat
HOOTE NANNY with Don MacSorley
Washington
RAMBLIN' JACK ELLIOTT
Lisa Kindred
The Charles Quartet
HOOT
Carol Langstaff
Jackie Washington
Charles River Valley Boys
LEN CHANDLER
JERRY CORBETT
Jones hootenanny
LIMITED ENGAGEMENT
DOC WATSON
Charles River Valley Boys
Tim Hardin
Robert L. Jones
The Bach to Mozart Players
Lisa Kindred Hootenanny
Jackie Washington
Square Dance with MR. DUDLEY BRIGGS
CHARLES RIVER VALLEY BOYS
The Lilly Bros. & DON STOVER
carol langstaff
ROBERT L. JONES
Ray Pong Hootenanny
MONDAYS 9 p.m.
Jackie Washington
JERRY CORBETT

TOP: ***Boston Magazine,*** August 1987 [DBA]
BOTTOM: ***Broadside,*** February 5, 1964 [BCA]

THE
FUGS
ATLANTIC RECORDS
FINE ARTS THEATRE
80 NORWAY ST. · BOSTON, MASS.
phone 262-9876
1 WEEK · JULY 19 thru JULY 25
Two Performances Nightly 8:30 and 10:30 p.m.
Tickets Now On Sale at Fine Arts Theatre & Symphony Cinema Box Offices

Concert flyer, July 1967 [Courtesy of John Campoli]

QUICK GAY GUIDE
American Civil Liberties Union 227-9469
Boston Gay Youth 536-6197
Charles Street Meetinghouse 742-0450
Daughters of Bilitis 262-1592
Dignity/Boston, c/o 1105 Boylston St., Boston, Ma. 02215
Fag Rag 536-9826
Gay Community Center 491-5669
or 288-8765
Gay Community News (c/o Charles St. Meetinghouse)
742-0450
Gay Media Watch 868-5729
Gay Speakers Bureau 547-1461
Gay Way Radio (WBUR-FM) ....
(Contact Elaine Noble or John Lawrence)
Good Gay Poets 536-0826
Homophile Community Health Service 266-5477
Homophile Union of Boston 536-6197
Lavender Hour (WBCN-FM) 261-8528
(Contact Andy Kopkind or Littlejohn)
Lesbian Liberation 354-8807
(c/o the Women's Center)
Metropolitan Community Church 266-7491
Project Place 267-9150
Red River Dyke Collective
c/o 43 Willow St., Somerville, Ma. 02143
Fr. Paul Shanley 267-0764
Gallery coffee house
Charles Street Meeting House
OPEN 12 noon To 12 pm 7 days
-70 Charles St. Boston
GAY WAYS
WBUR
THURSDAYS AT 9:00 p.m.
FRI. NITES 9:00 - 1:00 Charles Street Meeting House
GAY DANCES

Boston Coalition for the Liberation of Southern Africa

The Boston Coalition for the Liberation of Southern Africa (BCLSA) is made up of individuals and organizations opposed to U.S. government and corporate support for white domination in Southern Africa. The African National Congress of South Africa, Boston Organizing Committee and Boston Club (NNMLC) are organizational members. Work consists of educational events in communities, workplaces, churches and on campuses. Literature, films, slide shows and other materials on Southern Africa and the U.S. role in South Africa, Zimbabwe and Namibia are available. A major campaign in the past two years has been directed against the First National Bank of Boston which has an affiliate in South Africa and carries out discriminatory and anti-working class policies in New England. Material support drives have provided tons of clothing for Zimbabwean refugees.

People interested in working with BCLSA or in learning more about its activities in the Boston area should contact:

B.C.L.S.A.
P.O. Box 8791
BOSTON, MA 02114

BOYCOTT FIRST NATIONAL BANK OF BOSTON!
NO TO RACISM AND APARTHEID!!

TOP: ***Gay Community News,*** July 12, 1973 [THP]
BOTTOM: **Amandla concert program,** July 21, 1979 [BCA, courtesy of Janine Fay]

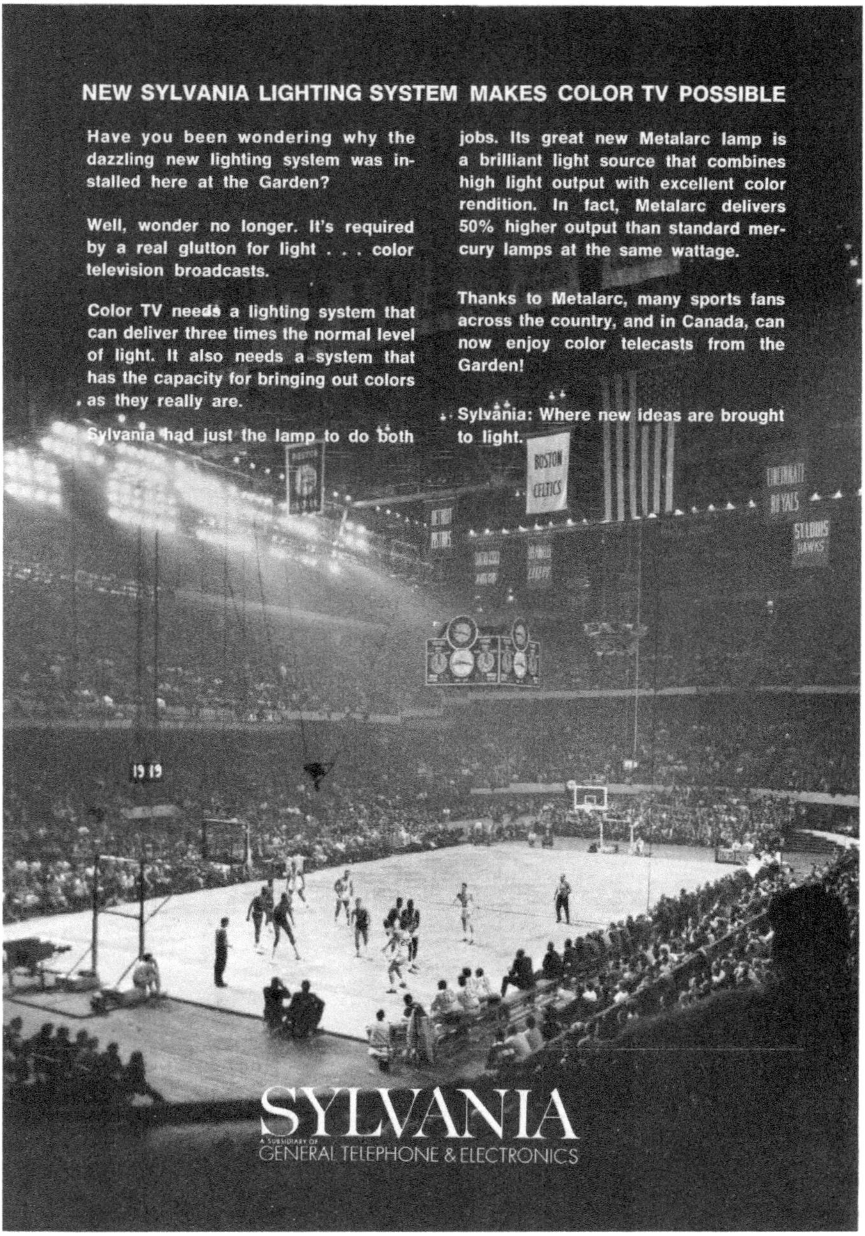
NEW SYLVANIA LIGHTING SYSTEM MAKES COLOR TV POSSIBLE
Have you been wondering why the dazzling new lighting system was installed here at the Garden?
Well, wonder no longer. It's required by a real glutton for light . . . color television broadcasts.
Color TV needs a lighting system that can deliver three times the normal level of light. It also needs a system that has the capacity for bringing out colors as they really are.
Sylvania had just the lamp to do both jobs. Its great new Metalarc lamp is a brilliant light source that combines high light output with excellent color rendition. In fact, Metalarc delivers 50% higher output than standard mercury lamps at the same wattage.
Thanks to Metalarc, many sports fans across the country, and in Canada, can now enjoy color telecasts from the Garden!
Sylvania: Where new ideas are brought to light.
BOSTON CELTICS
SYLVANIA
GENERAL TELEPHONE & ELECTRONICS

Boston Bruins program, 1967–1968 season [BCA]

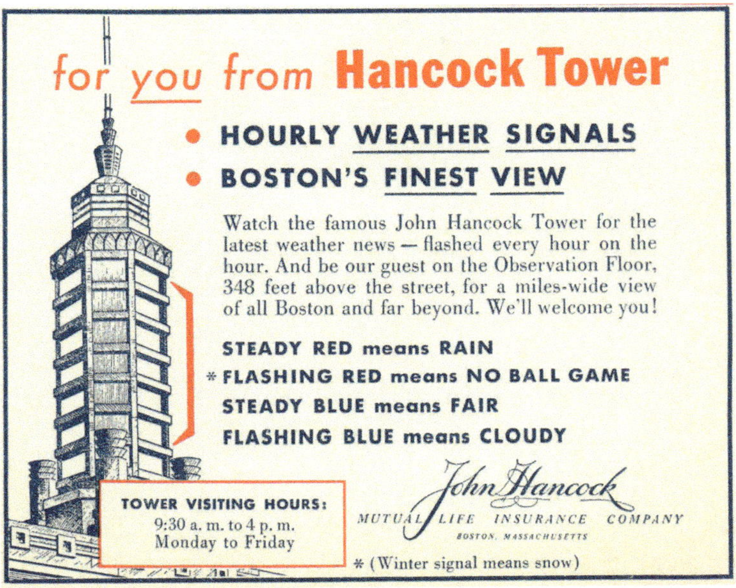
for you from Hancock Tower
• HOURLY WEATHER SIGNALS
• BOSTON'S FINEST VIEW
Watch the famous John Hancock Tower for the latest weather news — flashed every hour on the hour. And be our guest on the Observation Floor, 348 feet above the street, for a miles-wide view of all Boston and far beyond. We'll welcome you!
STEADY RED means RAIN
* FLASHING RED means NO BALL GAME
STEADY BLUE means FAIR
FLASHING BLUE means CLOUDY
TOWER VISITING HOURS:
9:30 a. m. to 4 p. m.
Monday to Friday
John Hancock
MUTUAL LIFE INSURANCE COMPANY
BOSTON, MASSACHUSETTS
* (Winter signal means snow)

POOR THOREAU
He couldn't live in the Walden Square Apartments.
But you can. For just $158 a month you can live in a brand new, sunny, one bedroom apartment in Cambridge. Your rent includes all utilities (except phone), free parking , plus a downstairs laundromat, food store, and adult center.
OFFICE HOURS 12 NOON to 6 P.M. 7 DAYS A WEEK
492-3020
saunders & associates
tors • 229 Newbury St. • Boston 02116 • 617-536-1620
EQUAL HOUSING OPPORTUNITY

TOP: **Boston Red Sox program,** 1962 [BCA]
BOTTOM: ***Somerville Journal,*** August 16, 1973 [BCA]

Come to
COM' Chev's
Open House
John Pesky
Come see John Pesky pick the winners of The Caribbean Trip from 10 A.M. — 12 Noon.
April 10, 1974
• GRAND DRAWING — For the Caribbean Trip
• PRIZES: RADIOS & BASEBALL TICKETS
• FREE REFRESHMENTS • SUPER VALUES
SEE THE CAR THAT'S RIGHT FOR YOU
CORVETTE DEPT.
'74 Corvette Coupe
Yellow with black interior, 4 sp. trans., p.s., p.b., am-fm radio, 6700 mi.
'73 Corvette Coupe
10,000 mi., am-fm stereo, turbo hydramatic trans., p.s., p.w., orange with black leather interior.
'73 Corvette Conv.
Turbo hydramatic trans., blue with white top, 19,000 mi. Sharp car.
'72 Corvette
White with saddle interior, 4 sp. trans., 29,000 mi., am-fm radio. Like new condition.
'72 Vega
2 Dr., 4 sp., 18,000 mi. Like new cond.
$2295
'70 MG Midget
Conv., 35,000 mi., 4 sp. trans., radio.
$1795
COMMONWEALTH CHEVROLET
1065 COMMONWEALTH AVENUE, Boston, Mass.
254-0450
Open Evenings

Chez Vous
Rollerway
Boston's Friendliest Skating Rink
Where Everyone Has Fun!
* Repairs Skates
* Skates Sold
* Special Rates for Parties and Organizations
11 Rhodes St.
Dorchester, Mass.
436-2332

TOP: ***Boston Herald American,*** April 9, 1974 [BCA]

BOTTOM: ***New England Teen Scene,*** May/June 1967 [ELA]

THE SHEAR CROPPERS ROOM
at the
BEAUTY PAVILION
1912 BEACON ST.,
CLEVELAND CIRCLE
566-9527
OPEN MON-SAT
THURS & FRI NITE
WHERE WHAT YOU WANT IS WHAT YOU GET
·BLOW CUTS·
·BLOW DRYING·
SUNBURSTING· BODY WAVING
10% DISCOUNT WITH THIS AD

Your Grandfather and perhaps
your Great Grandfather dined with us too!
MARKET DINING ROOMS
EAST VIEW OF FANEUIL HALL MARKET
1827
ESTABLISHED BEFORE YOU WERE BORN
In the Shadow of Faneuil Hall

TOP: ***Real Paper,*** December 27, 1972 [DBA]
BOTTOM: ***Real Paper,*** June 24, 1978 [DBA]

Boston Gay Guide

BARS

Bamboo Lounge	30 Avery	338-8342
Boston-Boston	15 Lansdowne	262-2424
Chaps	15 Blagden	266-7778
Citadel	22 Avery	482-9040
Club Max	54 Park Sq.	262-0750
Club 76	76 Batterymarch	542-3377
Delivery Entrance	12 Wilton	783-5701
Eagle	88 Queensberry	247-9586
Harry's Place	45 Essex	338-8116
Herbie's Ramrod	12 Carver	338-8280
Jacques	79 Broadway	338-7502
Napoleon Club	52 Piedmont	338-7547
119 Merrimac	119 Merrimac	523-8960
Paradise Cafe	180 Mass. Ave., Camb.	864-4130
Playland	21 Essex	338-7254
Somewhere	295 Franklin	423-7730
Sporters	228 Cambridge	742-4084
Styx	31 Huntington	247-3910
The Bar	252 Boylston	247-9308
Together	110 Boylston	426-0086
Twelve Càrver	12 Carver	338-8577
1270	1270 Boylston	261-1257

BATHS

Club Boston	4 LaGrange	426-1451
The Regency	11 Otis	338-7975

MASSAGE PARLORS

Jupiter in Aries	283 Dartmouth	267-7590

MOVIES

Art Cinema	204 Tremont	482-4661
South Station 1 & 2	23 South	423-4340

PUBLICATIONS

Esplanade	143 Albany St., Camb.	492-0056
GCN	22 Bromfield	426-4469

RESTAURANTS

Club Max	54 Park Sq.	262-0750
Fan Club	77 Warrenton	357-5050
La Trattoria	288 Cambridge	227-0211
The House	12 Wilton	783-5701

Courtesy of Esplanade Paperback
107 Charles Street, 523-2361

Pamphlet, 1978 [THP]

Garland

Sweaters for college girls at all the principal stores and smart shops in Boston and Cambridge

PIERRE'S

Continental Coiffures

1731 Beacon Street, Brookline

For professional Coiffures, friendly atmosphere, Luxury of Air Condition Dryers, Air Conditioned etc., at moderate prices visit Pierre's Continental Coiffures.

As an International Des Coiffeures Des Dames Member, Pierre travels to the fashion capitol, Paris, France and to other countries to attend the style shows; he is the first to bring back the new line in hair fashion.

For your new coif let Pierre style the one most becoming to you.

CALL AS 7-8588

Pierre
I.C.D. Member

—YOUR NEAREST **FORD** DEALER—

Sales and Service

FORD MADE PRODUCTS

GALAXIE — THUNDERBIRD — FALCON — FAIRLANE

Fine Selection of A-1 Used Cars

SALVI FORD SALES, Inc.

2 BLOCKS NORTH OF PORTER SQUARE

2067 MASSACHUSETTS AVE. CAMBRIDGE

UNiversity 4-5800

Collegiate Guide to Greater Boston (Harvard Crimson), 1963 [VACCA]

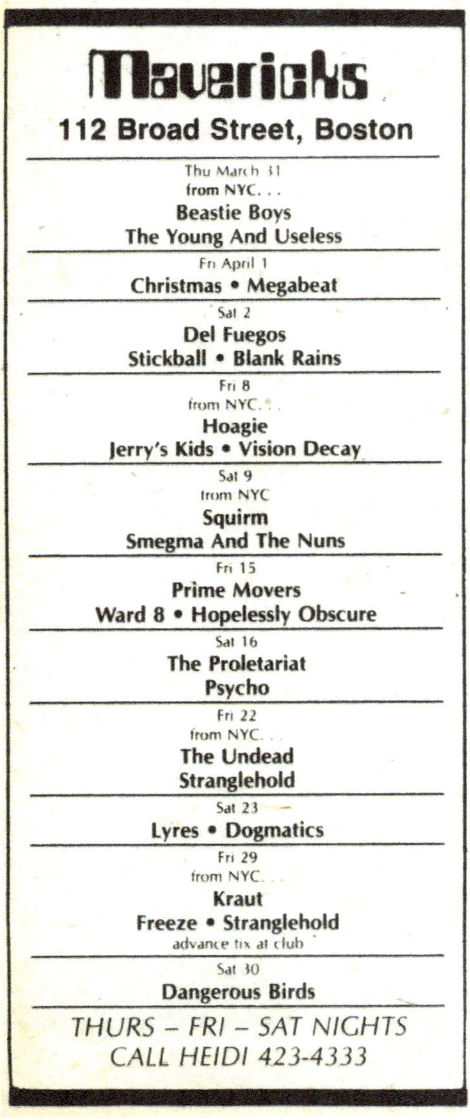
Mavericks
112 Broad Street, Boston
Thu March 31
from NYC. . .
Beastie Boys
The Young And Useless
Fri April 1
Christmas • Megabeat
Sat 2
Del Fuegos
Stickball • Blank Rains
Fri 8
from NYC. . .
Hoagie
Jerry's Kids • Vision Decay
Sat 9
from NYC
Squirm
Smegma And The Nuns
Fri 15
Prime Movers
Ward 8 • Hopelessly Obscure
Sat 16
The Proletariat
Psycho
Fri 22
from NYC. . .
The Undead
Stranglehold
Sat 23
Lyres • Dogmatics
Fri 29
from NYC. . .
Kraut
Freeze • Stranglehold
advance tix at club
Sat 30
Dangerous Birds
THURS – FRI – SAT NIGHTS
CALL HEIDI 423-4333

Boston Rock, March 1983 [DBA]

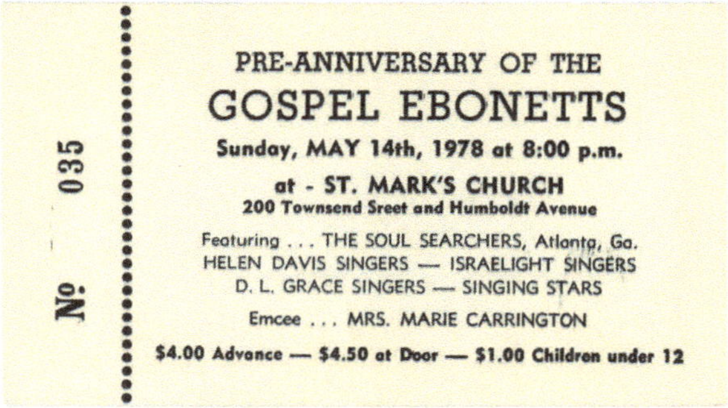
PRE-ANNIVERSARY OF THE
GOSPEL EBONETTS
Sunday, MAY 14th, 1978 at 8:00 p.m.
at - ST. MARK'S CHURCH
200 Townsend Sreet and Humboldt Avenue
Featuring . . . THE SOUL SEARCHERS, Atlanta, Ga.
HELEN DAVIS SINGERS — ISRAELIGHT SINGERS
D. L. GRACE SINGERS — SINGING STARS
Emcee . . . MRS. MARIE CARRINGTON
$4.00 Advance — $4.50 at Door — $1.00 Children under 12
№ 035

WE ... HERE AT WBCN 104.1 F.M. ... IN Addition to LAYING OUT Adult STEREO ROCK HAVE SOME SPECIAL GOODIES LIKE
JIM BYRD
SOUL MUSIC
SUNDAY 9-12 MIDNIGHT
AND
OLDIES
LITTLE WALTER
WED NES DAY
12-2 A.M.

TOP: **Concert ticket,** May 1978 [BCA]
BOTTOM: ***Boston After Dark,*** November 12, 1969 [DBA]

Records
Gangstarr
Posse
has just released
their new 12" single
It's How
Ya Cope b/w
Young Girls
featuring Joe Byrd, Jr.
Now available in record
stores all over Boston!
For booking information contact:
Bob Winstead
Globe Advertising Agency
(617) 267-5800 or 247-9141

***Source* magazine,** March 1989 [MHHA]

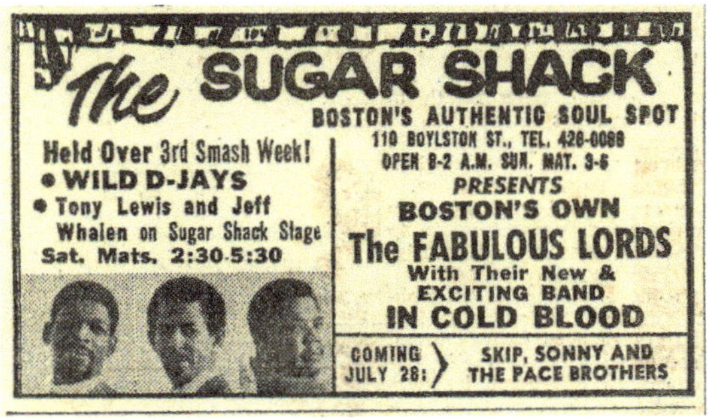
The SUGAR SHACK
BOSTON'S AUTHENTIC SOUL SPOT
110 BOYLSTON ST., TEL. 426-0080
OPEN 8-2 A.M. SUN. MAT. 3-6
PRESENTS
BOSTON'S OWN
The FABULOUS LORDS
With Their New & EXCITING BAND
IN COLD BLOOD
Held Over 3rd Smash Week!
• WILD D-JAYS
• Tony Lewis and Jeff Whalen on Sugar Shack Stage
Sat. Mats. 2:30-5:30
COMING JULY 28:
SKIP, SONNY AND THE PACE BROTHERS

Ralph Abernathy—SCLC
David Hilliard—Black Panther Party
Roy Innis—CORE
Roy Wilkins—NAACP
SPEAK FOR BLACK AMERICA
MONDAY, DECEMBER 8, 1969
– 7:30 P.M. –
ROBERT'S CENTER – Boston College
– ADMISSION FREE –
WILL YOU LISTEN?
presented by cultural committee undergraduate government–boston college

TOP: ***Boston Record American,*** July 17, 1969 [BCA]
BOTTOM: ***Boston After Dark,*** December 3, 1969 [DBA]

"Good night, good night!
Parting is such sweet sorrow,
That I shall say good night
till it be morrow!"
It's impossible to be a convincing
Romeo in the costume of a
Pagliacci. Do you look the part you
play, socially and in
business? To make sure they do, many
highly successful men wear
hand tailored clothes
by Walter-Morton fitted
for the "Louis look."
Louis
470 Boylston Street,
Boston
Men's and
students' apparel
Ladies Corner

Colonial Theater program, August 1961 [BCA]

Sammy White's
KING'S ROW
16 Soldiersfield Road
Brighton, Mass.
a great little place!
featuring
The SUN COMPANY
LENNIE'S
TONIGHT!
With Matinee Today 4-7
RAHSAAN ROLAND KIRK
and the VIBRATION SOCIETY
Coming Feb. 22 — 2 Weeks
JAMES COTTON
BLUES BAND
4 Nites — March 7-8-9-10
STAN KENTON
RESERVE NOW!
ON THE TURNPIKE, RT. 1
W. PEABODY 535-9806
OLIVER'S
62 Brookline Ave.
Sun. Happy Hour
Enjoy Doherty
from 3 'Til 2 A.M.
Free Buffet
Mon. Happy Hour
prices
Both with
DICK DOHERTY
"everybody's SWEETHEART"
Tues. Avant Garde
Great Place Great Entertainment
PAUL'S MALL
Catch the "LATE SHOW"
10 P.M. to 2 A.M.
STARTS TONITE
JIMMY HELMS
with RHYTHM
No Cover Sun.-Thurs.
following the Gershwin Show
JAZZ WORKSHOP
TONITE
SAM RIVERS
Cecil McBee
Norman Connors
MAT. 4-7
opens MON.
JOE HENDERSON
Quintet
Feb. 22 MOSE ALLISON
733 BOYLSTON ST., BOSTON
The Groggery
NIGHTLY
SAD BIRDS
SUNDAY HAPPY HOUR
JOHN MORGAN
MONDAY HAPPY HOUR PRICES
CORNER OF HARVARD &
CAMBRIDGE STS., ALLSTON
COMING MON. ONE WEEK
MASON DIXON
and the Line
NOW—THE CHOSEN FEW
THURSDAY MINI PRICES
Odee's
450 Rindge Ave.
CAMBRIDGE
492-6620
Members-Guests

Boston Herald Traveler, February 14, 1971 [DBA]

FREE CONCERT
NOON - 6
ROCK AGAINST REAGAN
BOSTON COMMON SAT 14TH
MDC
CRUCIFUCKS
DRI
THE DICKS
plus MORE
ALAN ANDERSON

Event flyer, May 1983 [Courtesy of Patty Lederer]

SKYCAP presents a
CARIBBEAN and AMERICAN NIGHT
EVERY FRIDAY
From 9 p.m. - 2 a.m.
Music by Two Best D.J.'s Mixing with a New Style!
GRAND MASTER WOODY SUPER STAR
MIX MASTER MIKE ROCK
AT THE SKYCAP PLAZA
575 WARREN STREET — DORCHESTER
Admission: $5 At the Door and FREE before 11 p.m.
FOR MORE INFORMATION CALL: WOODY MUSIC 427-8757 ★ MIKE ROCK 442-3076 ★
SKYCAP 442-3131
I.D. and PROPER DRESS is required. Tight Security

Event flyer, late 1980s [courtesy of DJ Bobby Taylor]

Play a set of bubbles
All the tennis you want in the most exciting place to play – under the bubbles at Government Center, Boston. Six indoor Plexi-Cushion courts, 11 for the outdoor season. Indirect lighting, saunas, restaurant and lounge, locker rooms, teaching pros, tournaments and clinics. Ample indoor parking. Single, married, family and corporate memberships available.
Charles River Park Tennis Club
35 Lomasney Way
at Government Center, Boston
call 742-8922 or 742-8913

MIKE'S CUSTOM LEATHER
because it feels SO-O GOOD
119 MERRIMAC STREET
BOSTON, MASS. 02114
Open 8p.m. to 2a.m. Wed. thru Mon.
Lubricated Condoms 5 for $1.oo
conveniently located at "119 MERRIMAC" browse while you enjoy your favorite beverage

TOP: ***Boston Magazine,*** September 1977 [DBA]
BOTTOM: ***Guide To The Gay Northeast,*** November 1987 [BCA]

Touraine
SUPER SUMMER SEPARATES
A perfect little polo shirt by Bobbie Brooks pairs up with Juniormates' snappy button-front skirt to create summer's cutest all occasion outfit. Top - S, M, L $10
Skirt - sizes 5 to 13 $13.
At your nearest Touraine Store
Arlington • Brookline • Cambridge • Saugus • Stoneham • Dedham • Natick • Shrewsbury • Leominster • Salem • Quincy • Brockton • Hanover • Danvers • Nashua &
Salem, N.H.

***Boston Phoenix* (Summer Preview),** June 1973 [BBR]

FILENE'S
CORPORATE IMAGE
Foresight and attention to detail have made my consulting firm quite a success. For spring, the success I see is this Chanel-style suit from Castleberry Knits.
I strongly recommend the authoritative look of its jacket with braided trim, straight, belted skirt, and soft polyester bow blouse. Natural with khaki trim. Of polyester-acrylic, sizes 6-16. $195.
Leather briefcase, $150.
In Corporate Image — fourth floor Boston, Chestnut Hill, and Southshore.
Call Tina Sutton at Filene's Executive Service in Boston, 357-2649.
Filene's Executive Service can save you time and energy. Our Personal Shopping Consultant, Tina Sutton, will be pleased to help you assemble a new wardrobe or coordinate, accessorize, and update your existing one.

Boston Magazine, January 1980 [DBA]

CUT OUT TO
Katy's
KENMORE SQUARE
LIVE ROCK TOP40
RON ROBIN'S DISCO
GOOD FOR ONE FREE ADMISSION
DURING THE MONTH OF AUGUST
(SAVES YOU AS MUCH AS $2)
In redeeming this ad for free admission to Katy's, I affirm I am 18 years of age or over. Valid for one free admission to Katy's Monday through Thursday evenings . . . and for one free admission with one paid admission on Friday, Saturday and Sunday . . . August 6-31, 1973.
MEMBERS
GUESTS

Paul's Mall
Jazz Workshop
733 Boylston St. 267-1300
MON. APR. 7 ONLY
KRAFTWERK
on Mercury Records
WED.–SUN. (Apr. 9-13)
DUKE AND THE DRIVERS
MON. APR. 14
PASSPORT
COMING APR. 18–20
JANIS IAN
OPENS MON.–THURS. (Apr. 7–10)
KENNY RANKIN
on Warner Bros. Records
APR. 18–20
THE HEADHUNTERS

TOP: ***Real Paper,*** August 1, 1973 [DBA]
BOTTOM: ***Real Paper,*** April 9, 1975 [LOCO]

BADGER ...
IT SPEAKS
FOR ITSELF.
ROBERTS/NEUSTADTER
69 NEWBURY STREET, BOSTON 267 2063

AFTER PARTY – ADMIT ONE
№ 1199
H.C.M. PRODUCTIONS
PRESENTS
"THIRD ANNUAL CELEBRITY AWARDS SHOW"
"The Night Hollywood Comes To You"
Friday, October 15, 1982 — 7:00 p.m.
JOHN HANCOCK AUDITORIUM
180 Berkley Street, Boston
ADVANCE TICKET: $12.00
AWARDS SHOW – ADMIT ONE
№ 1199

TOP: ***Boston Magazine,*** December 1977 [DBA]
BOTTOM: **Event ticket,** October 1982 [KBA]

What is printing? One of a series.

printing is a servant

. . . for the artist, for the writer, for the creative team that sets out to illustrate an idea and surround it with words . . . to persuade, to sell a commodity, to inform. The graphic arts are a *service* industry dedicated to quality and performance. All of us at Spencer subscribe to this idea.

Printing is Spencer!

SPENCER PRESS Inc.

90 INDUSTRIAL PARK ROAD, HINGHAM, MASS. 02043

749-5000

Boston Magazine, January 1970 [DBA]

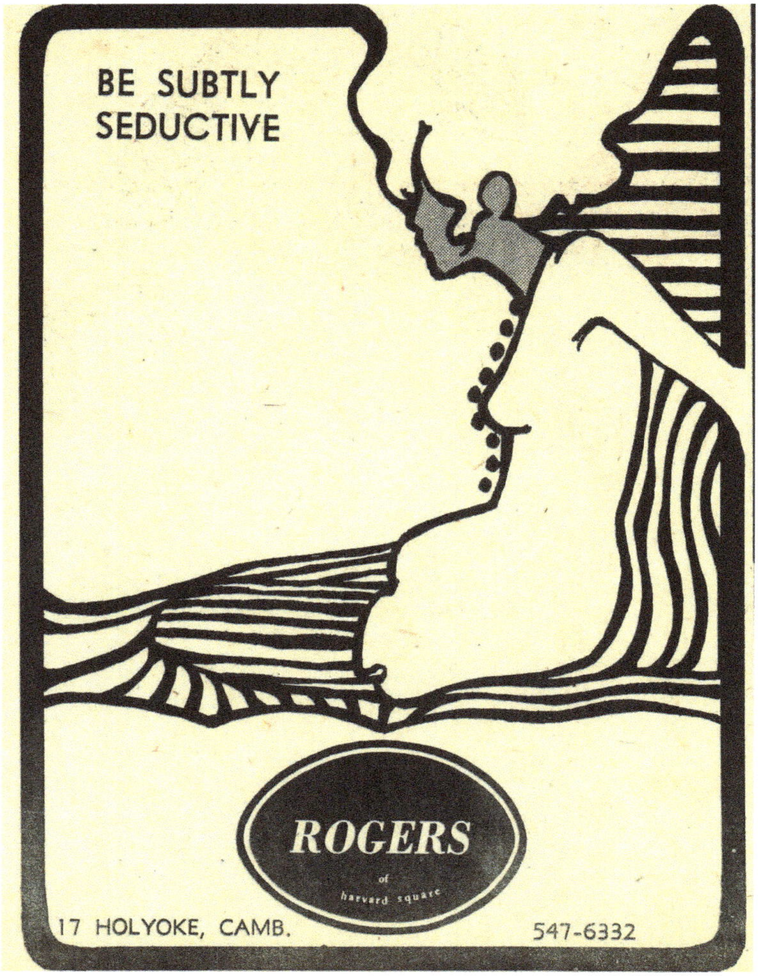
BE SUBTLY
SEDUCTIVE
ROGERS
of
harvard square
17 HOLYOKE, CAMB.
547-6332

Boston After Dark, September 17, 1969 [DBA]

DISCO
LESSONS
SUDDENLY You're DANCING
Tango
ChaCha
Rhumba
Hustle
Jitterbug
Waltz
Foxtrot
Classes every week. Beginner and Advanced. Featuring classes afternoons, evenings, weekends. Get Saturday Nite Fever Style any nite of the week.
5 Week Course
$25
call for further info.
BOSTON BALLROOM
CALL 536-8770 for SPECIAL OFFER!
367 BOYLSTON STREET, BOSTON
At Arlington Station — No Contracts Required

Real Paper, June 24, 1978 [DBA]

CUT · UPS
Richie
Larry
Donna
John
GEOMETRIC
UNISEX CUTS
CUTS
89 Charles Street
Boston, Mass.
523-8477

Boston Phoenix, June 21, 1972 [BCA]

PROPOSITION
A Circus/Theatre for children is coming to town. Improvised with music for anyone 10 and under. Every other Sunday, at The Proposition, beginning February 22 at 2 pm. Inman Square, Cambridge. 876-0088 $1.25. (Why not bring your birthday party?)
MURDER IN THE CATHEDRAL
by T. S. ELIOT
THEATRE CO. OF BOSTON
LESLIE LINDSEY CHAPEL
EMMANUEL CHURCH
15 NEWBURY STREET
NOW THRU APRIL 4
Tues, Wed, Thurs 8:30
Sat. 6, Sun. 5 & 8:30
$2.50, 3.50, 4.50
Fri. 8:30, Sat. 9:30
$3.00, 4.00, 5.00
Tel. res.: 261-2323
TEL. RES. 261-2323

Boston After Dark, March 18, 1970 [DBA]

STAND UP
FOR
SOMERVILLE!

WE ARE
THE
ALL AMERICA CITY!
DISPLAY AN ALL-AMERICA
CITY BUMPER STICKER —
NOW AVAILABLE AT MAYOR RALPH'S
OFFICE IN CITY HALL ; OR
CALL 625-6600 & ASK TO HAVE ONE
SENT TO YOU

1972 — 1973
SOMERVILLE, MASS.
ALL AMERICA CITY
WE, THE PEOPLE, TAKE PRIDE!

Somerville Journal, April 26, 1973 [BCA]

ALWAYS ON THE GO
WNAC-TV NEWS
BOSTON
AROUND THE TOWN
BOSTON
WNAC-TV NEWS
TO BRING YOU UP-TO-THE-MINUTE
WITH THE
EARLY NEWS 6:15 P.M.
LATE NEWS 11:00 P.M.
AN RKO GENERAL STATION
WNAC-TV
channel 7

Wilbur Theatre program, December 18, 1961 [BCA]

Ed George
FINAL4
Jim Butch
566-1657
Restaurant/Lounge
15 New Chardon St., Boston, MA 02114
(617) 723-8371
Bunratty's
Booking
CHRIS PORTER
(617) 254-9804
186 Harvard Ave.
Allston, MA 02134
BRIAN WASHBURN
Local Agent
(617) 451-6262
THE CHANNEL
Boston's best live rock
25 Necco St. Boston, MA 02210
Telephone
(508) 757-0001
Fax Phone
(508) 753-2930
HEART of the COMMONWEALTH
MARK MILLICH
261 Main Street • Worcester, Massachusetts 01608
DAVID T. GIAMMATEO
Entertainment & Promotions Manager
Bunratty's
"BOSTON'S BEST MUSIC-NIGHTLY!"
186 HARVARD AVE.
ALLSTON, MASS.
254-9820
Phil Bannatyne,
Proprietor
"Because fresh beer is best"
Cambridge Brewing Company
One Kendall Square, Bldg. 100 · Cambridge, MA 02139 · 617 494 1994
BONNEY BOULEY
T. T. The Bears Place
10 Brookline Street
Cambridge, MA 02139
Tel. 492-0082
280 GREEN STREET - CAMBRIDGE, MA. 02139
GREEN STREET GRILL
at
CHARLIE'S TAP
JAZZ CLUB
Formerly Tabasco Grille - On the Wild Side
(617) 876-1655
(617) 492-9723
John Clifford
186 Harvard Avenue
Allston, MA 02134
LOCAL 186
MICHAEL T. FORD
MANAGER
617-351-2660
617-351-2670
THE OUTER LIMITS ROCK CLUB
Booking / Promotions
29 Hancock Street
Quincy, MA 02171
John DeYoung (617) 328-1500
Michael DeYoung (508) 586-3035
C-LINE #61217
BUSINESS CARD

Chuck White Business Card Collection, 1980s–1990s [CWA/DBA]

Congratulations to N.E. Teen Scene

Jimmy "Early" Byrd

Radio Station

WILD

1090 on your dial

5:30 - 9:30 A.M. 2:00 - 3:00 P.M.

" The man that brought Nitty Gritty to the Bean City "

New England Teen Scene, January/February 1967 [ELA]

LIVE
CLASSICAL
MUSIC
NIGHTLY
AT THE ORSON WELLES
RESTAURANT
AND BAR
1001 Mass. Avenue
Cambridge, Mass. 02138
JLH '73

Boston Phoenix, April 24, 1973 [DBA]

WAKE UP AMERICA!
IT'S YOUR FAULT
Choose
Your
Leader into 1984
AT: PUNKT/DATA GALLERY
156 HANOVER ST North End
March 1-4th (primary day) SAT+SUN 7-11 til
*** OPENING MARCH 1 8:00 ********** April 1

Event flyer (design by Margaret Bailey Rosenbaum), March 1980 [FLYNN]

WRECK Lounge and the BOLAY Room
JAZZ
FOR 7--BIG NITES--7 ★ Plus Big Sun. Mat. at 3:00 p.m.
Direct from Birdland HELD OVER! BUCCI At The Organ
WITH
JOE RIDDICK ON DRUMS
ADA LEE JAZZ FESTIVAL STAR
CORNER, HARVARD AVE. AND CAMBRIDGE ST., ALLSTON AL 4-9400

TRACY COY VIVACIOUS DANCING LOVELY
BILLY PARKER COMEDY M.C.
RENA SAUNDERS DYNAMIC SONGSTRESS
CONTINUOUS ENTERTAINMENT 8 P.M. to 1 A.M. & DANCING NIGHTLY
FOR XMAS PARTIES RESERVE NOW PHONE FRAN CI 7-9001
BROWN DERBY
1358 BOYLSTON ST. BOSTON
NEAR FENWAY PARK
GUY MORRELL His Guitar and Songs

BRIGHT SPOT
Rates for Parties & Banquets
MAKE RESERVATIONS NOW FOR CHRISTMAS PARTIES
2—SHOWS EVERY NIGHT—2
PEGGY DAVIS SINGING STYLIST
GEORGIE HOLIDAY M. C.
BARBETTE ORIENTAL DANCER
298 Washington St. BRIGHTON ST 2-1612

Pony Room at CIRCLE Inn
469 NEPONSET AVE. at Neponset Circle, DORCHESTER
14th SMASH HIT WEEK!
APPEARING NIGHTLY TONY RAND
THE FABULOUS "MR. 7-11" of Columbia Recording Fame
PLENTY OF FREE PARKING

BIG JIM MELLEN'S SHANTY Lounge
Featured Nitely
The SENSATIONAL
NOBLE WATTS
His TENOR SAXE and ORGAN TRIO
COMING DEC. 2
The JOLLY JAX
• NO COVER • NO MINIMUM
1781 WASHINGTON ST.

• TONIGHT thru SUNDAY
Also Sunday Matinee 3-7
GEORGE BRAITH
Blue Note Record Star
and His Combo
NO COVER • NO MINIMUM
CONNOLLY'S STAR DUST ROOM
1184 TREMONT ST.
(Near RUGGLES ST.) GA 7-9831

LENNIE'S On-the-Turnpike Rt. 1 W. Peabody
Held Over Thru Sun. Dec. 1
HOWARD McGHEE TRIO
With PHIL PORTER • CANDY FINCH
Matinee Sun. — Dec. 1-4-7
Now Accepting Holiday PARTY RESERVATIONS
Res. JE 1-9622

CLOSED FOR ALTERATIONS
Reopening FRIDAY, NOV. 29
WITH A GALA SHOW!
1233 HOUSE
1233 Bennington St.
EAST BOSTON

ENJOY The Fabulous
FAY McKAY
for "Laffs in Song"
AL LEWIS and TONY HERNON "MINSTREL MEN"
HERBIE'S CACTUS ROOM
88 QUEENSBERRY ST. COR. KILMARNOCK
ONLY 2 BLOCKS FROM FENWAY PARK

To order an ad to Buy, Rent, Sell or Exchange — Telephone LIberty 2-4000.

Boston Record American, November 25, 1963 [BCA]

Just think.
You've got your
whole life
ahead of you.
It's up to you. You make the choices.
All we're telling you is to think before you act. Get the facts and make your own decisions. And when you come up against the really tough questions — sex, drugs, alcohol — it's always a good idea to talk about them. Talk to your mom or dad. Talk to your brothers and sisters and teachers. Talk to your friends. And if you feel you want to talk some more, call the Teen Line. Just call 424-5700, and we'll refer you to resources that deal with your particular question.
Just think. You've got your whole life ahead of you. So make the most of it. Starting now.
The Teen Line
424-5700
Sponsored by the HCHP Foundation, Inc.

Promotional campaign flyer, December 1985 [ELA]

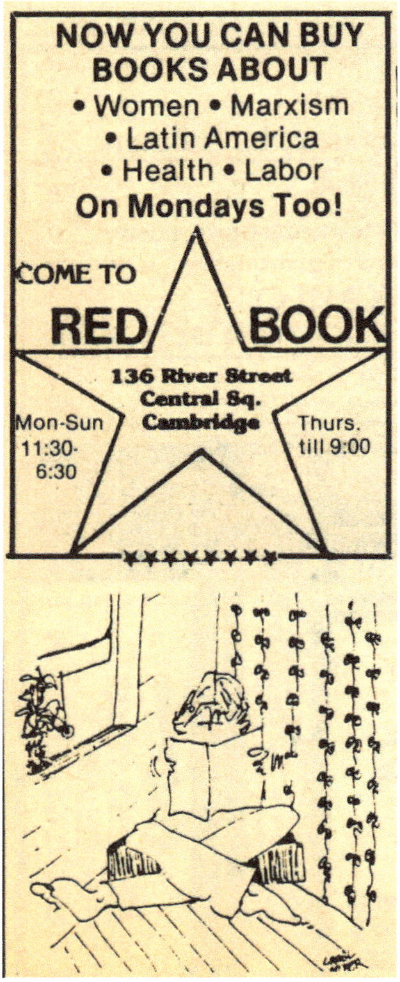
NOW YOU CAN BUY
BOOKS ABOUT
• Women • Marxism
• Latin America
• Health • Labor
On Mondays Too!
COME TO
RED BOOK
136 River Street
Central Sq.
Cambridge
Mon-Sun
11:30-
6:30
Thurs.
till 9:00

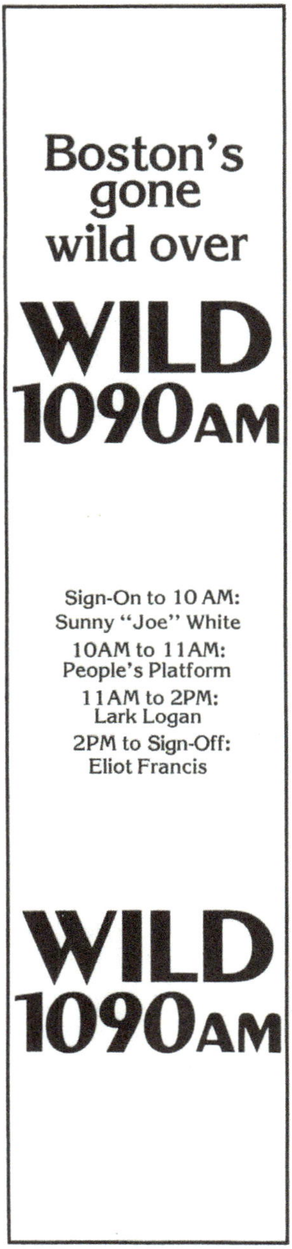
Boston's
gone
wild over
WILD
1090AM
Sign-On to 10 AM:
Sunny "Joe" White
10AM to 11AM:
People's Platform
11AM to 2PM:
Lark Logan
2PM to Sign-Off:
Eliot Francis
WILD
1090AM

LEFT: ***Sojourner* magazine**, September 1981 [BCA]
RIGHT: ***Nightfall,*** October 1977 [DBA]

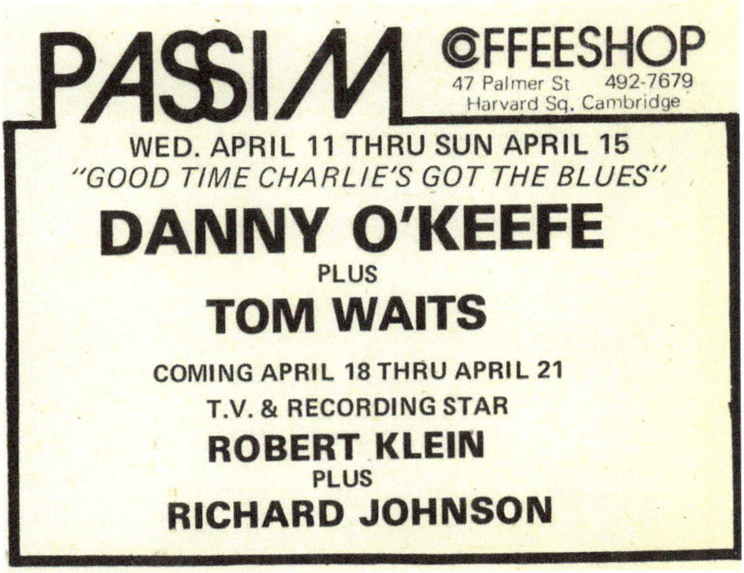
PASSIM
COFFEESHOP
47 Palmer St 492-7679
Harvard Sq. Cambridge
WED. APRIL 11 THRU SUN APRIL 15
"GOOD TIME CHARLIE'S GOT THE BLUES"
DANNY O'KEEFE
PLUS
TOM WAITS
COMING APRIL 18 THRU APRIL 21
T.V. & RECORDING STAR
ROBERT KLEIN
PLUS
RICHARD JOHNSON

UNICORN
COFFEE HOUSE
EVERY MONDAY NIGHT
the
DICK SUMMER
SHOW
THROUGH JUNE 4
THE SACRED
MUSHROOM
825 Boylston St. Boston
dial: UNICORN
June 6-18 RICHIE HAVENS / June 20 - July 2 THE GRATEFUL DEAD

TOP: ***Boston Phoenix,*** March 1, 1972 [BCA]
BOTTOM: ***Broadside,*** May 24, 1967 [BCA]

BOSTON CLUB
PRESENTS
THURS. MAY 3
FANNY
—on Warner Bros. Records
TUES. MAY 8 - THURS. MAY 10
GENYA RAVAN
—on Dunhill Records
COMING MAY 22
BERMUDASTROLLERS
Our policy is to bring to you national entertainment along with the best prices!
Coming Soon!
CHAMBERS BROTHERS / FABULOUS RHINESTONES
FOCUS / SPRING FEVER
the Garage
969 COMMONWEALTH AVENUE, BOSTON
PHONE 542–1550
Page 2
NIGHT LIFE

Night Life, May 1973 [DBA]

dummy's*

so called because we charge

25¢ Beer 12 oz.
50¢ Drinks
25¢ Hot Dogs

Huge Dance Floor

Great Sound & Lights

Except Friday & Saturday
50¢ Beer 12 oz.
1.00 Drinks
50¢ Hot Dogs

Wed Nite Free Beer
$2.00 Cover Charge

*The queen, the Pope, Batman and Robin, Frankenstein, Dracula, Alice in Wonderland and many, many more life-like dummies from the London Wax Museum will be there.

dummy's
967 Comm. Ave., Boston
Formerly The Boston Club

Boston Phoenix, September 21, 1976 [DBA]

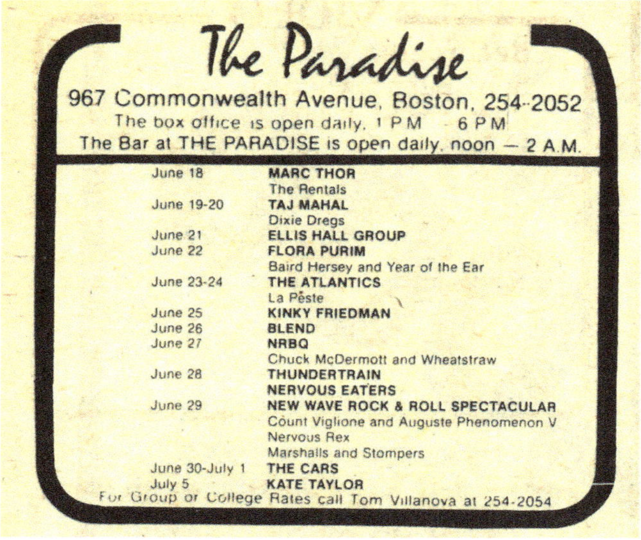
The Paradise
967 Commonwealth Avenue, Boston, 254-2052
The box office is open daily, 1 PM - 6 PM
The Bar at THE PARADISE is open daily, noon — 2 A.M.
June 18 MARC THOR
The Rentals
June 19-20 TAJ MAHAL
Dixie Dregs
June 21 ELLIS HALL GROUP
June 22 FLORA PURIM
Baird Hersey and Year of the Ear
June 23-24 THE ATLANTICS
La Peste
June 25 KINKY FRIEDMAN
June 26 BLEND
June 27 NRBQ
Chuck McDermott and Wheatstraw
June 28 THUNDERTRAIN
NERVOUS EATERS
June 29 NEW WAVE ROCK & ROLL SPECTACULAR
Count Viglione and Auguste Phenomenon V
Nervous Rex
Marshalls and Stompers
June 30-July 1 THE CARS
July 5 KATE TAYLOR
For Group or College Rates call Tom Villanova at 254-2054

BOSTON City Club
BOSTON'S LARGEST SINGLES CLUB
WEDNESDAY
Rock Festival 1970 featuring the finest in contemporary Rock and Soul Bands.
THURSDAY
MIKE LANDERS & THE PROFESSIONALS
A sound to satisfy all tastes.
FRIDAY—Sweet and Soul. Eddie Barden Orch. Brute Force, con't ent.
SATURDAY—Con't entertainment. The Attractions. Eddie Barden Orch.
SUNDAY—
EDDIE BARDEN ORCHESTRA
8-2 nightly 8-1 Sat.
free parking MBTA stops at front door
for parties banquets and functions call 542-1550
967 COMMONWEALTH AVENUE
MEMBERS GUESTS

TOP: ***Real Paper,*** June 24, 1978 [DBA]

BOTTOM: ***Boston Herald Traveler,*** April 26, 1970 [DBA]

The Land of OZ
Boston's Largest Private Gay Disco Club
VALENTINE'S DAY
Costume DRAG AND DANCE CONTEST
FREE! CHAMPAGNE & BUFFET
$500. IN CASH PRIZES!
WED. FEB. 11 ★ Fri. & Sat. $1. ADMISSION
SUN. thru THURS. NO COVER
The Land of OZ
Largest Dance Floor * Live Shows * Discotheque
969 COMMONWEALTH AVE.
BOSTON (NEAR COMM. ARMORY)
"Support Your Gay Disco Club"

Event flyer, most likely 1976 [THP]

Jacques
FREAKERS
Dance Contest
(couples only)
1st place — $50 cash prize
Thursdays 10pm
79 Broadway, Bay Village

TAKE YOUR PHONE WITH YOU
Dial Phone goes anywhere ■ Full dialing capability in a completely portable, all-solid state telephone
Attaché
MOBILE TELEPHONE CO.
Waltham • 617-890-0154

LEFT: ***Hit Parade of Boston,*** November 1978 [DBA]
RIGHT: ***Boston Magazine,*** September 1973 [DBA]

This is not
Bette Midler.
This is one of the impressionists
in the extraordinary Revue
"French Dressing". It is an
evening of incredible
illusions—Judy Garland,
Liza Minnelli, Julie Andrews,
Barbara Streisand,
Bette Midler and more—
it's music, it's dancing,
it's like nothing
you've ever seen before
You've got to see it
to believe it!
DINNER & SHOW
Coming Jan. 9
Reserve Your Table
Now For Best Seating!
Call 879-5300
and Charge It.
Bank Americard • Mastercharge
American Express • Diners Club
Chateau de Ville
Dinner
Theatre
FRAMINGHAM

South Middlesex News, January 6, 1976 [BCA]

KUUMBA
Reception
Presented by Members of the
BAAA
Boston Afro-American
Artists Association
MUSIC • DANCE
POETRY • FOOD
and MORE
featuring
BLACK FOLKS THEATER CO.
AFRICAN UNITY DANCE TROUPE
"LIFT HIM UP" MINISTRY PRODUCTIONS
FRED WOODARD JAZZ QUARTET
Tuesday, December 5th
5:30 p.m. to 9:00 p.m.
UMASS / CPCS
CAMPUS GALLERY
100 Arlington St., Boston, Mass.
ADMISSION FREE
J. Barbour

Event flyer, most likely December 1989 [KBA]

A PHOENIX SUCCESS STORY

Since long before "Fuzz," starring Burt Reynolds and Raquel Welch opened at the Cheri Theatre Complex on Wednesday, June 14, Sack Theatres has been trying to find an answer to the April issue of Cosmopolitan.

Finally they placed the following ad in the June 21 issue of the Phoenix:

Looking for a MALE "FUZZ" model.

Must be willing to pose in the nude. Mail photo to

"FUZZ" 539 Washington St. Boston, Mass. 02111

SUCCESS AT LAST!

This photo was produced on Wednesday, June 28!
Whatever you are searching for no matter how unique or unusual, use the Phoenix to help you!

CITADEL
2nd FLOOR MEN'S LOUNGE
gay DISCO IS HERE
Starting Tues., Dec. 16
D.J. Raving Ron's Dancing Machine
Tuesday thru Friday Every Week
New Light Show
New Sound
22 AVERY ST.
BOSTON
338-9634

TOP: ***Boston Phoenix,*** July 5, 1972 [BCA]
BOTTOM: **Event flyer,** late 1970s [THP]

mammoth
RECORDS
Steve Balcom
Label Manager
MARK MELOCCARO
PRESIDENT
VILD
RECORDS, INC.
185 COREY RD
BOSTON, MA 02146
(617) 566-3339
ANNA STATMAN
Marketing Director
RECORDS
7381 Beverly Blvd.
Los Angeles, CA 90036
(213) 937-4660
RELATIVITY
IN-EFFECT
COMBAT
Peter Kang
TOUR PROMOTION
TAANG!
RECORDS
P.O. BOX 51
AUBURNDALE, MA 02166
PH (617) 965-5673
FAX (617) 527-1647
METAL BLADE
RECORDS
LORI MEADOWS
Artist Relations
729 7th Avenue • 14th Floor • New York, NY 10019
212 • 921 • 4370 FAX 212 • 869 • 2040
BLACK&BLUE
RECORDS
"MUSIC TO MAKE YOUR EARS HURT"
(401) 949-4887
PETER YARMOUTH
LARRY EVILELF
Suite 152
400 D. Putnam Pike
Smithfield, RI 02917
Coyote
RECORDS
STEVE DALY
P.O. BOX 112 • UPTOWN HOBOKEN • NEW JERSEY 07030
(212) 995-0648
21ST CIRCUITRY
RECORDS
396 Waller Street
San Francisco
California 94117
Don Blanchard
415.252.9578
(617) 442-3284
B. DOWN RECORDS
(HOME OF GANGSTARR POSSE)
19 Wyoming St.
P.O. Box 35
BOSTON, MA 02121
JUDITH L. JOHNSON
PRESIDENT
C-LINE #61217
BUSINESS CARD

Chuck White Business Card Collection, 1980s–1990s [CWA/DBA]

IT'S A HAPPENING
And it's at Lechmere in Cambridge and Dedham where you can select
SUNN AMPLIFIERS
SLINGERLAND DRUM SETS
FARFISA ORGANS
VEGA BANJOS
BOGEN AMPLIFIERS
All are designed to fit young pocketbooks and all are in stock at both Lechmere stores. Choose also from a complete line of accessories from the most complete selection in New England. . . and . . . wouldn't you know it even a happening is priced Lechmere's way.
CAMBRIDGE
88 FIRST ST.
Tel. 491-2000
LECHMERE
where you pocket the difference
DEDHAM
ROUTE 1
Tel. 329-2200

New England Teen Scene, July 1968 [ELA]

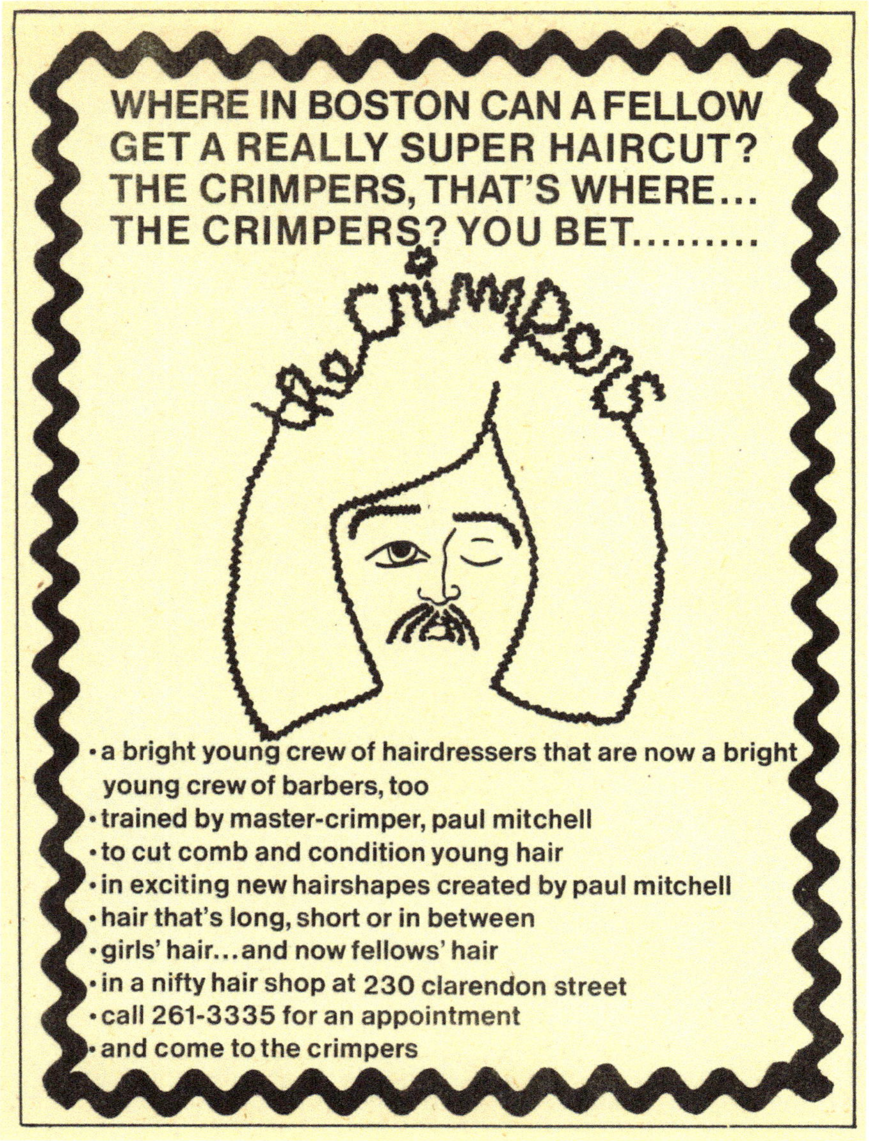
WHERE IN BOSTON CAN A FELLOW
GET A REALLY SUPER HAIRCUT?
THE CRIMPERS, THAT'S WHERE...
THE CRIMPERS? YOU BET.........
the crimpers
• a bright young crew of hairdressers that are now a bright young crew of barbers, too
• trained by master-crimper, paul mitchell
• to cut comb and condition young hair
• in exciting new hairshapes created by paul mitchell
• hair that's long, short or in between
• girls' hair...and now fellows' hair
• in a nifty hair shop at 230 clarendon street
• call 261-3335 for an appointment
• and come to the crimpers

Boston Phoenix, December 1, 1971 [BCA]

MORE JAZZ, MORE OF THE TIME, AND BETTER
ON WBUR, 90.9 FM
WBUR – WE HAVE EVERYTHING BUT COMMERCIALS

Jazz New England, October 1974 [VACCA]

UNIVERSAL PRODUCTIONS
Presents In Concert
DWAYNE
OMARR
Also Appearing
• Young Generation
• Chocolate Kisses
• Gospel Singer Peaches Evans
• Calypso Pan Player Mickey
• Next Generation
• Acappella Singer Stacey Brown
• Male Vocalist Brian Delouch
• Comedian Jef Tarpley
• Female Vocalist Raynya Conway
Strand Theatre
282 Columbia Road
April 18, 1986 • 8:00 pm - until
Advance Tickets $10.00 • At the Door $12.00
Miss this event and blame yourself!
UNIVERSAL PRODUCTIONS
DWAYNE OMARR
Strand Theatre
April 18, 1986 • 8:00 pm

two
O'Clock
Club
642 Washington Street
Boston
CONTINUOUS
ENTERTAINMENT
2 PM – 2 AM
THE LONGEST BAR
IN MASSACHUSETTS
Call 426-6610 for
Bachelor Party
Arrangements
Featuring
Crystal Blue
"Miss Persuasion"
Also: MACHINE GUN KELLY

TOP: **Concert ticket,** April 1986 [BCA]
BOTTOM: ***Boston Phoenix,*** April 17, 1973 [BCA]

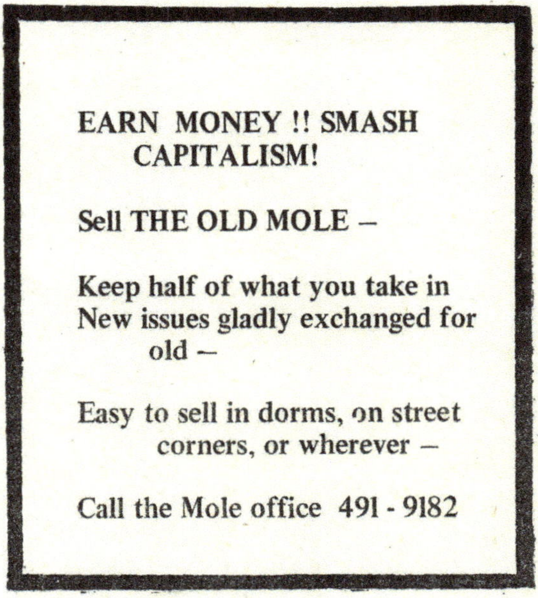
EARN MONEY !! SMASH CAPITALISM!
Sell THE OLD MOLE –
Keep half of what you take in
New issues gladly exchanged for old –
Easy to sell in dorms, on street corners, or wherever –
Call the Mole office 491 - 9182

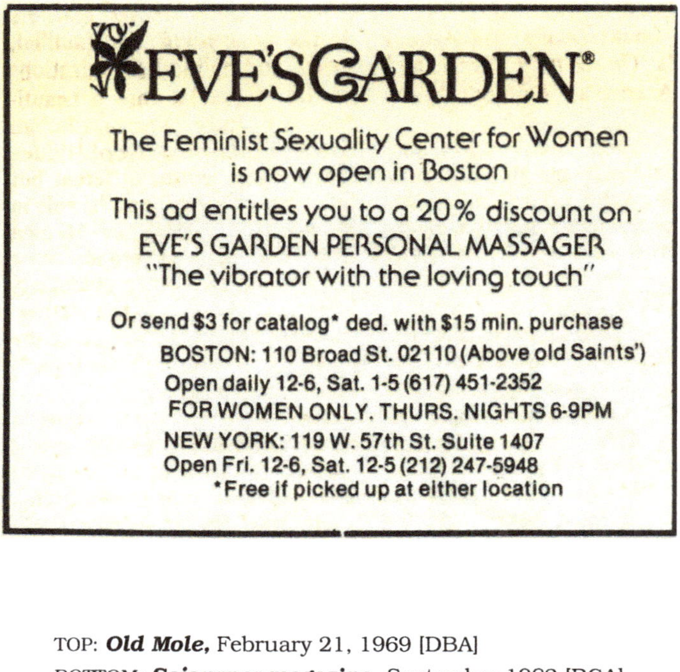
EVE'S GARDEN®
The Feminist Sexuality Center for Women is now open in Boston
This ad entitles you to a 20% discount on EVE'S GARDEN PERSONAL MASSAGER
"The vibrator with the loving touch"
Or send $3 for catalog* ded. with $15 min. purchase
BOSTON: 110 Broad St. 02110 (Above old Saints')
Open daily 12-6, Sat. 1-5 (617) 451-2352
FOR WOMEN ONLY. THURS. NIGHTS 6-9PM
NEW YORK: 119 W. 57th St. Suite 1407
Open Fri. 12-6, Sat. 12-5 (212) 247-5948
*Free if picked up at either location

TOP: ***Old Mole,*** February 21, 1969 [DBA]
BOTTOM: ***Sojourner* magazine,** September 1982 [BCA]

NEIGHBORHOOD MOVIE DIRECTORY FOR SATURDAY

NOW! At Reduced Prices!
SYMPHONY I
HUNT. at MASS. 262-8820
Free Glasses!
The Stewardesses
STEREOVISION
3D
POSITIVE ADULT IDENTIFICATION REQUIRED
THE UNPUBLISHABLE NOVEL IS NOW AMERICA'S MOST CONTROVERSIAL FILM!
RATED X
EASTMANCOLOR
WITH
CHRISTINA HART • MICHAEL GARRETT
EXECUTIVE PRODUCER LOUIS K. SHER • WRITTEN AND DIRECTED BY ALF SILLIMAN JR.

ESQUIRE THEATRE GUIDE
Rte.3 CINEMA CITY CHELMSFORD 256-0611
1 Wuthering Heights
2 WALTER MATTHAU "A New Leaf"
3 "LITTLE BIG MAN"
4 LOVE STORY
All Shows Sun-Thur 7&9:30; Fri & Sat 7&10

NO. STATION CINEMA 227-6651 opp. BOSTON GARDEN
"SENSUAL PRACTICES IN SWEDEN" X

garden 536-9477 ARLINGTON ST.
GLENDA JACKSON "WOMEN IN LOVE" 1:15-3:25-5:30 7:40-9:45

CAPITOL BROCKTON 961-2114
1 VANISHING POINT
2 "LOVERS & OTHER STRANGERS"

Winthrop Cinema 846-3440
THUNDERBALL JAMES BOND YOU ONLY LIVE TWICE

PLAZA DERRY, N.H. 432-2576
X "He and She" X

BACK BAY
SENSUAL PRACTICES

BELMONT
STUDIO CINEMA (R) 484-1706
"I LOVE MY WIFE" 7:00 9:00
Mat. Only "KING KONG ESCAPES" & "EVIL OF FRANKENSTEIN" — Children 75c

BROCKTON
SKYVIEW 3 SMASH HITS
HOUSE THAT SCREAMED
"HORROR HOUSE"
3rd "DIE MONSTER DIE"

CHELMSFORD
CHELMSFORD DRIVE-IN • Rte. 110
"THUNDERBALL" 7:30
"YOU ONLY LIVE TWICE"

CHELSEA
Rte. 1-1A PARKWAY PLAZA Free Parking
884-6557 James Bond in "THUNDERBALL" (GP)
2:00 and 6:30
"YOU ONLY LIVE TWICE" (GP)
4:00 and 9:00

DORCHESTER
E.M. LOEW'S PARK 436-2100
AMPLE ADJACENT PARKING
1524 DORCHESTER AVE.
DOUBLE SEAN CONNERY 007 SPECTACULAR
"THUNDERBALL" (GP) 2:30 & 8:40
"YOU ONLY LIVE TWICE" 12:30 & 6:45

EVERETT
PARK "LADY IN CEMENT" 7:30
"THE GREAT WHITE HOPE" 9:00
"BIKINI BEACH" Co-hit 1:15

GLOUCESTER
NO. SHORE 1&2 283 1936
"Little Big Man" 7 & 9:30
"Love Story"

HYDE PARK
NU PIXIE CINEMA EVE. 7:45 361-6111
"WOODSTOCK" (R)

NEPONSET—REVERE—SUFFOLK—V.F.W.—NATICK
CLEVELAND CIRCLE—LAWRENCE—DEDHAM

7 ACADEMY AWARD NOMINATIONS
INCLUDING
BEST PICTURE
BEST ACTOR
BEST ACTRESS
BEST SUPPORTING ACTOR
BEST DIRECTOR
LOVE STORY by ERICH SEGAL
ALI MACGRAW RYAN O'NEAL
GP
SHOWN: 1:30 3:30 5:30 7:30 9:50
Circle THEATRE AT CLEVELAND CIRCLE
566-4040 • FREE PARKING • ROCKING CHAIR SEATS
AT THE INTERSECTION OF BEACON ST. AND CHESTNUT HILL AVE. ONLY 1 MIN. FROM EITHER RT. 9 OR COMMONWEALTH AVE. VIA CHESTNUT HILL AVE. ALSO EASILY ACCESSIBLE VIA M.B.T.A.

SHOWCASE CINEMAS 1 AND 2
AT ROUTES 114 AND 495, LAWRENCE 686-2121
"Wonderfully Funny" —Globe
Walter Matthau Elaine May A New Leaf G
WEEKDAYS 7:30-9:30
SAT. & SUN. 1:40-3:30-5:40-7:40-9:40
"RACY DRAMA" —Globe
BARRY NEWMAN VANISHING POINT GP
WEEKDAYS 7:40-9:40
SAT. & SUN. 1:30-3:30-5:30-7:30-9:30

DRIVE-IN THEATERS
CHILDREN UNDER 12 FREE
ELECTRIC IN-CAR HEATERS
MON. THRU THURS. 7:30 P.M. —FRI. & SAT. CONT. 7 P.M. —SUN. & HOL. CONT. 6:30 P.M.
DEDHAM RTES. 1 & 128 326-3800
SUFFOLK OPP. TRACK 567-7900
REVERE RTE. C1 & 60 284-5700
V.F.W. 325-6000 PARKWAY RT. 1 W. ROXBURY
NEPONSET AT NEPONSET CIR. 282-3500
NATICK RT. 9 & 30 FRAMINGHAM LINE 653-0800
1st RUN THE HOUSE THAT SCREAMED
JANE FONDA SPIRITS of the DEAD
PLUS WHAT A THIRST! COUNT YORGA vampire
DOUBLE BOND THRILLER
SEAN CONNERY "THUNDERBALL"
PLUS SEAN CONNERY IS JAMES BOND YOU ONLY LIVE TWICE
3rd Feature at Revere, VFW and Neponset Only
BURT LANCASTER THE SCALP HUNTERS

MEDFORD
FREE GAS
STARTS 7 P.M.—SUN.—6 P.M.
EX 5-3400
MEADOW
GP BONDED ENTERTAINMENT
"THUNDERBALL"
"YOU ONLY LIVE TWICE"
3rd HIT—DANGER ROUTE
ELECTRIC HEATERS
GLEN
GP THE SUSPENSE IS SHEER TORTURE
THE HOUSE THAT SCREAMED
2. BLACK SUNDAY
3. DUNWICH HORROR

MEDFORD TWIN DRIVE-IN
WINTER POLICY!
$4.00 per CARLOAD
WELLINGTON (GP)
"WOODSTOCK"
"HARPER"
(XXX) CIRCLE
"THE THREESOME"
"JULIE IS NO ANGEL"
"TURN TO LOVE"
STARTS DAILY 7 P.M. • SUN. 6 P.M.

BURLINGTON
BR2-0860 Route 128
JCT RTE 128 & 3 EXIT 41S
E.M. LOEWS DRIVE INS
Sean Connery as James Bond · color
"THUNDERBALL"
YOU ONLY LIVE TWICE color
PINEHURST 667-7911
RTE 38 EXIT 41N ON 128
Barbra Streisand · Geo Segal
OWL and the PUSSYCAT color
"VIRGIN SOLDIER"
R

CANTON
$3.00 PER CARLOAD
BLUE HILLS DRIVE-IN 828-2122
Rte. 138, Canton
EASY RIDER
LOVING
CORRUPTION 7:00
OPEN FRI. SAT. SUN.

NORTH WEYMOUTH
ELECTRIC IN CAR HEATERS
WEYMOUTH
"BULLITT" Steve McQueen
"GREEN BERETS" John Wayne
DRIVE-IN Open 6:30 337-3500 SOUTH SHORE Route 3A
"THE HOUSE THAT SCREAMED"
"SPIRITS of the DEAD"
"SCREAM and SCREAM AGAIN"

MEDFORD
CINEMA I & II 395-9499 MEDFORD SQ.
"THUNDERBALL" 7:00 Plus
"YOU ONLY LIVE TWICE" 9:00
"LOVERS AND OTHER STRANGERS" 7-9
"HELLO DOWN THERE" 1:30

NATICK
NATICK Loew's
TODAY 1:30-3:30 5:30-7:30-9:35

SCITUATE
PLAYHOUSE 1&2
LOVE STORY 1:30 7:00 9:30 GP
LITTLE BIG MAN 1:30 7:00 9:30 GP

Boston Record American, April 10, 1971 [BCA]

the Molls
Interplanetary Rock
Performing at:
The Rat, Kenmore Sq.
Date: Mon- Wed, Jan 10-12
The Molls screamed and hissed above them. "They're coming again," the girl managed to gasp.
Call 787-5420 for info

Concert flyer, January 1977 [Courtesy of Tristram Lozaw]

DEL FUEGOS
DOGMATICS
SPEARHEAD, GO!
PRIME MOVERS
SUMMER DANCE PARTY
ALL AGES
SAT. JULY 10
GALLERY EAST
ADMISSION $4.00 6pm.-10pm.
SPECIAL ADDED ATTRACTIONS

Concert flyer, July 1982 [VALDEZ]

KATY'S
thru June 22
margo thunder
June 23-29 Allston Funk
METAXA FESTIVAL Tues-Wed-Thurs
TUESDAY, KING OF CLUBS NIGHT
KATY'S: A wonderful world with beatuiful people
KENMORE CLUB KENMORE SQ. BOSTON 536-1950

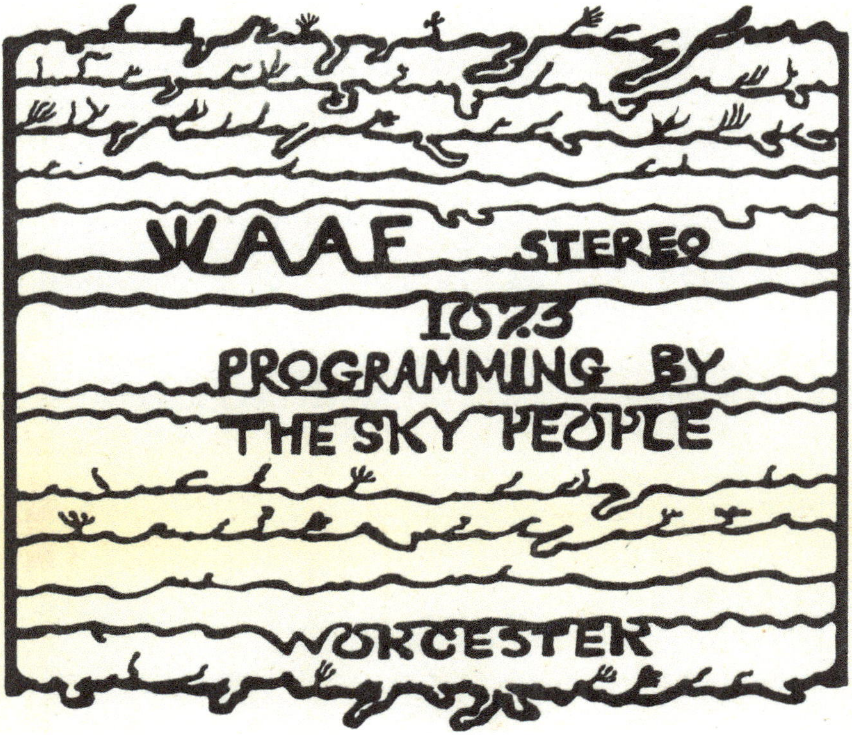
WAAF STEREO
107.3
PROGRAMMING BY
THE SKY PEOPLE
WORCESTER

TOP: ***Real Paper,*** June 18, 1975 [DBA]
BOTTOM: ***Free Paper (Cambridge Phoenix),*** October 14, 1970 [DBA]

Get all your licks in!
J.P. Licks delicately hand-rolls Danish Sundae ice cream cones . . . BIG, CRISP and FRESH. You choose two generous scoops (from very possibly the finest 25 flavors anywhere) like: Kahlúa, Amaretto, White Coffee, Carrot Cake and top with homemade bittersweet hot fudge, butterscotch (made with creamy butter), fresh cut strawberries, or choose from 10 LICKS MIXES like: Crushed Reese's, Heath Bars and M&M's, and finish with a crown of fresh whipped heavy cream.
J.P. Licks
HOMEMADE ICE CREAM CO.
1225 Cambridge Street
Inman Square Cambridge
486 Centre Street
Jamaica Plain
The Next Time You Need An Ice Cream Fix . . . Drop By And Lick for Yourself!

***What's New* magazine,** late 1983 [DBA]

Before:
After:
"The Either/Orchestra
changed my whole outlook!"
Either/Orchestra:
Thursdays in Sept.
Ryles, Inman Sq.

Concert poster, September 1987 [GERSHON]

station wagon. Call evenings 547-1141 or 547-3789.

Super Cheap-moving & hauling, 868-8853.

Moving? Person with truck and lower rates. Call after 6-266-5991.

Media Movers: "Something in the way we move." 354-2374 ask for Michael.

Muscle Movers: Big men for a big job. Call 262-6892 ask for David.

This is what we're all about

PHASE 2 – Boston's largest and most popular computer dating service. For free info. and an application dial 266-2138 (anytime).

Phase 2

Gene's DATSUN

SEDANS • WAGON • PICKUP • SPORTS CARS

Repairs on all other makes.

'57 Austin Healy 100-4 completely reconditioned

'67 VW fastback 14,000 miles

1280 Cambridge St. Cambridge 354-9046

HELP WANTED

Financial Partner needed for new enterprise in Boston: benefit to enlightened community and profitable. Mr. Erdmann, 432 Broadway, Cambridge 02138.

THE SANCTUARY IN CAMBRIDGE

STREET PEOPLE'S PROBLEMS

492-2000 • 24 hrs.

BOUTIQUE de OPTIQUE

REGISTERED DISPENSING OPTICIANS

EYEWEAR FROM THE WORLD OVER & THE LATEST FASHION TINTS

WE WILL CUSTOM MAKE ANY SHAPE FRAME YOU WANT

LAB ON PREMISES. EMERGENCY REPAIRS DONE WHILE YOU WAIT.

227-3676

89 Charles Street

Copyright Oct. 13, 1970 — The Phoenix; Oct. 14, 1970 — The Free Paper.

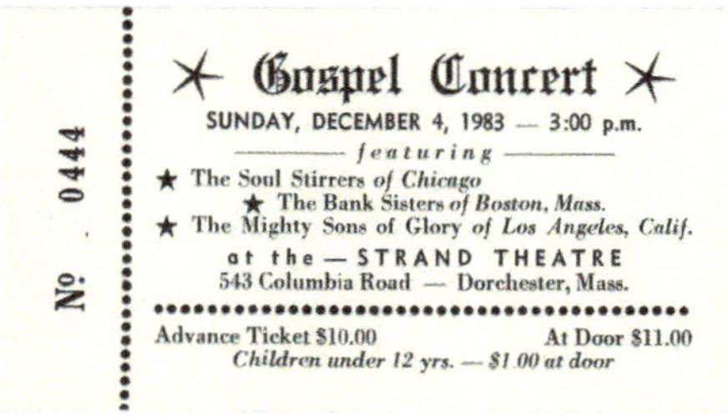
No 0444
Gospel Concert
SUNDAY, DECEMBER 4, 1983 — 3:00 p.m.
featuring
The Soul Stirrers of Chicago
The Bank Sisters of Boston, Mass.
The Mighty Sons of Glory of Los Angeles, Calif.
at the — STRAND THEATRE
543 Columbia Road — Dorchester, Mass.
Advance Ticket $10.00
At Door $11.00
Children under 12 yrs. — $1.00 at door

TOP: ***Free Paper (Cambridge Phoenix),*** October 14, 1970 [DBA]
BOTTOM: **Concert ticket,** December 1983 [BCA]

ARMADILLO
will knock you out
and that's no jive
A Clothing and Shoe Store
for Adventurous Men
and Sporting Ladies
Till 8 o'clock
thru December
134 Newbury St.
Boston

Boston Phoenix, December 10, 1974 [DBA]

IBA
Areito presenta
Obra teatral escrita y dirigida por: Jorge Arce.
Desarrollada por el taller de improvisación AREITO.
viernes 30 de Junio 8:P.M.
(1989)
CENTRO CULTURAL VILLA VICTORIA
ENTRADA LIBRE!!
UN REGALO PARA MAMÁ
A GIFT FOR MOMMY
play, written and directed by Jorge Arce.
performed by the Improvisation workShop AREITO.
Friday, JUNE 30th at 8:p.m.
Free admission.
Este Proyecto se hace posible con Fondos de: Heritage MASS Council of Art and the Humanities.

Theater flyer, June 1989 [Courtesy of Snell Library at Northeastern University]

FOXBORO
TUES. NITE:
Miss New England
BEAUTY
PAGEANT
You!-The Fans are the JUDGES!
ON ROUTE 1 easy to reach from ROUTE 95 Exit 28 from BOSTON • From PROVIDENCE Exit 30 • Post Time 8 P.M.
"THE BIG EXACTA" ON 7th & 8th RACES
PLUS 2 PERFECTAS NIGHTLY • FOURTH AND LAST RACE

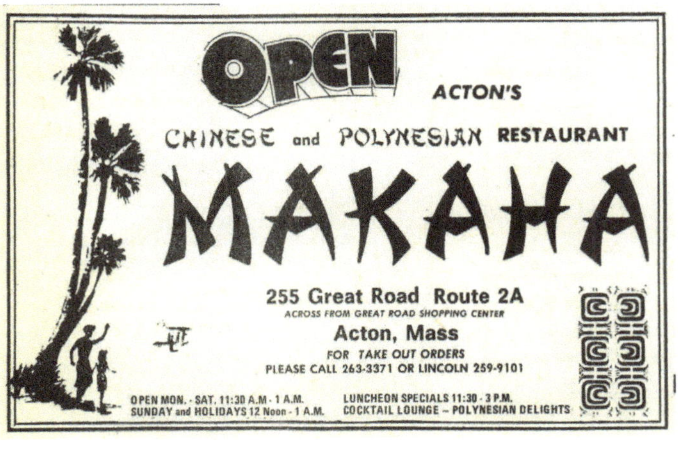
OPEN
ACTON'S
CHINESE and POLYNESIAN RESTAURANT
MAKAHA
255 Great Road Route 2A
ACROSS FROM GREAT ROAD SHOPPING CENTER
Acton, Mass
FOR TAKE OUT ORDERS
PLEASE CALL 263-3371 OR LINCOLN 259-9101
OPEN MON. - SAT. 11:30 A.M - 1 A.M.
SUNDAY and HOLIDAYS 12 Noon - 1 A.M.
LUNCHEON SPECIALS 11:30 - 3 P.M.
COCKTAIL LOUNGE – POLYNESIAN DELIGHTS

TOP: ***Boston Herald Traveler,*** July 21, 1969 [BCA]
BOTTOM: ***Sudbury Citizen,*** June 20, 1974 [BCA]

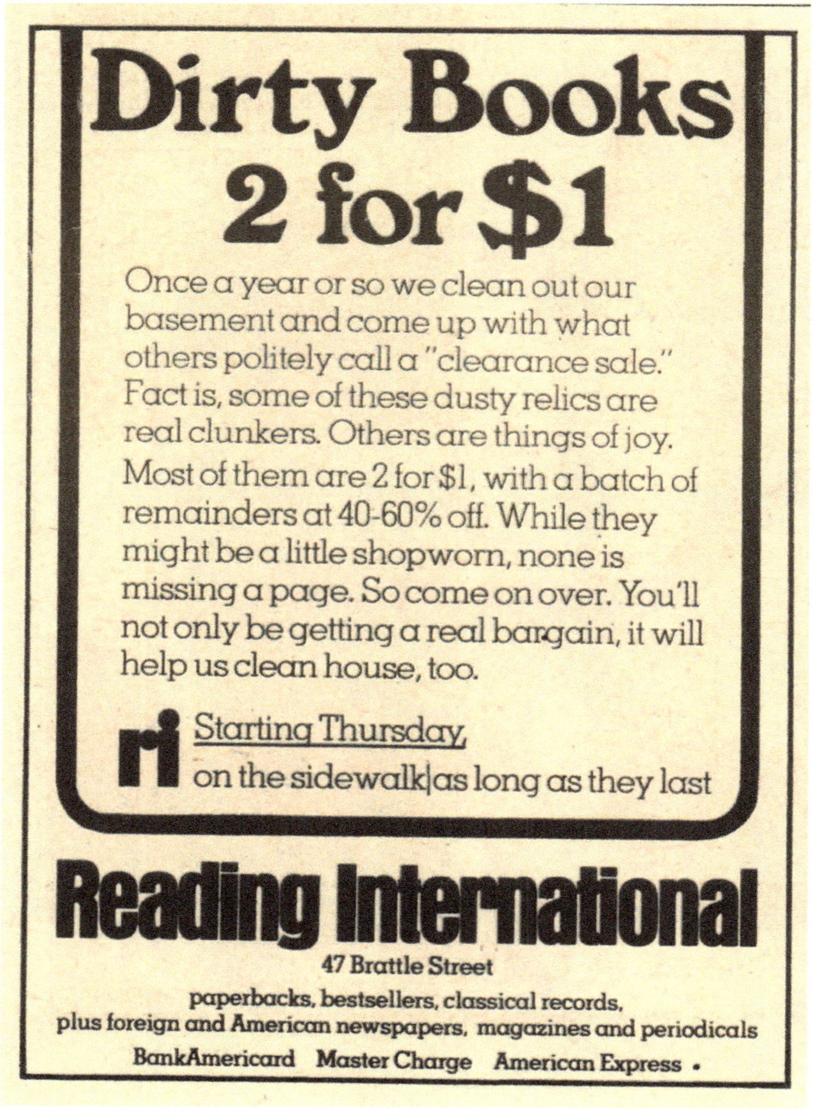
Dirty Books
2 for $1
Once a year or so we clean out our basement and come up with what others politely call a "clearance sale." Fact is, some of these dusty relics are real clunkers. Others are things of joy. Most of them are 2 for $1, with a batch of remainders at 40-60% off. While they might be a little shopworn, none is missing a page. So come on over. You'll not only be getting a real bargain, it will help us clean house, too.
Starting Thursday,
on the sidewalk|as long as they last
Reading International
47 Brattle Street
paperbacks, bestsellers, classical records,
plus foreign and American newspapers, magazines and periodicals
BankAmericard Master Charge American Express •

Real Paper, September 18, 1974 [BCA]

Eat,
Drink & Be
Literary.
Pâtés • Home-made Soups
Hot Entrées & Seasonal Specials
Delicious Salads • Assorted
Sandwiches • Cheeses • Fresh
Fruits • Espresso • Apértifs, Beers
& Wines
Harvard
Book Store
Café
Breakfast through Late Supper
190 Newbury Street at Exeter, Boston • 536-0095
Open Monday thru Saturday 8-11
Open Sunday 12-6 During Christmas Season

Boston Phoenix, December 7, 1982 [DBA]

Stereo Jack's
we buy & sell the widest selection of new & used LP's in New England
1704 MASS. AVE.
497-9447
CAMBRIDGE, MA 02138

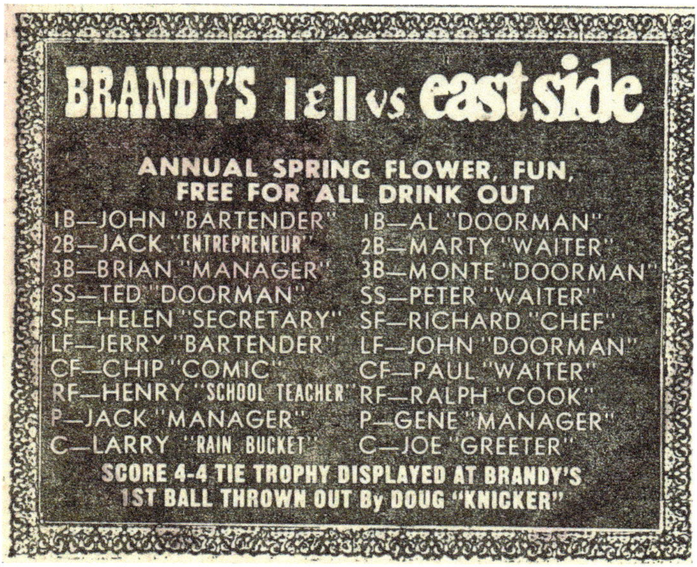
BRANDY'S I & II vs. east side
ANNUAL SPRING FLOWER, FUN, FREE FOR ALL DRINK OUT
1B—JOHN "BARTENDER"
2B—JACK "ENTREPRENEUR"
3B—BRIAN "MANAGER"
SS—TED "DOORMAN"
SF—HELEN "SECRETARY"
LF—JERRY "BARTENDER"
CF—CHIP "COMIC"
RF—HENRY "SCHOOL TEACHER"
P—JACK "MANAGER"
C—LARRY "RAIN BUCKET"
1B—AL "DOORMAN"
2B—MARTY "WAITER"
3B—MONTE "DOORMAN"
SS—PETER "WAITER"
SF—RICHARD "CHEF"
LF—JOHN "DOORMAN"
CF—PAUL "WAITER"
RF—RALPH "COOK"
P—GENE "MANAGER"
C—JOE "GREETER"
SCORE 4-4 TIE TROPHY DISPLAYED AT BRANDY'S
1ST BALL THROWN OUT By DOUG "KNICKER"

TOP: ***Boston Phoenix,*** December 7, 1982 [DBA]
BOTTOM: ***Boston Herald Traveler,*** April 26, 1970 [DBA]

DANCERS
GOOD PEOPLE
RAP SESSION
SPECIAL PRESENTATIONS
SPEAKERS
POETRY
GOSPEL MUSIC
Faishon & Hair styles by Daishiki Village
REFRESHMENTS
AFRICAN WOMEN'S DAY
Sunday
Febuary 14TH, 1971
10AM – 5⁰⁰PM
All SisTers welcome!
Arlington st CHURch
355 Boylston st.
Boston, MASS

Event flyer, February 1971 [KBA]

GEORGE WEIN Presents ....

NEWPORT JAZZ FESTIVAL

FENWAY PARK BOSTON / NEW ENGLAND

FRIDAY • SATURDAY JULY 27 • 28

FRI., JULY 27 8:00 P.M. WAR, *"The World Is a Ghetto"* / RAY CHARLES & All Star Orchestra, Raeletts / HERBIE MANN / DAVID NEWMAN / STAPLE SINGERS / BILLY PAUL

SAT., JULY 28 8:00 P.M. STEVIE WONDER / B. B. KING / DONNY HATHAWAY / FREDDIE HUBBARD 5 / CHARLES MINGUS 6 / RAHSAAN ROLAND KIRK

Tickets $5.50, $6.50, $7.50 • All Seats Reserved. On sale at all Ticket Agencies: Hub, Tyson, A Nubian Notion Inc.; 146 Dudley St. & 53-A Humboldt Ave., Roxbury, 5 Central Sq., Cambridge; Minuteman Records, Soundscope Records, Out-of-Town Tickets, TICKETRON: All locations 237-9748; Red Sox Advance Sale Ticket Office at Fenway Park; and Boston Office of Newport Jazz Festival/NE, 121 Newbury St., Boston, Mass. 02116 – Phone for information: (617) 262-1665 • Mail Orders.

NEWPORT FOLK FESTIVAL
JULY
24
1965
Saturday Evening at 8:00
FESTIVAL FIELD
CONNELL HIGHWAY
Newport, Rhode Island
ADMISSION PRICE $5.50 TAX EXEMPT
NO REFUNDS OR EXCHANGES
SEC.
SEAT
1A
5
GLOBE TICKET COMPANY

TOP: ***Real Paper,*** July 18, 1973 [DBA]
BOTTOM: **Concert ticket,** July 1965 [VALDEZ]

Starts Friday!
SWEET SWEETBACK'S BAADASSSSS SONG
ORIGINAL SOUNDTRACK ALBUM AVAILABLE EXCLUSIVELY ON STAX RECORDS
A film of MELVIN VAN PEEBLES
YOU BLED MY MOMMA
YOU BLED MY POPPA
BUT YOU WONT BLEED ME
X
NO ONE UNDER 18 CAN OR WILL BE ADMITTED! A UNIFORMED ATTENDANT WILL CHECK ALL I.D.'S
Music Hall
423-3300
268 TREMONT
ENDS WEDNESDAY!
ROD STEIGER • WATERLOO
LAST SHOW TODAY AT 3:00 P.M.

Boston Herald Traveler, May 2, 1971 [DBA]

1270
Every Tuesday
You Have
A Double Date
Visit Spinoff, The Roller Disco, And Receive
A Pass Good For Free Admission to 1270
Come To 1270 And Receive A Complimentary
Roller Skate Rental At Spinoff
Spinoff
145 Ipswich St., Boston
1270
1270 Boylston St., Boston

Hit Parade of Boston, November 1979 [DBA]

Court Street News 81 Court Street Brockton, MA 02401
• ADULT MAGAZINES
• ADULT VIDEOS
• ADULT MOVIE RENTALS
• RUBBER GOODS & NOVELTIES
EVERYTHING FOR THE ALL AMERICAN BOY
DROP BY!
Open 7 Days! 10a.m. - 10 p.m.

FRIENDS SOCIAL CLUB
(Formerly North Station Cinema)
276 Friend Street, Boston
(Opposite Boston Garden)
Always the Latest and Hottest in All Male Videos.
Showing on Our Giant Screen!
★ Triple Features ★ Film Festivals
★ Thursdays – Membership Request Day
For Membership Information and Current Feature Titles Call
(617) 720-4979
We Welcome New Members

Guide To Gay New England, May 1986 [BCA]

PUnktDATA
presents
The most inspiring
human
seXual response
and
UNNATURAL axe
AT
BAC
320
NEWBURY
FRI.
SEPT.
FIRST 9:30

Concert poster (design by Dini Lamot), September 1978 [FLYNN]

WMBRs' LATE RISERS' CLUB PRESENT
LIVE WRESTLING
-ON WARM LEATHERETTE-
CRYSTAL CANdy VS RUDE BOYZ
FEB 4,6,8 AT 88.1 FM
10:50 am

Boston Rock, June 1980 [DBA]

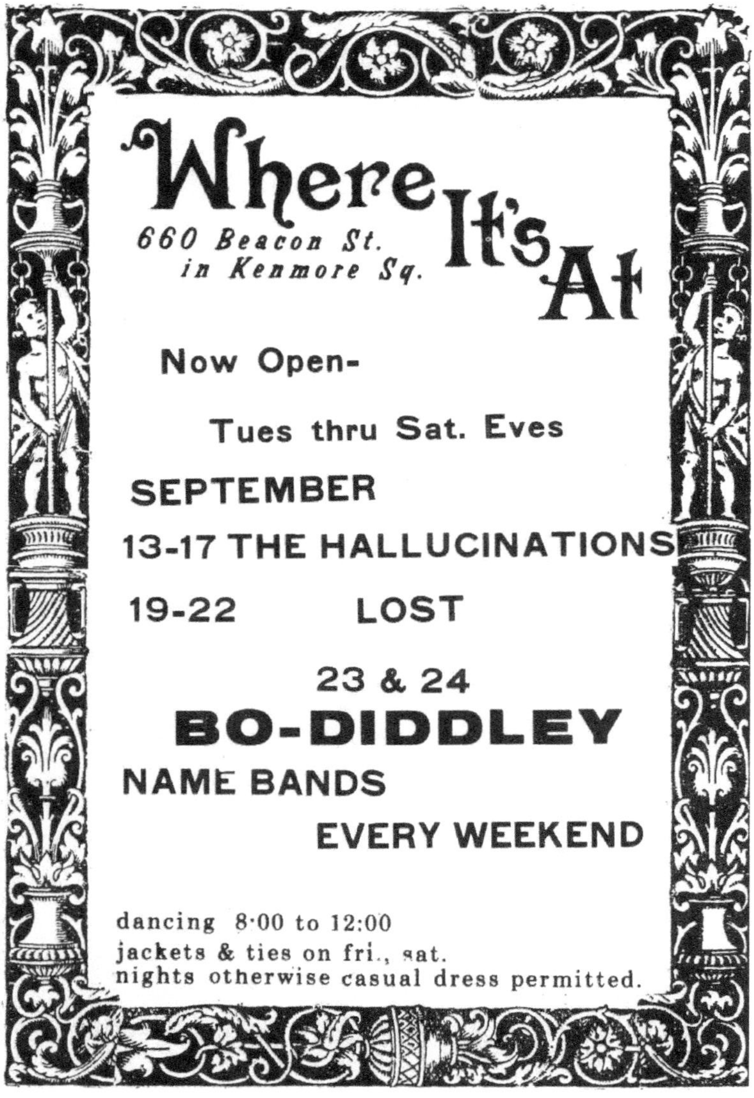
Where It's At
660 Beacon St.
in Kenmore Sq.
Now Open-
Tues thru Sat. Eves
SEPTEMBER
13-17 THE HALLUCINATIONS
19-22 LOST
23 & 24
BO-DIDDLEY
NAME BANDS
EVERY WEEKEND
dancing 8·00 to 12:00
jackets & ties on fri., sat.
nights otherwise casual dress permitted.

Broadside, August 31, 1966 [BCA]

Berklee
College
of Music
presents
HYPERTENSION
directed by
Steven Jenkins
Wednesday, October 24, 1979, 8:15 pm
Berklee Performance Center, Mass. Ave. at Boylston, Boston

Nº 426
IN PERSON
JOE SIMON
AND HIS
REVUE
CARVER AUDITORIUM
Nº 418
IN PERSON
JOE SIMON
AND HIS
REVUE
CARVER AUDITORIUM
80 TALBOT AVE. -- DORCHESTER, MASS.
Saturday, July 3, 1982 — 9 p.m. 'til 2 a.m.
Advance Admission $10.00
At Door $12.00
Nº 418

TOP: **Concert program cover,** October 1979 [KBA]
BOTTOM: **Concert tickets,** July 1982 [BCA]

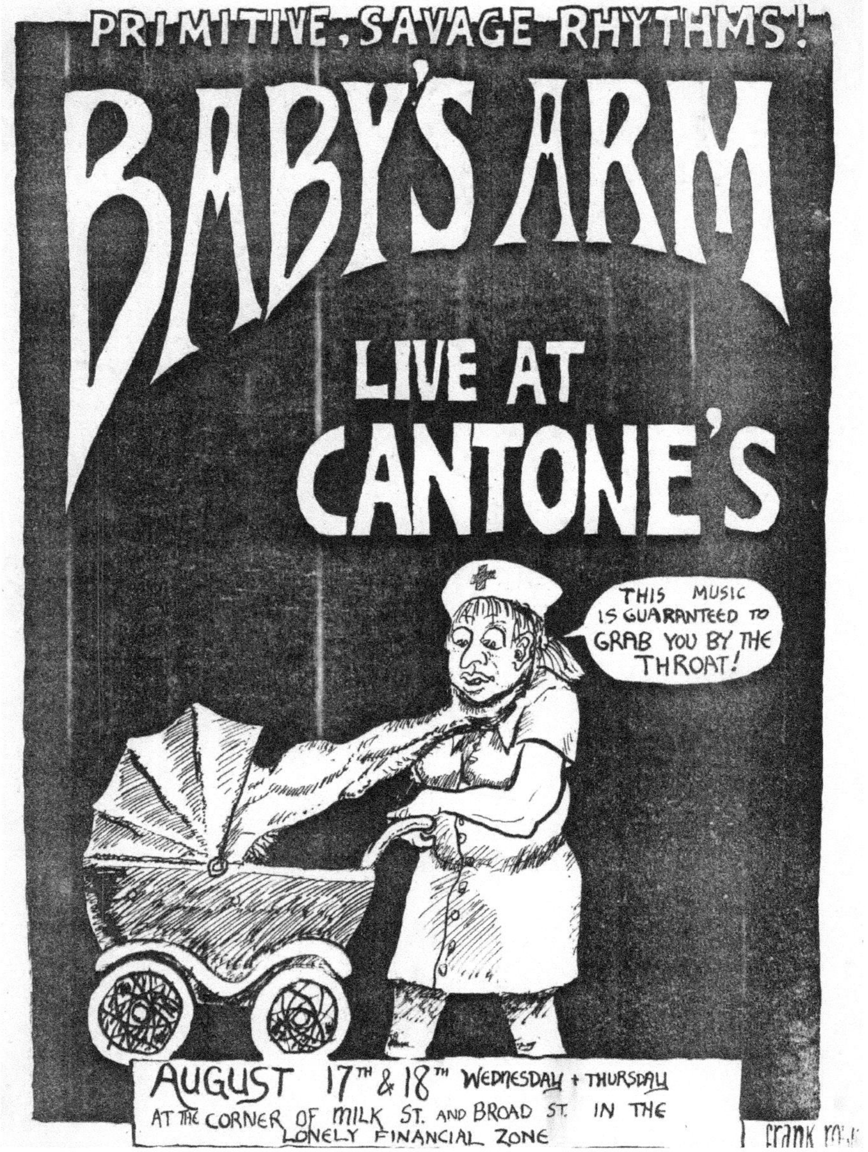
PRIMITIVE, SAVAGE RHYTHMS!
BABY'S ARM
LIVE AT CANTONE'S
THIS MUSIC IS GUARANTEED TO GRAB YOU BY THE THROAT!
AUGUST 17TH & 18TH WEDNESDAY + THURSDAY
AT THE CORNER OF MILK ST. AND BROAD ST. IN THE LONELY FINANCIAL ZONE

Concert flyer (artist: Frank Rowe), August 1977 [LOCO]

NOW IN PAPERBACK
H. RAP BROWN'S
explosive political autobiography
DIE NIGGER DIE!
$1.95
A DIAL PRESS PAPERBACK
Distributed by DELL
Scott

PHONES

AFSC	864-3150
Bad Trips	423-5868
Birth Control	536-8790
Black Panther Party	442-0100
Bread & Roses	492-4130
Cambridgeport Free Clinic	876-0284
Caravan Theater	491-9579
Committee Returned Vol.	868-8293
Ecology Action	876-7085
GBCTC	536-2840
Mass. Lawyers Guild	742-4256
Medical Comm. Human Rights	734-MCHR
Mid-East Group	354-2670
NAC	354-3082
New Mobe	492-6717
Newsreel	864-2600
New England Free Press	536-9219
Problem Pregnancies	527-7188
Project Place	267-5280
Student Health Org.	423-4725
Student Homophile League	868-0706
Women's Liberation	492-4130

Working Women's Conference

hy are we paid less than men?
hy do we have to work all day and come home and work some more?
hy don't we have a union that fights for women's rights?
hy do we pay the most rent for the worst houses?
hy does the cost of living go up faster than our wages?
hy aren't there any free nurseries?
hy aren't there good neighborhood health clinics?
hy do we have the worst, most boring jobs where we work – in offices, department stores, factories, hospitals?
THER PEOPLE AREN'T GOING TO CHANGE THINGS FOR US.
en aren't going to fight for women's rights. We have to get together to build something better for ourselves.

Working Women's Conference
Saturday and Sunday, May 2 & 3 at U. Mass, Boston, 100 Arlington St. (Rm. 222) Registration: 9 am Sat.
ay Care available at U. Mass. For more information or transportation, call:
Connie: 547-8546 Janet: 868-7995 Meredith: 492-7665

CUBAN FLICKS

DISCUSSION WITH BRIGADE MEMBERS

CHARLES ST. MEETING HOUSE
April 23 at 7:30
CONTRIBUTION $1.50

THE MILLION
VAL

Old Mole, April 17, 1970 [DBA]

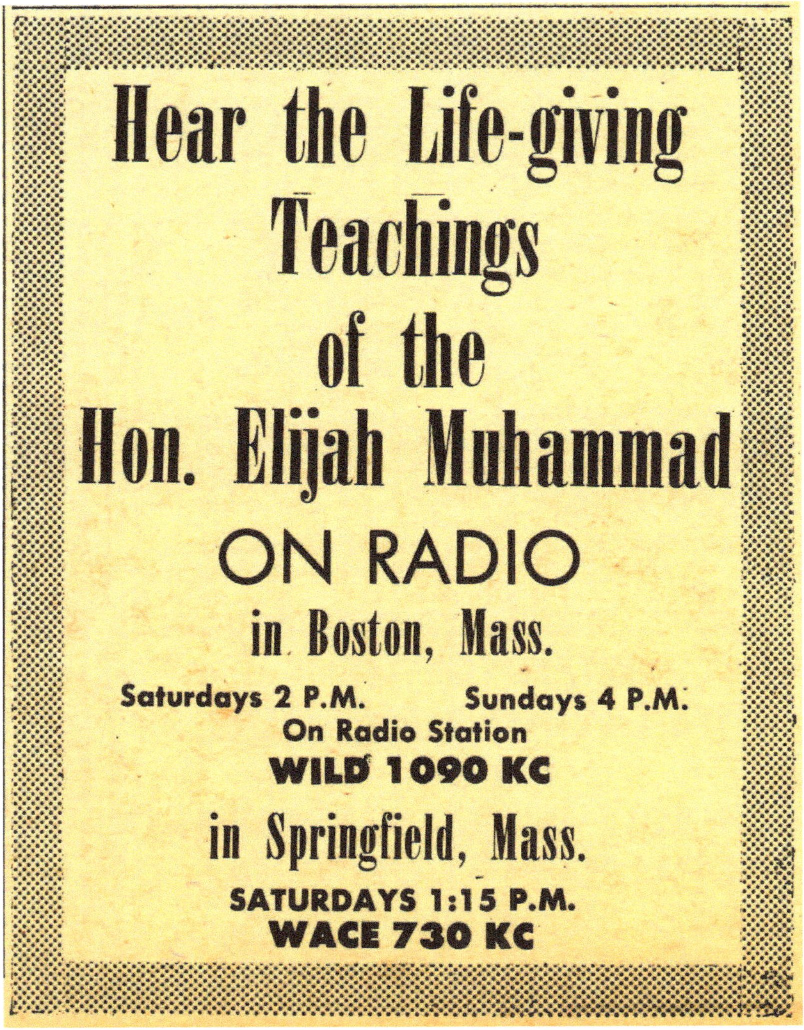
Hear the Life-giving Teachings of the Hon. Elijah Muhammad

ON RADIO

in Boston, Mass.

Saturdays 2 P.M. Sundays 4 P.M.

On Radio Station

WILD 1090 KC

in Springfield, Mass.

SATURDAYS 1:15 P.M.

WACE 730 KC

***Muhammad Speaks* newspaper,** July 5, 1968 [BCA]

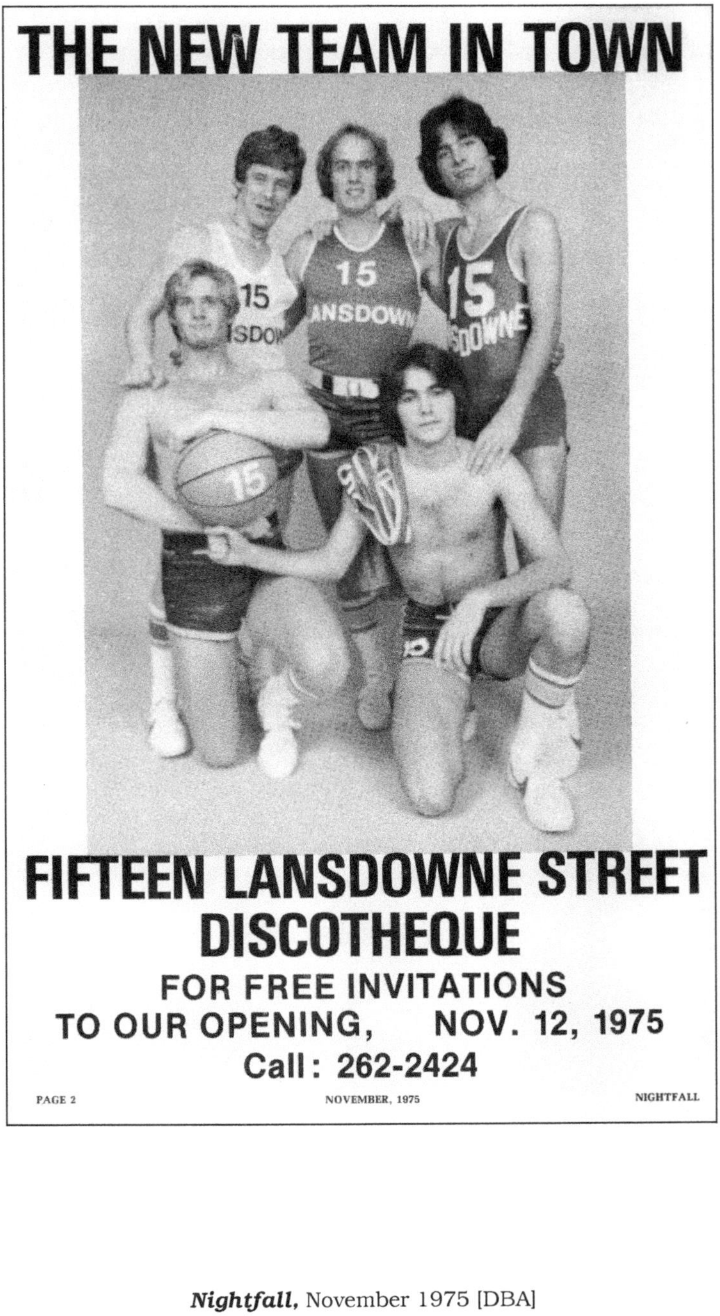
THE NEW TEAM IN TOWN
15
15 LANSDOWN
FIFTEEN LANSDOWNE STREET
DISCOTHEQUE
FOR FREE INVITATIONS
TO OUR OPENING, NOV. 12, 1975
Call: 262-2424
PAGE 2
NOVEMBER, 1975
NIGHTFALL

Nightfall, November 1975 [DBA]

Change the 12 days of Christmas
to 12 months.
Give everybody
Boston Magazine.
(They'll love you all year).
Boston
Boston
Boston
Boston
Boston
Boston
Boston
Boston
Boston
Boston
Boston
Boston
The Young Doctors Revolt
The Angry Young Jocks
The Coming Revolt of the Working Girl

Boston Magazine, December 1972 [DBA]

afro·fashions·silks.
handmade tribal garments & sandals
WOULD YOU BUY AN AMALA FROM THIS MAN?
J. EKWUGHA AMAECHI
THE WINDOW TO WATCH
2276 Washington Roxbury
442-2892
Present this ad and 10% of your purchases will be donated to the Biafra Relief Fund.

Spectrum India
157 NEWBURY ST.

organic whole grain
imported beans, seaweeds
flours·stone ground daily
fresh organic vegetables
erewhon trading company
342 newbury street 262 - 3420

Boston After Dark, July 9, 1969 [BCA]

Deborah A. Catalano
Public Relations
Consulting • Press Kits • Press Releases • Writing • Etc.
P.O. Box 665, Winchester, MA 01890, (617) 226-2378
New England Performer magazine
(617) 395-7055
11 Riverside Ave. Suite 4
Medford, MA 02155
DEBORAH A. CATALANO
Public Relations/
Staff Writer
SEARCHING FER SLOANE
WENDY L. SHLENSKY
P.O. BOX 1562
BOSTON MA 02205
617-787-9861
EVANGELISTS FOR UNITY
PUBLICATIONS, PRODUCTIONS, ET. AL.
PHOENIX MEDIA/COMMUNICATIONS GROUP COMPANIES:
THE BOSTON PHOENIX
THE PROVIDENCE PHOENIX
THE WORCESTER PHOENIX
STUFF MAGAZINE
WFNX-FM 101.7
GRAPHIC SERVICES
MASS WEB PRINTING
TELE-PUBLISHING INC
Phoenix
MEDIA/COMMUNICATIONS GROUP
DAVID BIEBER
Director of Special Projects
126 BROOKLINE AVE. BOSTON, MA 02215
617-859-3302 FAX 617-536-1463
The Boston Globe
P.O. Box 2378 Boston, MA 02107-2378
STEVE MORSE
MUSIC WRITER
(617) 929-2810
Berklee
COLLEGE OF MUSIC
Robert J. Jaczko
Assistant Chair
Music Production and Engineering Department
1140 Boylston Street • Boston, Massachusetts 02215-3693
(617) 747-8253 • Fax: (617) 247-6878
Internet address: rjaczko@berklee.edu
Hirsh Gardner
Productions
102 Union Street
North Andover, MA 01845
(508)683-1190
REC MOOD FOOD RDS
Kurt G. Underhill
1381 Kildaire Farms Road • Suite 246 • Cary, NC 27511
(919) 557-8311
Fax (919) 557-7922
EMail: Moodfoodnc@aol.com
SoundFood for your MusicMood. . .
Thank you
for
celebrating
my Birthday
with me!
Kayley Rachel Brodrick
1/28/2001
AMERICA'S
SOUP KITCHEN
ON
WHEELS
Andrew Hoffman
P.O. Box 390074 Cambridge, MA 02139
(617)666-3646
C-LINE #61217
BUSINESS CARD

Chuck White Business Card Collection, 1980s–1990s [CWA/DBA]

Now 300% more exclusive.
Cambridge Imported Cars is the only factory authorized dealer in the Greater Boston area that leases, services, and sells Mercedes-Benz automobiles exclusively. And now we're adding 125,000 square feet to our dealership. We'll have state-of-the-art equipment, 35 work bays for prompt and efficient service, and a spacious new showroom. Cambridge Imported Cars—as exclusive as the cars we represent. 259 McGrath Highway, Somerville, MA 02143, (617) 666-4100.
Cambridge Imported Cars
259 McGrath Highway, Somerville, MA 02143 666-4100
MERCEDES-BENZ
CAMBRIDGE IMPORTED CARS, INC.

Boston Magazine (25th Anniversary Supplement), 1987 [DBA]

take it! magazine
With a free Flexi-Disc Record in every issue.
WHERE THE SHIT HITS THE FAN.
Monthly Columns:
Sports by Richard Meltzer
L.A. by Gregg Turner
Books by Ira Kaplan
Poolside Pep Talk by Byron Coley
Also: Film Cartoons, Poetry, N.Y., Boston and more.
6 issues $8.00
12 issues $15.00
Sample Copy $1.50
Send to: Take It! Magazine
196 Harvard Ave., Suite 5
Boston, MA 02134
FOR SUBSCRIBERS ONLY: Specially designed picture sleeves for each Flexi-Disc included with your issue.

***New York Rocker* magazine,** July/August 1981 [BCA]

HYPNOSONICS
SUBSONIC REVUE
FAREWELL, EARTH:
THE LAST REVUE
NO. 16 DEC. 15 AT
THE PLOUGH
WITH LOVE FROM THE SUBSONIC ARMY:
The Cubist and The Fauve loyal soldiers manning the tantric horn
extensions untyiringly Jon Hilt master of the wooden symbol
what happened to Vince now the hypnosonically inclined Michael Ike
Rivard Tamara Jenkins Gospel Ranch Don K-Bar rewriting classical
music history songbird Connie "honey" White Sir Frederic Bernstingle
Earl and Eli Latrobe Cloaca Tony Highbrow Brothers Kendall Skand
Joe Harvard Jerome Deupree El Matador The Singing Carney Twins Afro
Cupids Al From Michigan Dan and Mary (your bartenders) + the Man of Sand

Events flyer, December 1987 [RIVARD]

Restaurants

Make no misteak.
★ ★ ★ ★
"In a great tradition one of America's choice steakhouses."
—FOOD & WINE MAGAZINE
"Boston's best steakhouse."
—BOSTON MAGAZINE
Scotch 'n Sirloin
77 N. Washington Street off Causeway Street
Near Boston Garden, Government Center and Faneuil Hall. · Valet Parking 723-3677
the EUROPEAN Restaurant
BOSTON'S OLDEST ITALIAN RESTAURANT
All Italian Dishes our specialty
PIZZA AT ITS BEST
CHOICE WINES • LIQUORS
218 Hancock St., Boston
523-5694
Boston's Most Abundant Salad Bar
SOUPER SALAD
• Super Sandwiches • Quiches
• Beer and Wine • Sensational Desserts • Chicken Teriyaki
Simply Super!
"The Garage" at Harvard Square
119 Newbury St., Boston
524 Commonwealth Avenue, Boston
South Shore Plaza – Braintree
Souper Salad Express – Burlington Mall
Boston Globe Calendar ★ ★ ★ ★ "This is the Best."
Super caterers for every occasion – for every size. Call 964-8710
Continue your enjoyment after the game at......
T's Pub
THE PLACE TO MEET
DJ ENTERTAINMENT
Thursday, Friday & Saturday
HAPPY HOUR Friday, 3:30-7:30
SUPER 12-FOOT TV SCREEN
973 Commonwealth Ave. Boston, Mass. 254-0807
M•O•N•T•A•N•A•S
In the Back Bay.
● Elegant Dining ● Casual Café
● Live Jazz
160 Commonwealth Ave. Boston, MA 536-3556
CASA ROMERO
"the best Mexican food this side of Taxco... the cuisine at Casa Romero is as sophisticated as the decor..."
Gourmet Magazine
Mexican Cuisine
Open Monday thru Saturday from 5:00 PM
Closed Sundays
30 Gloucester Street Back Bay, Boston Reservations: 536-4341
The Black Rose
Mother Sweeney's Sunday Buffet
Luncheon and Dinner
Live Irish Entertainment 7 Nights a Week
RÓISÍN DUBH
Boston's Original
IRISH ENTERTAINMENT PUB
160 STATE ST., BOSTON, MA 02109
523-8486 / 742-2286
A new place, that's on the right track.
Trolleys welcomes you to Boston's newest restaurant experience, where casual elegance and fine dining make it the perfect lunch or dinner stop.
11:30 A.M. – 2:00 A.M. 7 Days
Across from Haymarket Station
Entertainment Nightly
Daily Lunch, Dinner, Cocktails and Sunday Brunch
Visa
Master Charge
American Express
367-8126
Valet Parking
55 Canal Street, Boston, MA 02114
TROLLEYS

***Red Sox Yearbook*, 1983 [BCA]**

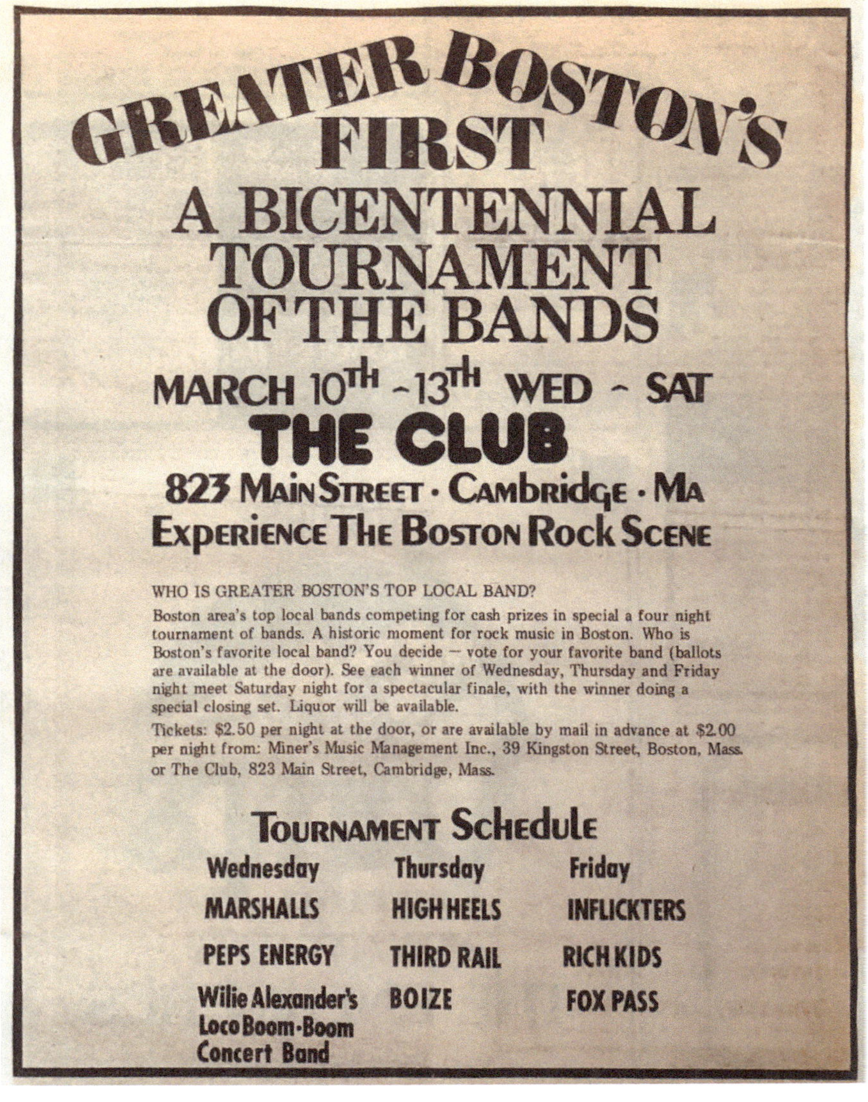
GREATER BOSTON'S
FIRST
A BICENTENNIAL
TOURNAMENT
OF THE BANDS
MARCH 10TH ~13TH WED ~ SAT
THE CLUB
823 MAIN STREET · CAMBRIDGE · MA
EXPERIENCE THE BOSTON ROCK SCENE
WHO IS GREATER BOSTON'S TOP LOCAL BAND?
Boston area's top local bands competing for cash prizes in special a four night tournament of bands. A historic moment for rock music in Boston. Who is Boston's favorite local band? You decide — vote for your favorite band (ballots are available at the door). See each winner of Wednesday, Thursday and Friday night meet Saturday night for a spectacular finale, with the winner doing a special closing set. Liquor will be available.
Tickets: $2.50 per night at the door, or are available by mail in advance at $2.00 per night from: Miner's Music Management Inc., 39 Kingston Street, Boston, Mass. or The Club, 823 Main Street, Cambridge, Mass.
TOURNAMENT SCHEDULE
Wednesday
MARSHALLS
PEPS ENERGY
Wilie Alexander's Loco Boom-Boom Concert Band
Thursday
HIGH HEELS
THIRD RAIL
BOIZE
Friday
INFLICKTERS
RICH KIDS
FOX PASS

Real Paper, March 10, 1976 [LOCO]

Fancy This
1134 Mass. Ave., Cambridge
281 Main St., Falmouth

***Fusion* magazine,** April 14, 1969 [ELA]

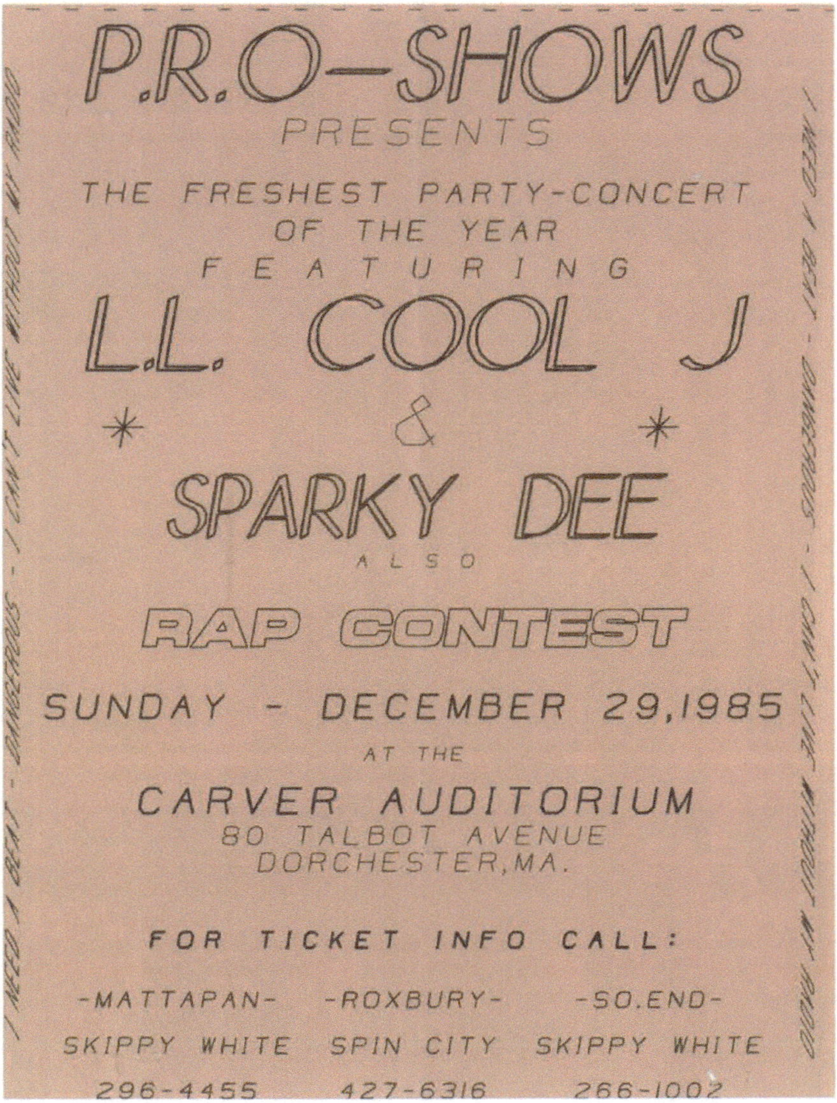
P.R.O-SHOWS
PRESENTS
THE FRESHEST PARTY-CONCERT
OF THE YEAR
FEATURING
L.L. COOL J
&
SPARKY DEE
ALSO
RAP CONTEST
SUNDAY - DECEMBER 29,1985
AT THE
CARVER AUDITORIUM
80 TALBOT AVENUE
DORCHESTER,MA.
FOR TICKET INFO CALL:
-MATTAPAN- -ROXBURY- -SO.END-
SKIPPY WHITE SPIN CITY SKIPPY WHITE
296-4455 427-6316 266-1002
I NEED A BEAT - DANGEROUS - I CAN'T LIVE WITHOUT MY RADIO
I NEED A BEAT - DANGEROUS - I CAN'T LIVE WITHOUT MY RADIO

Concert flyer, December 1985 [Courtesy of Jed Hresko]

Collàge, Ltd.
presents it's First Annual
Designers Display
Competition
Sunday, February 22, 1981
6:00 p.m.
John Hancock Auditorium
180 Berkeley Street, Boston

Event program cover, February 1981 [Courtesy of Yvonne & Tony Rose]

INN-SQUARE MEN'S BAR
LADIES INVITED.
1350 Cambridge St. Inman Sq.
491-9672
CRAFTS

in conclusion...

What can I say, summer's coming to an end. Izzy is back from summer camp. It won't be long before it's too cold to take my Sea Eagle out on Mystic Lake. Hey, I can honestly say that I had a great summer.

Those of you that haven't sent in the poll from last issue still have time to get it in(the deadline is Aug 30). I was thinking of doing a set of trading cards on the winners of the poll, but I'm unsure about it now. Who knows, I'll do something for the winners. They'll be listed in the next issue.

This months plug goes to MOVIE MACABRE hosted by ELVIRA(Sat. nights 10:30 ch 68). Our hostess digs up the worst horror flicks of all time and keeps interrupting the action to get her two bit jokes in. But the main attraction is just getting to look at Elvira. She wears a low-cut, high slit black tight dress and sprawls herself out on a couch. Her breasts are perfect specimens for use of the special effects in a 3-D movie. So while I'm waiting for some accidental exposure, I hope you all enjoy the rest of your summer.

Thanks to Tanya Rose and the rest of the contributers to this, our 3 year anniversary issue.

T. Max

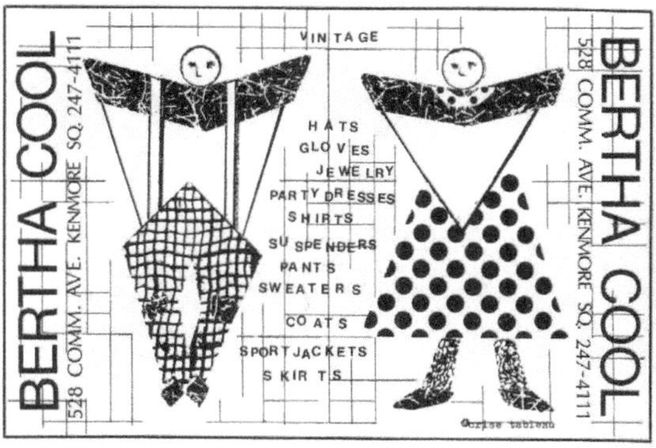
BERTHA COOL
528 COMM. AVE. KENMORE SQ. 247-4111
VINTAGE
HATS
GLOVES
JEWELRY
PARTY DRESSES
SHIRTS
SUSPENDERS
PANTS
SWEATERS
COATS
SPORTJACKETS
SKIRTS
BERTHA COOL
528 COMM. AVE. KENMORE SQ. 247-4111

REWARD - $50
CHILDREN of PARADISE seeks
band practise space
CALL: 864-8647

SOMEDAY
YOU'LL
LEARN
HOW
TO
DO
THE MARY
STEPS #3 & 4

down avenue

HERBOLIC & SCORPIO PRODUCTION
presents . . . IN CONCERT
Jamaica's Internationally acclaimed Recording Artist
LEROY SMART
Featuring Bands – SONS OF CREATION from New York
THE PERFIDIANS from New York
Guest Appearances – LENKY ROY
LOVE JOY & RAS PIPPIN
Musically – WORLD WIND I-FI
SATURDAY
MAY 3rd
10:00 P.M. - SHARP
TENNIS-UP
100 MASS. AVE. (at Newbury St.) BOSTON, MASS.
TICKETS: $7.00 ADVANCE
$8.00 AT DOOR
Tickets Available at: ALL SKIPPY WHITE STORES
ALL NUBIAN NOTION STORES – ALL STRAWBERRY RECORDS LOCATIONS
CODMAN SQUARE BAKERY, 521 Washington St., Dorchester
SCORPIO RECORD, 628 Washington St., Dorchester – 436-9726
PLUS
A SMART AFTER PARTY
DISCO's: SIR "D" MEET INNER CONTROL I-FI
LENA PARK COMMUNITY CENTER
150 AMERICAN LEGION HWY. – DORCHESTER, MASS.
DONATION: $3.00 per Person

Concert poster, May 1980 [DBA]

The Biggest, Wildest, Dancingest Honky-Tonk in Mass.
Ride the Wild Bull at
CELEBRATION
533 Commonwealth Ave * Boston * 536-1950
NARCISSUS
the ultimate dance club
533 Commonwealth Avenue
536-1950

***City Limits* magazine,** February 1981 [DBA]

JIMMY'S
WORLD FAMOUS FOR
SEAFOOD SPECIALTIES
also Prime Meats
Open Daily except Sunday
11:30 A.M. to 9:00 P.M.
HARBORSIDE RESTAURANT
ON HISTORIC BOSTON FISH PIER: 242 NORTHERN AVE.
• HA 6-6444
• HA 6-5343
Winner of Holiday Magazine's Dining Distinction Award for Seven Consecutive Years: 1957 - 1963
BOSTON'S FINEST
MOTOR HOTELS
the FENWAY
1271 BOYLSTON ST.
the FENWAY NORTH
On the Northeast Expwy.
QUALITY COURTS
THE FENWAY Commonwealth
COMMONWEALTH AVE. AT KENMORE SQ.
NEW,
wonderful accommodations
are NOW in Boston!
Superb accommodations designed for people on the go, whether it's for business or pleasure. Ideal accessibility to downtown and suburban areas. Free parking.
For Room Reservations
call COpley 7-8300

Panorama, December 29, 1963 [VACCA]

November at Mirage.

4 Disco DJ's Headline
"Dance Your Ass Off Sunday"

Four of Boston's top disco DJ's will spin out at Mirage on Nov. 16 & 30, *"Dance Your Ass Off Sunday". ,ay"*

Mirage's own Joe Carvello, emcee, will host along with 3 other top Boston Disco DJ's.

"This line-up of super-DJ's," said manager Big Al, "will make Mirage the jumpingest night spot on the east coast. We even expect a good crowd from New York."

The festivities will include record giveaways, flowers at the door, and free munchies. Plan now to be there.

Dance Your Way to
$10,000 Disco Dance Contest

A fabulous week for two at the famous Club Mediterranee is the grand prize in Mirage's first annual *Let-It-All-Hang-Out Disco Dance Contest.*

Mirage will give away prizes valuing nearly ten thousand dollars.

The Contest will run every Monday and Tuesday nights through November. Weekly winners will be awarded ski trips, record albums, and cash prizes (ski trips will be total packages at Sugarloaf and Killington). Each week's winners will become eligible for the grand finals on November 24 & 25.

"Boston is the best disco city in the country," said Big Al, "and the country's best disco dancers will be found at Mirage."

If you'd like to enter (and with those prizes who wouldn't), ask for details today.

Joey Carvello's
"Super Sunday
Disco Matinee Marathon"

An all day,
all night Dance Party

Starting at 2pm
Nov. 9 & 23

Mirage
590 Comm. Ave. Kenmore Sq. 266-7050
Parking at the door.
DISCO/RESTAURANT/PUBLIC & PRIVATE PARTIES

NIGHTFALL NOVEMBER, 1975 PAGE 45

Nightfall, November 1975 [DBA]

T

★★½ **THE THREEPENNY OPERA (1931).** Bertolt Brecht and Kurt Weill's powerful musical was adapted to the screen by G.W. Pabst in a fog-enshrouded, expressionistic style full of gloomy chiaroscuro, soft edges, and swirling wreaths of smoke and dust. Infuriated by the blunted satire and apolitical ambiance of the film, Brecht, along with Weill, sued the producers for altering the work's content (the pair lost the case). The picture seems more significant now for its stylistic beauties, which are considerable. *Coolidge Corner.*

★★★**TWO FOR THE ROAD (1967).** Frederick Rafael's witty, innovative screenplay cuts this story of Albert Finney's

STARTS WED.! DOUBLE FEATURE
Sorority Sweethearts
2nd Smash Week
xXx
red hot pounding action
LISA DE LEEUW
BRIDGETTE MONET
LINDA SHAW
PREMIER ENGAGEMENT
EXCLUSIVE 1st RUN!
WEST END PUSSYCAT CINEMA
75 CAUSEWAY ST
523 4050
Cont fr 10 A M
xXx
WE DARE YOU TO RESIST
Irresistible
STARRING EROTIC AWARD WINNERS!
SAMANTHA FOX AND RICHARD PACHECO
PLUS 2nd FEATURE Starring: John C. Holmes Laurien Dominique
XXX
WIDE SCREEN VIVID COLOR
"SUPERSTAR"
PUSSYCAT CINEMA
STUART & WASH
487-1350
Cont fr 9 30 A M

WEST NEWTON
CINEMA 1·2·3
1296 Wash. 964-6060
EATING RAOUL
7:30
9:30
2nd Week
R
WINNER ACADEMY AWARD
BEST FOREIGN FILM
2ND WEEK
MEPHISTO
4th and Final Week
Sun-Thu 8:00/Fri-Sat 7:20-9:45
A FILM BY JOHN SAYLES
4th Week
LIANNA
R

PARKWAY PLAZA Cinema 1&2
PARKWAY PLAZA SHOPPING CENTER
CHELSEA • OFF REVERE BEACH PARKWAY
CONTINUOUS PERFORMANCES
DAILY FROM 12 • SUNDAY FROM 1
ACRES OF FREE PARKING
THE COUPLES THEATRE
Phone 884-0088
ACTION PACKED
BATTLE OF THE SUPER STARS
SEKA vs. VERONICA HART
"TARA TARA TARA"
XXX
plus
JOHN C. HOLMES
GEORGINA SPELVIN
1st TIME EVER ON THE SCREEN! THINK OF THE POSSIBILITIES
The JADE Pussycat
PREMIERE ENGAGEMENT
100% ALL AMERICAN GIRLS! The perfect adult movie! Lots of girls, lots of sex and lots of style! Hustler Mag
100% ALL AMERICAN GIRLS! More seductive new bodies than I have ever seen before! Al Goldstein's Magazine
ALL AMERICAN GIRLS
plus 'a Scent of Heather"
xXx
• LATE SHOW FRI. & SAT. ONLY AT 11:45 • SEPARATE ADMISSION •
JOHN HOLMES ★★ MARILYN CHAMBERS
Insatiable

Cinema Brookline
Hearthstone Plaza
Rte. 9, Brookline Vill.
566-0007
the Patriot Cinemas, Inc.
Thru Thurs. 4/7
BASED ON A TRUE STORY.
JACK LEMMON
SISSY SPACEK
missing
(PG)
7:00-9:20
Sat. & Sun. 2:00-4:30
4 ACADEMY AWARD NOMINATIONS
Including BEST Picture Actor Actress
ALL SEATS $1.75
Garage Parking $1.00

Boston Phoenix, April 5, 1983 [DBA]

PHOTO BY – ROGER PERRON

Goody, Steve, Marvelous Marvin, Greg Litchfield (forehead), Hank and Pat

CONGRAULATIONS CHAMP!
From

THE DONUT HOLE, INC.

620 Washington Street
South Easton, Massachusetts 02375
Telephone (617) 238-6833

THE DONUT HOLE, INC., Proprietors Hank and Jean Barry

Supervisor: Norma Page

Employees:
Mary Hurley
Dale Anderson
Peggy Patterson
Narla McGill
Brian Groom
Kathy Farrell
Nicki Previti
Maura Farrell
Jim MacLoed
Shirley Souza
Joan Bonamici
Jack Pereira
Laurie DeCosta
Patty Tracy

Marvin Hagler vs. Fully Obel Boxing Program, January 17, 1981 [BCA]

Twin Lobster Special
MONDAYS & TUESDAYS
$12.99
available through May 31
Tia's
at Long Wharf
Adjacent to the Marriott
Not valid with coupons
Seafood Restaurant & Bar

GOOD LUCK BRUINS
Hood
SINCE 1846
Food For Fitness

TOP: ***Boston Magazine,*** May 1985 [DBA]
BOTTOM: **Boston Bruins program,** 1967–1968 season [BCA]

MUKASA RECORDS
509 COLUMBUS AVE SO END
WEST INDIAN & HAITIAN MUSIC
3 BLOCKS
FROM PRUDENT AL
CENTER BETW EN
MASS AVE & EWPORT

Subway News magazine, (artwork by Magnus Johnstone), Summer 1980 [BCA]

NEW SOUTH END
CYCLORAMA
MUSIC
IN AN
ENVIRONMENT
THAT MAKES
CONCERTS
MORE THAN
MERE
SURVIVAL
SOON!
Proceeds to benefit THE BOSTON MUSIC FOUNDATION.

***Nebula* magazine,** January 1972 [DBA]

EIGHT TRACK RECORDING
Fort APACHE
169 Norfolk Avenue
Roxbury, MA 02119
617 442 4026
Joe Harvard
617 876 4012
HEART PUNCH STUDIO
(617) 739-0948
8 TRACK RECORDING
! $15.00 per hour !
STATION STREET
BROOKLINE, MA
02146
PAUL MARTIN
(617) 755 5643
MCM
25 FOSTER STREET
WORCESTER MA 01608
MISSION CONTROL
545 BOYLSTON STREET
BOSTON, MA. 02116
262-2070
NEW ENGLAND SOUND
16 TRACK RECORDING
Call 617-376-5619
Normandy Sound
25 Market St. Warren, RI 02885
401 247 0218
24 TRACK

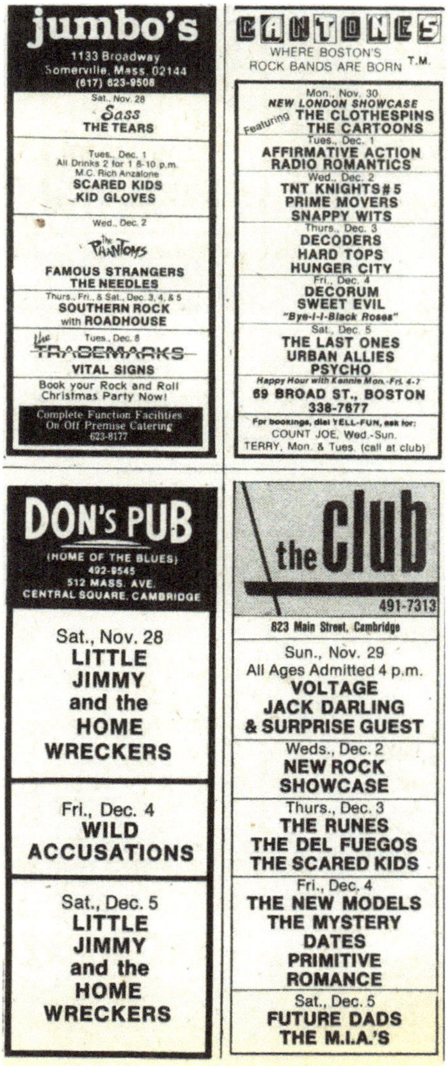
jumbo's
1133 Broadway
Somerville, Mass. 02144
(617) 623-9508
Sat., Nov. 28
Sass
THE TEARS
Tues., Dec. 1
All Drinks 2 for 1 8-10 p.m.
M.C. Rich Anzalone
SCARED KIDS
KID GLOVES
Wed., Dec. 2
The PHANTOMS
FAMOUS STRANGERS
THE NEEDLES
Thurs., Fri., & Sat., Dec. 3, 4, & 5
SOUTHERN ROCK
with ROADHOUSE
Tues., Dec. 8
the TRADEMARKS
VITAL SIGNS
Book your Rock and Roll
Christmas Party Now!
Complete Function Facilities
On Off Premise Catering
623-8177
CANTONES
WHERE BOSTON'S
ROCK BANDS ARE BORN T.M.
Mon., Nov. 30
NEW LONDON SHOWCASE
Featuring THE CLOTHESPINS
THE CARTOONS
Tues., Dec. 1
AFFIRMATIVE ACTION
RADIO ROMANTICS
Wed., Dec. 2
TNT KNIGHTS#5
PRIME MOVERS
SNAPPY WITS
Thurs., Dec. 3
DECODERS
HARD TOPS
HUNGER CITY
Fri., Dec. 4
DECORUM
SWEET EVIL
"Bye-I-I-Black Roses"
Sat., Dec. 5
THE LAST ONES
URBAN ALLIES
PSYCHO
Happy Hour with Kennie Mon.-Fri. 4-7
69 BROAD ST., BOSTON
338-7677
For bookings, dial YELL-FUN, ask for:
COUNT JOE, Wed.-Sun.
TERRY, Mon. & Tues. (call at club)
DON'S PUB
(HOME OF THE BLUES)
492-9545
512 MASS. AVE.
CENTRAL SQUARE, CAMBRIDGE
Sat., Nov. 28
LITTLE JIMMY and the HOME WRECKERS
Fri., Dec. 4
WILD ACCUSATIONS
Sat., Dec. 5
LITTLE JIMMY and the HOME WRECKERS
the Club
491-7313
823 Main Street, Cambridge
Sun., Nov. 29
All Ages Admitted 4 p.m.
VOLTAGE
JACK DARLING
& SURPRISE GUEST
Weds., Dec. 2
NEW ROCK SHOWCASE
Thurs., Dec. 3
THE RUNES
THE DEL FUEGOS
THE SCARED KIDS
Fri., Dec. 4
THE NEW MODELS
THE MYSTERY DATES
PRIMITIVE ROMANCE
Sat., Dec. 5
FUTURE DADS
THE M.I.A.'S

LEFT: ***The Beat,*** February 1986 [BCA]
RIGHT: ***Boston Phoenix,*** December 1, 1981 [DBA]

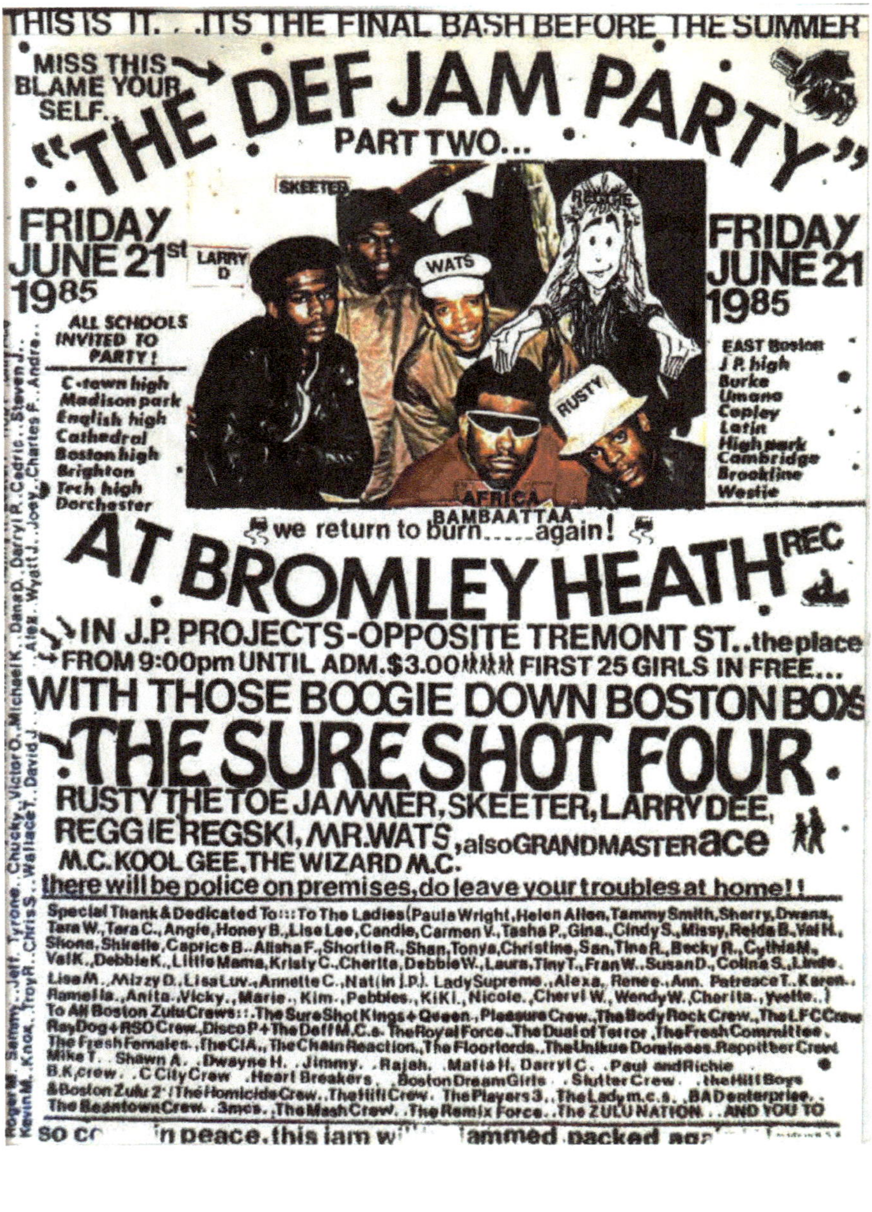
THIS IS IT. . .ITS THE FINAL BASH BEFORE THE SUMMER
MISS THIS BLAME YOUR SELF..
"THE DEF JAM PARTY"
PART TWO...
SKEETER
LARRY D
WATS
REGGIE
RUSTY
AFRICA BAMBAATTAA
FRIDAY JUNE 21st 1985
FRIDAY JUNE 21 1985
ALL SCHOOLS INVITED TO PARTY!
C-town high
Madison park
English high
Cathedral
Boston high
Brighton
Tech high
Dorchester
EAST Boston
J.P. high
Burke
Umana
Copley
Latin
High park
Cambridge
Brookline
Westie
we return to burn......again!
AT BROMLEY HEATH REC
IN J.P. PROJECTS-OPPOSITE TREMONT ST..the place
FROM 9:00pm UNTIL ADM.$3.00 FIRST 25 GIRLS IN FREE...
WITH THOSE BOOGIE DOWN BOSTON BOYS
THE SURE SHOT FOUR
RUSTY THE TOE JAMMER, SKEETER, LARRY DEE,
REGGIE REGSKI, MR.WATS, also GRANDMASTER ace
M.C. KOOL GEE, THE WIZARD M.C.
there will be police on premises, do leave your troubles at home!!
Special Thank & Dedicated To::: To The Ladies (Paula Wright, Helen Allen, Tammy Smith, Sherry, Dwana, Tara W., Tara C., Angie, Honey B., Lisa Lee, Candie, Carmen V., Tasha P., Gina., Cindy S., Missy, Reida B., Val H., Shona, Shirelle, Caprice B.. Alisha F., Shortie R., Shan, Tonya, Christine, San, Tina R., Becky R., Cythia M., Val K., Debbie K., Little Mama, Kristy C., Cherita, Debbie W., Laura, Tiny T., Fran W.. Susan D., Colina S., Linda. Lisa M., Mizzy D., Lisa Luv., Annette C., Nat (in J.P.). Lady Supreme., Alexa, Renee., Ann. Patreace T.. Karen., Ramella., Anita., Vicky., Marie., Kim., Pebbles., KiKi., Nicole., Cheryl W., Wendy W., Cherita., Yvette..)
To All Boston Zulu Crews::. The Sure Shot Kings + Queen., Pleasure Crew., The Body Rock Crew., The LFC Crew, RayDog + RSO Crew., Disco P + The Deff M.C.s. The Royal Force., The Dual of Terror, The Fresh Committee, The Fresh Females., The CIA., The Chain Reaction., The Floorlords., The Unikue Dominoes. Rappitber Crew, Mike T.. Shawn A.. Dwayne H.. Jimmy.. Rajah.. Mafia H. Darryl C.. Paul and Richie.. B.K. crew.. C City Crew .Heart Breakers. Boston Dream Girls. Stutter Crew. the Hill Boys & Boston Zulu 2 / The Homicide Crew.. The Hifi Crew. The Players 3.. The Lady m.c.s. .BA Denterprise.. The Beantown Crew. . 3mcs. The Mash Crew. The Remix Force. . The ZULU NATION. . . AND YOU TO
so c in peace, this jam w jammed packed ag

Concert flyer, June 1985 [MHHA]

Brattle Theatre 40 Brattle St

SUMMER REPERTORY, 1972

June 21-27
Wed-Tues

Marcel Carne's
CHILDREN OF PARADISE
5:15, 8:30

June 28-July 4
Wed-Tues

TWO FILMS BY INGMAR BERGMAN
SHAME
6:20, 9:30
plus
THE HOUR OF THE WOLF
8:00

July 5-11
Wed-Tues

THREE FILMS BY JEAN RENOIR
BOUDU SAVED FROM DROWNING
6:00, 9:35
plus
PICNIC ON THE GRASS
7:30
also
A DAY IN THE COUNTRY
8:55

July 12-18
Wed-Tues

Eric Rohmer's
LA COLLECTIONNEUSE
6:00, 9:30
plus
Jean-Luc Godard's
PIERROT LE FOU
7:40

July 19-25
Wed-Tues

TWO FILMS BY FEDERICO FELLINI
I VITELLONI
6:15, 9:30
plus
THE WHITE SHEIK
8:00

July 26-Aug 1
Wed-Tues

Eric Rohmer's
MA NUIT CHEZ MAUD
6:15, 9:30
plus
Jean-Luc Godard's
MY LIFE TO LIVE
8:05

Aug 2-8
Wed-Tues

Bernardo Bertolucci's
THE CONFORMIST
5:30, 9:25
plus
Lindsay Anderson's
IF . . .
7:30

Aug 9-15
Wed-Tues
BOGART IS BACK
Humphrey Bogart and Ingrid Bergman
in
CASABLANCA
6:00, 7:50, 9:35

Aug 16-22
Wed-Tues
Humphrey Bogart and Lauren Bacall
in
THE BIG SLEEP
5:30, 7:30, 9:30

Aug 23-29
Wed-Tues
Humphrey Bogart and Sydney Greenstreet
in
THE MALTESE FALCON
6:00, 7:50, 9:35

Boston Phoenix, June 21, 1972 [BCA]

"I can't believe all these famous designer labels.
What kind of a discount store is this?"
Miltons gives you 20% to 50% off
famous designer labels, every day.
MILTONS
HE'S GIVING DISCOUNTING
A GOOD NAME
Route 9, Chestnut Hill
• South Shore Plaza, Braintree
• Northshore Shopping Center, Peabody
• Route 5 (at I-95), Warwick, R.I.
Store Hours: Mon.-Sat., 10:00 AM-10:00 PM
Sun. 12 noon-6:00 PM
We accept the following credit cards, MasterCard, Visa, American Express.

Boston Globe, October 16, 1986 [BCA]

Mr. Bartley never gives you a bum steer!
MR. BARTLEY'S BURGER COTTAGE
1246 Mass Ave., Cambridge
"The Beethoven of Beef"
The Boston Globe, Boston Magazine, Real Paper, Harvard Crimson & Chomp agree.
We have the best burgers in Greater Boston.
TEL. 354-9830
FOR TAKE OUT
Large selection of salads

good for a gander
EXCLUSIVELY AT
Tello's
415 BOYLSTON STREET BOSTON
+W 10-8:30 • T,Th,F 10-6
TEL. 336-1365
STUDENT
CHARGE ACCOUNTS

TOP: ***Real Paper,*** October 5, 1975 [DBA]
BOTTOM: ***Boston After Dark,*** November 12, 1969 [DBA]

The University Shop
'the wide tie'
hand fashioned paisleys foulards and stripes, in colours to compliment your wardrobe.
"popular with dear old Dad in 1935."
SAKS FIFTH AVENUE
73 MT. AUBURN STREET, CAMBRIDGE.

DICKSON BROS
HARDWARE · HOUSEWARES · PAINT
The Most Complete Supply of Housewares
DICKSON BROS. CO.
26 Brattle Street, Cambridge
876-6760

Harvard Lampoon, April 1970 [DBA]

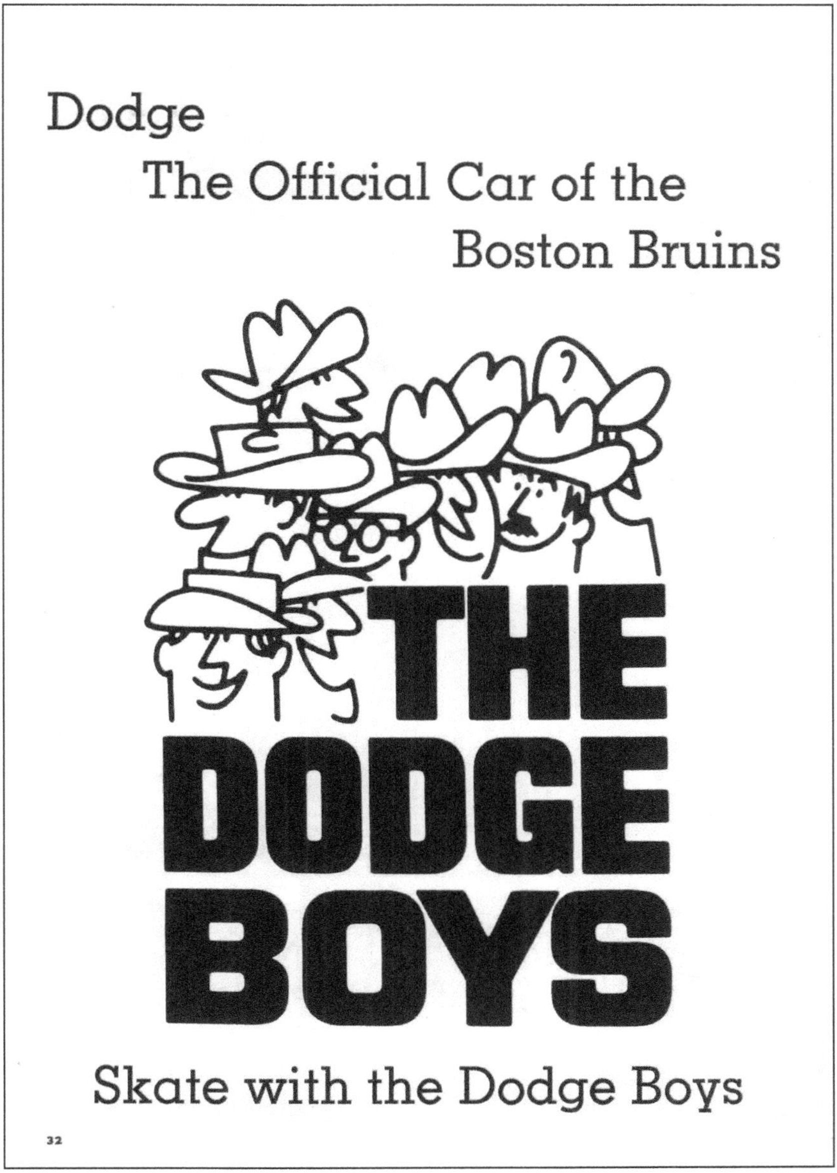
Dodge
The Official Car of the
Boston Bruins
THE
DODGE
BOYS
Skate with the Dodge Boys
32

Boston Bruins yearbook, 1974–1975 [BCA]

Come On.
This ain't no big come-on, high-pressure hard-sell hype. Only a soft-sell gentle nudge to get you to subscribe to the Real Paper. Just fill out the coupon below . . .
Real Paper
10 B Mt. Auburn St., Cambridge, MA 02138
□ 20 weeks for $4.00
□ 1 year for $10.00
□ 2 years for $18.00
Name
Address
City
State Zip
I enclose $
□ New □ Gift (Send donor's name on separate sheet.)

Real Paper, July 18, 1973 [DBA]

B. JONES
24
CELTICS
32
BIRD
33
ERVING
6
CELTICS
WE'RE PLEASED
TO TAKE YOU
TO COURT.
The First National Bank of Boston is proud to be one of the sponsors bringing you the Boston Celtics on WBZ-TV Channel 4.
1784
BANK OF BOSTON

Boston Celtics Media Guide, 1982–1983 [BCA]

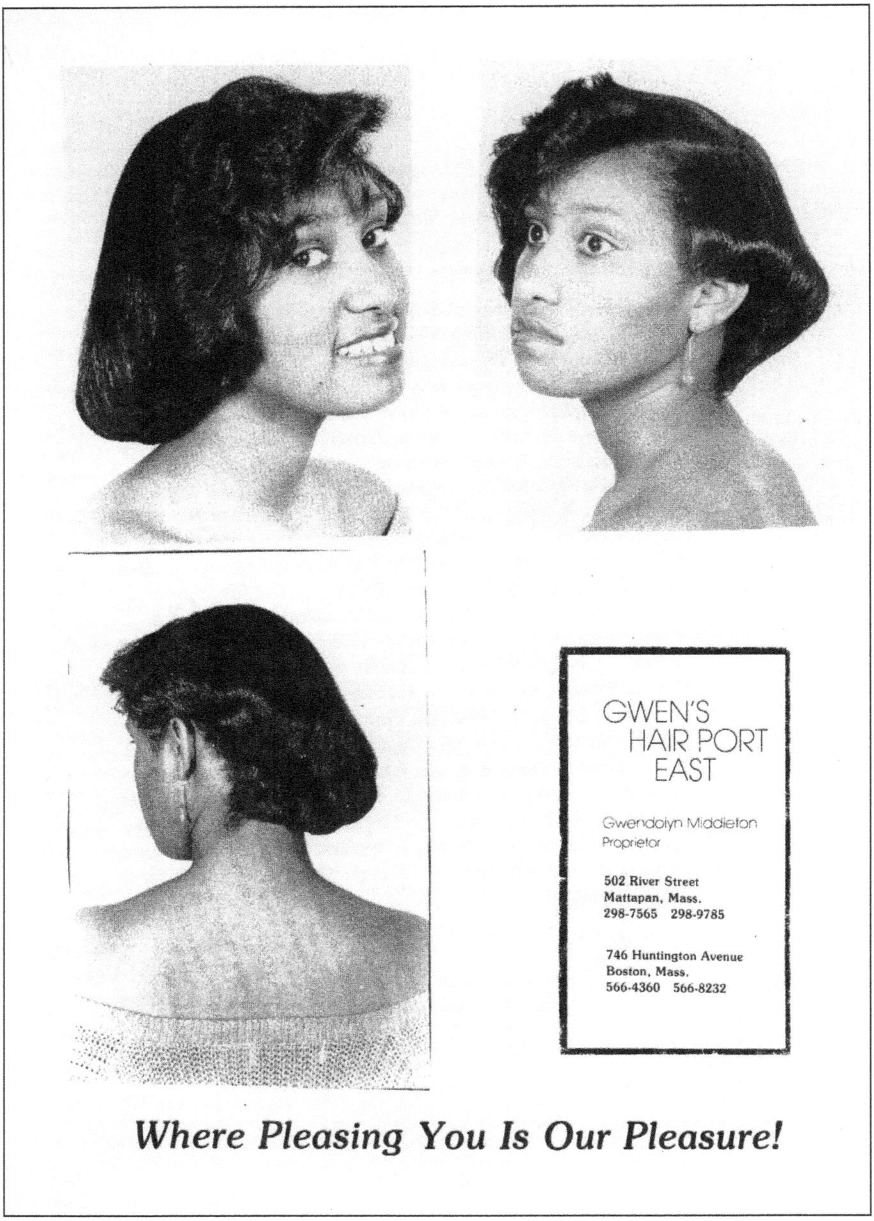
GWEN'S
HAIR PORT
EAST
Gwendolyn Middleton
Proprietor
502 River Street
Mattapan, Mass.
298-7565 298-9785
746 Huntington Avenue
Boston, Mass.
566-4360 566-8232
Where Pleasing You Is Our Pleasure!

Designer's Display Competition program, April 21, 1985 [KBA]

NEW LOCATION at 25 ESSEX ST.
NORMANDY LOUNGE
25 ESSEX ST. • 542-4558
UNIQUE MONIQUE
LAURA LADOUX
PHIL ALLEN
MICHEL LANE
ANITA CARI
CONT. ENTERTAINMENT 1 P.M. to 2 A.M.
TONIGHT
Boston's own
NORM CROSBY
Appearing thru March 13
Call (617) 536-7900 for reservations—and to book your special parties, too.
at Playboy of Boston
WE'RE COMING WITH MARCH
SONNY STANTON'S
TALK OF THE TOWN
835 Beacon Street, Boston (near Kenmore Sq.)
featuring
CLARENCE TATE
WE HAVE ARRIVED

OPENING MON. SURVIVORS LTD.
LAST DAY — THE BETTER WAY
MON. BIG NIGHT—THURS. MINI PRICES
TUES. LADIES' NIGHT—CHAMPAGNE
Odee's
450 Rindge Ave., CAMBRIDGE
492-6620
Members-Guests
MARCH 15 — THE SHIRELLES
MARCH 22—THE HAPPENINGS
TEDDY BEAR lounge
PARK SQUARE · BOSTON
Starring
SATAN's ANGEL
WELCOME BACHELOR PARTIES
WE CATER ALL KINDS OF PARTIES
Co-feature
CIELITO DARLING
The Cuban Bombshell
THE DANCING CUBS
floor shows 2 P.M. & 2 A.M.
COMING: MORGANA
THE
NINETIES
INTERNATIONAL RESTAURANT and LOUNGE
extends an invitation to join us and discover:
• The finest food prepared by a Cordon Bleu Chef and served 4 p.m. to 1:30 a.m. 7 days
• Nitely entertainment, including live & in concert Broadway Shows Sundays and Mondays at 9:30 & 11:30 p.m.
• Intimate atmosphere • Valet Parking
• All of the nicest people anywhere
• The RN place everyone is talking about
90 BROADWAY (Park Sq.),
BOSTON 542-0410

PAGE SEVEN — A
YUM.
NEXT TIME YOU'RE HUNGRY...
...BUY A RECORD.
POP - ROCK
BLUES & FOLK
6.98 NOW 4.19
5.98 NOW 3.69
4.98 NOW 2.99
STORE HOURS:
MON-SAT 9:30 am-MIDNIGHT
MAIL ORDERS:
35c 1st RECORD 15c EACH ADDITIONAL
discount records, inc.
STORES FROM COAST TO COAST
18 BOYLSTON STREET
CAMBRIDGE, MASS. 02138
PHONE: 492-4064-5
OFFER GOOD 'TILL OCTOBER 30TH.
THIS COUPON IS GOOD FOR 1 FREE HOT-DOG AT THE TASTY WITH ANY PURCHASE AT DISCOUNT RECORDS, CAMBRIDGE. BE SURE TO HAVE THE COUPON STAMPED AT THE TIME OF PURCHASE.
Tasty
Store Hours 7 A.M. - 1 A.M.
SANDWICH SHOP
TASTY HOT-DOG
DISCOUNT RECORDS 18 BOYLSTON ST.
BOYLSTON STREET

TOP: ***Boston Herald Traveler,*** March 7, 1971 [DBA]

BOTTOM: ***Free Paper (Cambridge Phoenix),*** October 14, 1970 [DBA]

Fat Albert's Disco
Have you ever sat in a 200-year-old barn while listening to and enjoying the latest disco light and sound show?
If the answer is no... you haven't experienced Fat Albert's!
Get away - from the city, the noise, and the traffic... Take a short drive through the countryside and unwind at Fat Albert's tonight!
Take Exit 4W off Rt.52 - go straight through the lights at Oxford Center. Left on Dudley Road - Go about 3 miles and bear left at the fork. Welcome!
Reservations are a definite necessity...
987-1214

Night Life, February/March 1979 [DBA]

bad trips
PROJECT PLACE
legal
medical
psychiatric help
24 hr. switchboard
call: 267-5280

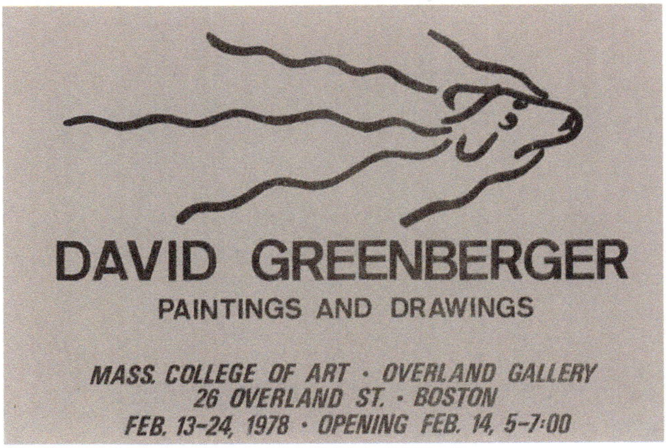
DAVID GREENBERGER
PAINTINGS AND DRAWINGS
MASS. COLLEGE OF ART · OVERLAND GALLERY
26 OVERLAND ST. · BOSTON
FEB. 13-24, 1978 · OPENING FEB. 14, 5-7:00

TOP: ***Boston After Dark,*** March 25, 1970 [DBA]
BOTTOM: **Event postcard,** February 1978 [BCA]

It's Playboy
Early or late.
Early: Cocktail hour with Bob Winter at piano. 5-8:30 PM nightly.
Late: Early-morning Steak & Eggs Breakfast beginning at 11:30 PM. $3.50 per person.
Special rates now available for business meetings and private parties.
Playboy
54 Park Sq./Boston/536-7900

Boston Magazine, September 1975 [DBA]

For the woman who
appreciates a gentleman's look.
That tailored look that has long turned your head will now turn his. Robert Todd's new line of women's clothing offers sweaters, slacks, suits, tailored shirts, blazers, and accessories that are a cut above all the rest. Natural fibers only. Only at Robert Todd.
ROBERT TODD LTD.
141 Newbury Street Boston, Mass. 02116 267-0650

Boston Magazine, September 1975 [DBA]

ADAM LEWIS
Music Director
(603) 899-5111 x 224
(603) 899-6448 Fax
WFPR 93.3 FM
Pond Scum Radio
Franklin Pierce College
Rindge, NH 03461
The Morning After Blues
WMFO
91.5 FM
Holly Harris
Disc Jockey / Producer
Emcee, Voice-Overs, Vocalist,
Musicologist, Production
P.O. Box 65
Medford, MA 02153
(617) 491-6989
(617) 381-3800
104 FM
WBCN
DAVID BIEBER
Creative Services Director
1265 Boylston Street, Boston, MA 02215 617-266-1111
FM 104
INFINITY BROADCASTING CORPORATION
66
JAMES D. K. WILLIS
Assistant Music Director
WVJV-TV
111 Speen Street
Framingham, MA 01701
(617) 350-6666
curt gowdy
broadcasting
corporation
wccm & fm 94cgy
33 franklin street
lawrence, ma 01840
(617) 683-7171
(617) 729-9470
ROCK 93
WCGY 93.7 FM
"Boston Music Showcase"
Sundays 6-10 pm
JOSEPH A. VIGLIONE
Music/Account Rep.
Lawrence: (508) 683-7171 Boston: (617) 729-9470
CURT GOWDY BROADCASTING
33 Franklin St. · Lawrence, MA 01840
WZLX
classic hits 100.7 fm
DR. K
Staff Musicologist
JOHN HANCOCK TOWER
200 CLARENDON STREET
BOSTON, MA 02116
(617) 267-0123
A Station of Cook Inlet Radio Partners, L.P.
413-538-2044
WMHC 91.5 FM
Mount Holyoke College, South Hadley, MA 01075
ELIZABETH RODENO, Music Director
C-LINE #61217
BUSINESS CARD
91.3 FM
WDJM
FRAMINGHAM STATE COLLEGE
MARYROSE ANSUPO
CONCERT CLUB LIAISON
HOME PHONE (617) 731-2002
100 STATE STREET
FRAMINGHAM, MA 01701
(508) 872-1321 - (508) 626-4622
WAAF
107 FM
Pamela Nolan
Promotion Coordinator
19 Norwich Street
Worcester, MA 01608-2498
(617) 752-5611

Chuck White Business Card Collection, 1980s–1990s [CWA/DBA]

Locke-Ober Cafe

3 and 4 WINTER PLACE
BOSTON

LI 2-1340 — Closed Sundays

Joseph's Restaurant

279 DARTMOUTH ST. and
147 NEWBURY ST.

CO 6-1502—Closed Sundays

(UNDER LOCKE-OBER MANAGEMENT)

(MEN'S BAR & GRILL ROOM)

EXETER KEnmore 6-7067

EXETER STREET THEATRE

AT THE HUB OF
THE HUB'S BEST DINING AND WINING…
THE BEST IN FILMS!

EXETER AND NEWBURY STREETS, BOSTON
(NEAR COPLEY SQUARE AND THE NEW PRUDENTIAL CENTER)

Rent Control Us

Kirkland Realty

1172 MASS. AVENUE
CAMBRIDGE
868-1130

Club Henry IV, Inc.

Delicious — Intriguing

FRENCH FOOD

Cuisine by Pierre

Chef and Owner formerly from
"The French Line"

Aperitifs and Imported Wines

[illegible]

96 WINTHROP ST.
HARVARD SQUARE

354-8388 — 864-9061

Pizza — Steaks — Spaghetti
Ravioli—Cacciatore Chicken
Choice Liquors

Served Until 12 p.m.

SIMEONE'S

Italian American Restaurant

21 Brookline St., Cambridge
off Mass. Ave.

Telephone: 354-9569

ASK ABOUT OUR STUDENT DISCOUNTS

Carte Blanche - American Express
Bank Americard

MANCHESTER GUARDIAN • ENCOUNTER • THE ECONOMIST • STATIST • FOREIGN AFFAIRS • PARIS MATCH •

LOS ANGELES TIMES • MONTREAL STAR

THEATRE, CONCERT
TICKETS
SYMPHONY HALL

OUT OF TOWN NEWS, INC.

KIOSK, HARVARD SQUARE
(Next to Subway Entrance)

FOREIGN NEWSPAPERS AND LITERARY PUBLICATIONS
BACK NUMBER SERVICES • SUBSCRIPTIONS
and
OUT OF TOWN THEATRE TICKET AGENCY

EL 4-7777

NEWSPAPERS·MAGAZINES

WASHINGTON POST • ST. LOUIS POST-DISPATCH • NEW YORK TIMES • MIAMI HERALD • LONDON OBSERVER •

LE MONDE • DIE SPIEGEL •

Harvard Lampoon, April 1970 [DBA]

RED
AUERBACH

RED AUERBACH'S
8th ANNUAL
BASKETBALL SCHOOL

Camp Milbrook

MARSHFIELD, MASS.

Boys 13 to 19 Years Old
August 25 thru August 31

A BASKETBALL SCHOOL RUN BY COACHES under the direction of Red Auerbach, Gen. Mgr. of the World Champion Celtics. Exclusively, Bill Russell, player-coach of the Celtics, and others.

Tuition includes excellent food, living accommodations, awards and individual instruction by the finest exponents of basketball.—**$150.**

FOR INFORMATION CONTACT:

Red Auerbach, Boston Celtics,
Boston Garden,
150 Causeway St., Boston, Mass. 02114

Jerry Volk, Director, Camp Milbrook
5 Pickwick Rd., West Newton, Mass. 02165
or Phone BIgelow 4-6741

BILL
RUSSELL

Boston Bruins program, 1967–1968 [BCA]

The BOSTON
sound
The sound of FLEETWOOD
The ACTION LINE..... 284-0750
Join our
growing list of
SATISFIED CLIENTS
MGM
EPIC
RIGHT!
BULLET
BIG BEAT
MERCURY
PLYMOUTH
SOUND CITY
KAMA SUTRA
ABC RECORDS
VERVE FORECAST
ELVIS PRESLEY MUSIC
New England's
ROCK
STUDIO
FLEETWOOD RECORDING STUDIOS
321 REVERE STREET
REVERE, MASS. 02151

COMPLIMENTARY
OPEN SEATING
KNIGHTS OF COLUMBUS
541 CAMBRIDGE STREET
ALLSTON, MASSACHUSETTS
FEB.
11
1978
Sat. Eve. at 8:00
La Peste
WITH THE
INFLIKTORS
ADMISSION $2.00
NO REFUNDS or EXCHANGES
GOOD ONLY
SATURDAY EVE.
FEBRUARY,
11
1978
KNIGHTS OF COLUMBUS
OPEN SEATING

TOP: ***New England Scene* magazine,** September 1968 [DBA]
BOTTOM: **Concert ticket,** February 1978 [LOCO]

SALSA IS HOT
SALSA NIGHT AT Mirage
LATIN MUSIC EVERY SUNDAY
beginning at 8 p.m.
Featuring
THE ELEVEN PIECE
Los Bravos Band
plus Salsa Disco
$4.00 at the door
590 Commonwealth Ave. Kenmore Sq.

80-MINUTE CD NO KIDDING
THE WORLD'S FIRST 80-MINUTE COMPACT DISC ALSO HAPPENS TO BE A CRUCIAL CHRONICLE OF ONE OF THE WORLD'S MOST IMPORTANT BANDS
They said it couldn't be done, but . . .
Rykodisc, The Company You'd Expect To Do This, announces a major breakthrough in digital technology: the first Compact Disc to break the sound barrier — 80 minutes of music on a single disc.
RCD 40072 • AAD
MISSION OF BURMA: an 80-minute document of the brilliant career of this brash, vital quartet — including two previously unreleased tracks.
Also out now:
BIRDSONGS OF THE MESOZOIC: SONIC GEOLOGY (RCD 20073 • AAD) 70 minutes of "punk jazz classical car-wreck music" (The Boston Globe).
Write for free catalogue.
RYKO
RYKODISC USA
Pickering Wharf, Bldg. C-3G
Salem, MA 01970
COMPACT disc DIGITAL AUDIO

TOP: ***Nightfall,*** March 1976 [DBA]

BOTTOM: ***Spin magazine,*** April 1988 [BBR]

FACING PAGE: ***Boston Rock***

(cover of debut issue, photo by Phil In Phlash), June 1980 [DBA]

BOSTON ROCK

June 1980
VOL. [illegible], #1
$1.00

The Neighborhoods

Rick Harte
Johnny Lydon, PIL

Providence Civic Center plays host to Styx on March 4th. L-R: Dennis DeYoung, Tommy Shaw, James Young, John Panozzo & Chuck Panozzo.

happenings and did just that by inking a new high energy group on the scene called **POWERHOUSE** February 27 thru March 11th for two big weeks. . . .**THE BARN DOOR** continues to feature T.N.T. every Wed., Fri. & Sat. but with a special added feature of **DAWN** (R.I.'s newest and most exciting vocal discovery) not to mention that she could be **NIGHT LIFE'S FOXE Of The MONTH** at anytime.

CONTINENTAL L.T.D.
123 MATHEWSON ST. PROV. R.I. 02903 401-421-4721
BEST SELECTION IN STAGEWEAR
FOR SHOW & ROCK BANDS
"TOP OF THE LINE"
EXCLUSIVE CUSTOM TAILORING
GROUP DISCOUNTS
ON STAGE
by CONTINENTAL L.T.D.
ALSO LOCATIONS AT:
621 WASHINGTON ST.
BOSTON, MASS. 02111
617-482-7340
721 PURCHASE ST.
NEW BEDFORD MASS.
617-992-3331
ON STAGE
by CONTINENTAL L.T.D.

Night Life, February/March 1979 [DBA]

Things Happen
when you wear
Eleganza!
FREE! Send for full-color catalog of the latest ELEGANZA fashions for men . . . from the world's largest mail order house of its kind. SEE eye-catching SLACKS: baggy legs . . . big flares . . . double-knits . . . dashing designs, fabrics, colors! SEE attention getting SUITS: walking suits, slack suits, shirt suits! SEE sensational SHIRTS, designed to make every head turn your way! SEE our exciting collection of imported shoes and boots from all over the world. See these and more — sold by mail only and unconditionally GUARANTEED!
THE BOLDEST COLLECTION OF DASHING APPAREL AND DRAMATIC IMPORTED FOOTWEAR ANYWHERE.
Suit $44.95
Shoe $27.95
Slacks $17.95
Slacks $16.95
Shoe $34.95
Eleganza
MAIL COUPON TODAY FOR EXCITING
NEW FREE CATALOG
Rush me your FREE full color catalog showing plenty more great styles like these!
Name
Address
City State Zip
Eleganza
23 Pearl Street, Brockton, Mass. 02403

***Hit Parader* magazine**, May 1973 [BBR]

HILLTOP BUTCHER SHOP
Frank Giuffrida
HILLTOP
BUTCHER
SHOP
IN REAR
★OUR STEAK HOUSE QUALITY
★AT WHOLESALE PRICES
★FOR RETAIL CUSTOMERS
★ AND NOW ★
HILLTOP
GENERAL STORE
AT. . .Frank Giuffrida's
HILLTOP BUTCHER SHOP
OPEN MON.-SAT. 9 A.M.-9 P.M.
HILLTOP
STEAK
HOUSE
ROUTE U.S. 1 SAUGUS, MASS.
OPEN EVERY DAY 11 A.M.-11 P.M.

Boston Magazine, August 1977 [BCA]

Serenely Eloquent...

Your unerring good taste is reflected in a decor
that bids 'welcome' to your family and friends
on so many different occasions—
be they casual or formal.
For an appointment with one of our designers,
phone 426-1500 Ext. 156

PAINE
FURNITURE
BOSTON • NATICK

Boston Magazine, September 1975 [DBA]

music is our thing
the american revolution
wbcn-fm 104
now on the air at 8:15 a.m.!
with remote studios at the boston tea party

***New England Scene* magazine**, July 1968 [ELA]

Good Luck Miss Black Fox
from

RIBS ON WHEELS
See Richie or Jimmy

240 CENTER, ROX. 522-8905

Compliments of Willie Hicks

HICKS AUTO BODY

10 TALBOT AVENUE DORCHESTER

Compliments of the

ENERGETICS
Boston's No. 1 Vocal Group

Call 536-5131 – or 427-2059

P & G ENTERPRISES 1824 WASH. BOSTON

Compliments of

EBONY MARKET

Specializing in all Kinds of
MEATS – GROCERIES – FISH & VEGETABLES

846 BLUE HILL AVENUE 436-9004

Best of Luck from

LOUIE'S LOUNGE
1788 WASHINGTON ST., BOSTON
HI 5-8288

Open Daily from 8 A.M. 'til 2 A.M.
"THE PLACE WHERE OLD FRIENDS MEET"

SEE CHICKIE OR PORTER

Congratulations from

THE NEW SUNRISE GROCERY STORE

OPEN FROM 8 A.M. to 6 P.M.
See Bob Murphy or Madison

256 WARREN STREET KINGWOOD

Compliments of

DECCO BEAUTY SUPPLIES
Located on Ruggles St. for 44 Years

Now Located at
390 BLUE HILL AVENUE 445-2312

Compliments of

ROSCOE'S LOUNGE

"The Soul Oassis in the Ghetto"
ENTERTAINMENT EVERY WEEKEND

Roscoe Gòrham, Prop.

1724 WASHINGTON STREET 247-8418

Congratulations Miss Black Fox
from

HITE
Radio & Television Co., Inc.

1672 WASHINGTON STREET KE6-0677

Best Wishes from

COLLIER'S BABY SITTING SERVICE

We Will Baby-Sit Five Days a Week
in My Home – Pick Up & Deliver in
Mattapan – Roxbury & Dorchester

66 ASTORIA STREET, MATTAPAN 296-6772

John Seagraves 986 BLUE HILL Av.
DORCHESTER, MASS.

J & S CATERERS
Restaurant & Function Room!
CATERING FOR ALL OCCASIONS
IN OUR DINING ROOM OR YOURS

282-8639

Compliments of

CHICO'S NEWS & VARIETY STORE
SOUTH END'S ONLY 24 Hr. STORE

1923 WASHINGTON STREET 247-8119

Miss Black Fox event program, May 27, 1973 [KBA]

HERBIE'S RAMROD ROOM
266-2986
photo by richard lahart
1254 BOYLSTON,
BOSTON

Hit Parade of Boston (photo by Richard Lahart), November 1979 [DBA]

DANCE
YOUR ASS OFF
RHINOCEROS
NEAR BROAD ST. IN THE HEART OF BOSTON'S FINANCIAL DISTRICT
THE RHINOCEROS 295 Franklin St., Boston (617) 423-7730

Nightfall, November 1975 [DBA]

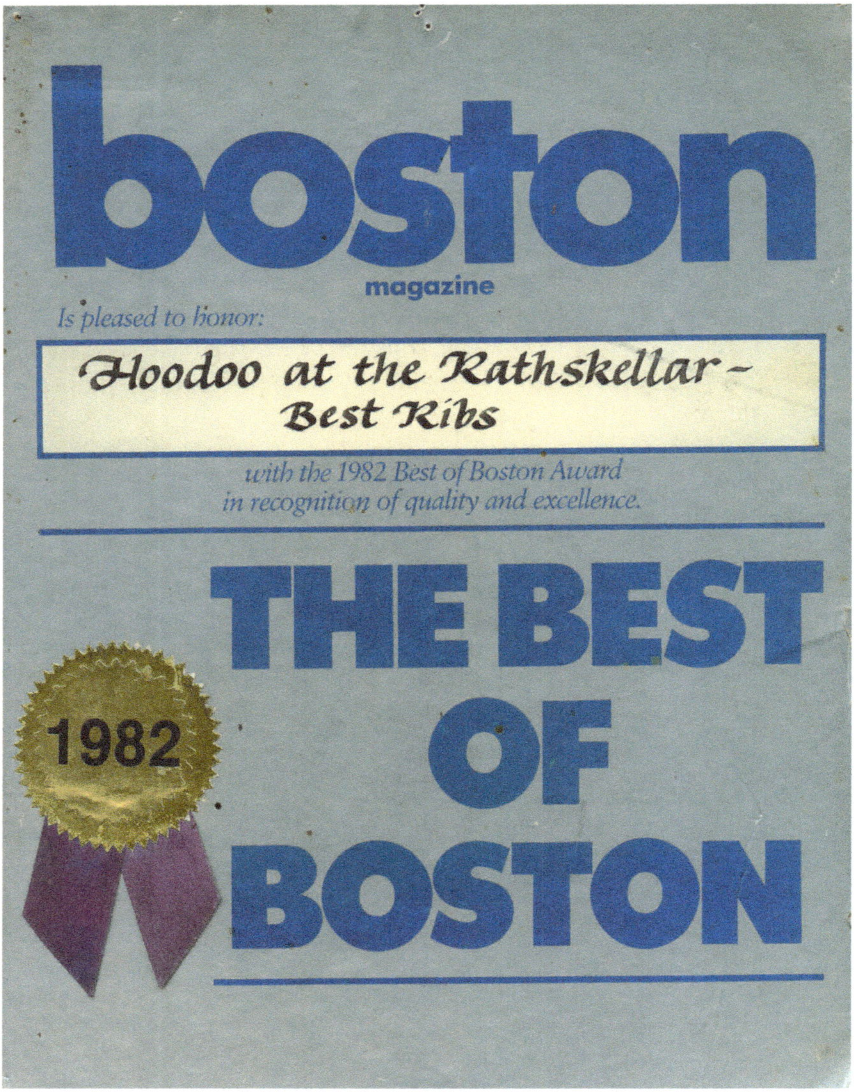
boston
magazine
Is pleased to honor:
Hoodoo at the Rathskellar -
Best Ribs
with the 1982 Best of Boston Award
in recognition of quality and excellence.
THE BEST
OF
BOSTON
1982

***Boston Magazine* "Best Ribs" award,** 1982 [VALDEZ]

JACK'S
DRUM
SHOP
INC.

New England Teen Scene (artist: Ronn Campisi), October 1967 [ELA]

PRINCE CHARLES
AND
THE CITY BEAT BAND
HIT CITY MANAGEMENT
TONY ROSE
1-617-436-1238
A KID LYRICON AND
DR. FUNK N CHAIN
MONSTER P FUNK A THING
FUNSHIP ADVENTURE

Promotional flyer/photo, early 1980s [KBA]

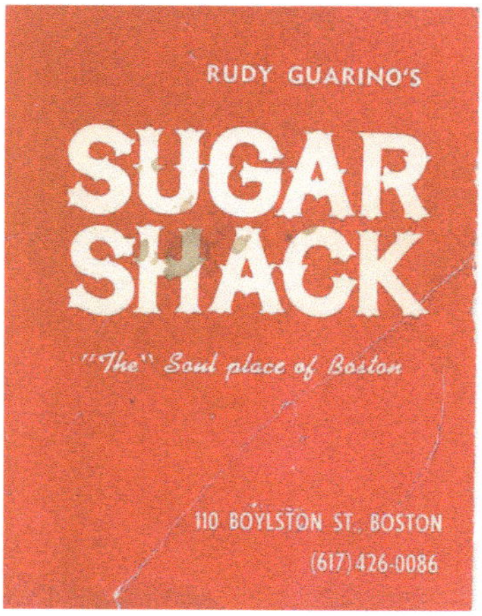
RUDY GUARINO'S
SUGAR SHACK
"The" Soul place of Boston
110 BOYLSTON ST., BOSTON
(617) 426-0086

192
8th ANNUAL
Miss Black Fox Beauty
Contest - Show & Dance
169
8th ANNUAL
Miss Black Fox Beauty
Contest - Show & Dance
FRIDAY, NOV. 16th,1979 — 7:30 p.m.
TRAVELODGE AT BROOKLINE
CRYSTAL BALLROOM
1200 Beacon St., Brookline, Mass.
Advance Tickets: $10.00

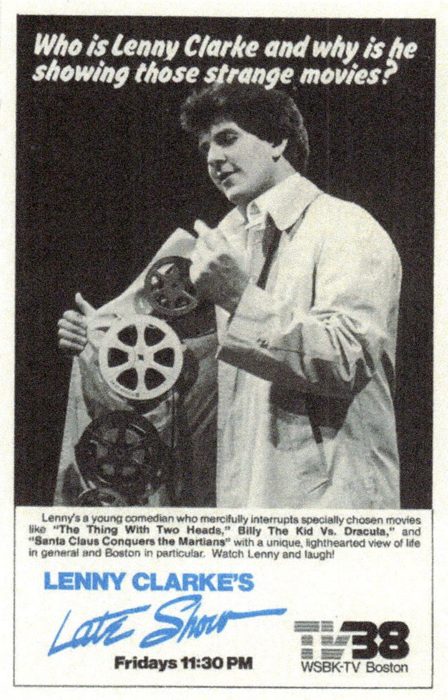
Who is Lenny Clarke and why is he showing those strange movies?
Lenny's a young comedian who mercifully interrupts specially chosen movies like "The Thing With Two Heads," Billy The Kid Vs. Dracula," and "Santa Claus Conquers the Martians" with a unique, lighthearted view of life in general and Boston in particular. Watch Lenny and laugh!
LENNY CLARKE'S
Late Show
Fridays 11:30 PM
TV38
WSBK-TV Boston

LANES OF MATTAPAN
1354 BLUE HILL AVE
presents
MAURICE
STARR
RCA RECORDING ARTIST
Talent Nite
Every Tues.
what ever you do. .
this is for you.
FOR INFORMATION CALL
298-4850

UPPER LEFT: **Matchbook,** Late '60s [Rudy Guarino's Sugar Shack Facebook page]
UPPER RIGHT: **Event Ticket,** November 1979 [BCA]
LOWER LEFT: **General Cinema Theatre Guide,** December 1981 [DBA]
LOWER RIGHT: **Event Flyer,** Early 1980s [KBA]

JEROME CARLHIAN
22 HEATHS BRIDGE RD.
CONCORD MASS 01742
CLUB 47 INC.
47 PALMER STREET
HARVARD SQUARE
CAMBRIDGE 38, MASSACHUSETTS
U. S. POSTAGE
PAID
Boston, Mass.

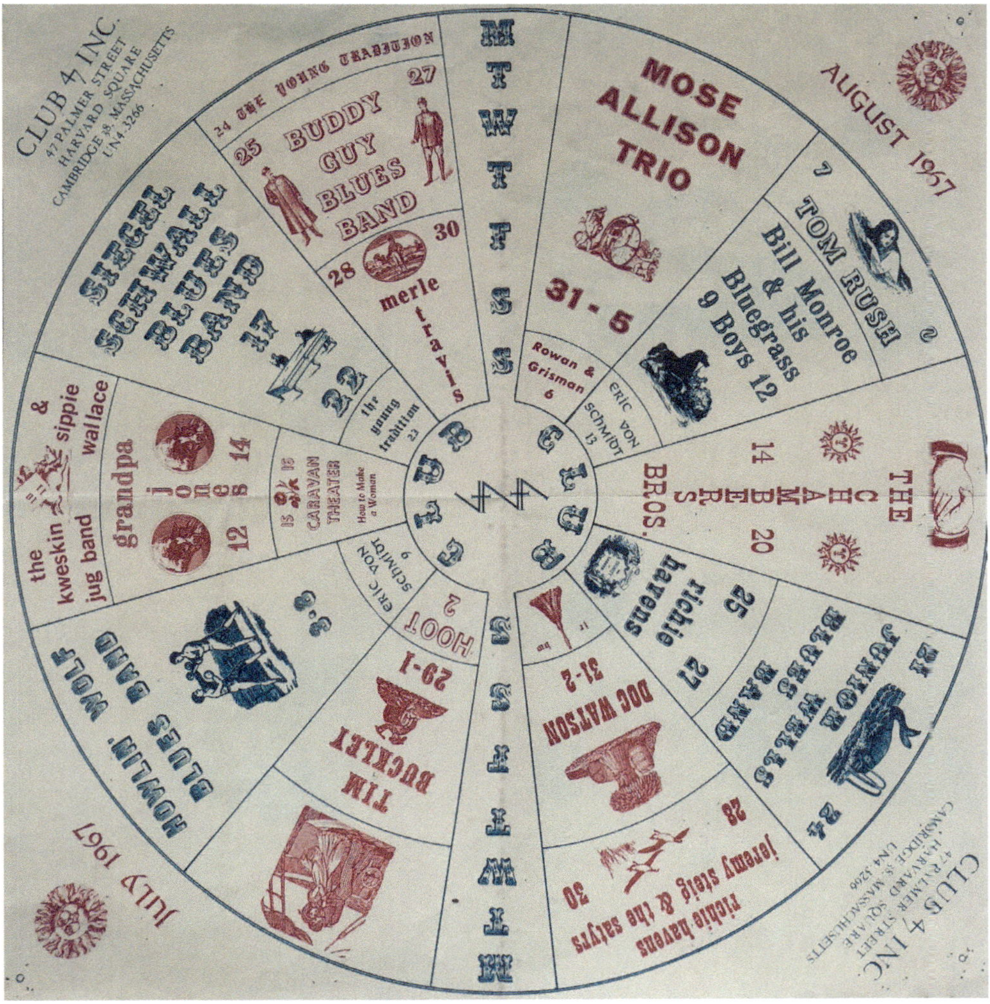
CLUB 47 INC.
47 PALMER STREET
HARVARD SQUARE
CAMBRIDGE 38, MASSACHUSETTS
UN4-3266
AUGUST 1967
MOSE ALLISON TRIO
31 - 5
7 TOM RUSH 9
Bill Monroe & his Bluegrass Boys 12
Rowan & Grisman 6
ERIC VON SCHMIDT 13
THE CHAMBERS BROS. 14 20
25 richie havens 27
21 JUNIOR WELLS BLUES BAND 24
DOC WATSON 31-2
28 jeremy steig & the satyrs
richie havens 30
HOOT 2
ERIC VON SCHMIDT 9
TIM BUCKLEY 29-1
HOWLIN' WOLF BLUES BAND 3-8
July 1967
the kweskin jug band & sippie wallace
grandpa jones 12 14
15 16 CARAVAN THEATER How to Make a Woman
SIEGEL SCHWALL BLUES BAND 17 22
the young tradition 23
24 THE YOUNG TRADITION
25 BUDDY GUY BLUES BAND 27
28 merle travis 30
M T W T F S S
CLUB 47

BOTH PAGES: **Events calendar** (front and back, quad-fold)
July/August 1967 [VALDEZ]

Saave!!
You're a winner on the road with fine automotive products from Zayre. You can keep your car in top shape all season long with this great selection of famous names at famous low Zayre prices. Look for this heavy-hitting team of automotive products at 65 Zayre stores all over New England. Get it all...at Zayre.
Zayre
15

Red Sox Scorebook, 1980 [BCA]

RENT A MAGICIAN

RONDAR E. GOODE
89 Blue Hill Ave., Roxbury, 445-8960. Magician, ventriloquist. Needs a few days notice but will perform anytime; has a number of different acts. Other magicians available.

Real Paper, April 11, 1973 [BCA]

THANK YOU!

One thing I love is that my Thank Yous are a lot longer this time around. I had a pretty tight archival circle before *Volume 1* hit, and the length of this list means that a lot of amazing people have helped and supported me over the past two years.

I will start with my incredible wife Margot Edwards, who allows more piles and boxes around our home than most kind and forgiving people would. My family also always has my back and I love 'em for it: Rich & Sally Coleman (aka Mom and Dad), Darcie, Jenna, Hope, Sadie, Raziyah, Paula, Alexis, Janet, Louise, Nate and Elena.

Next up are my "Usual Suspects," because they have been in my corner since before the first volume: David Bieber, Kay Bourne, Chuck White, Lance Salemo, Jeannie Smith, Reebee Garofalo, Wayne Valdez and Pacey Foster (UMass Boston & the amazing Massachusetts Hip-Hop Archive). Also big thanks to Dan Booth and Adam "Papa D" DeFalco, who helped me out in many ways as I conceptualized this crazy endeavor in 2018.

In the past two years I expanded my network of people to learn from and to borrow scanning fodder: Willie "Loco" Alexander (for allowing me the rare privilege of being able to absorb and scan his legendary Scrapbooks), Erik Lindgren, Mark Flynn (Punkt Data Gallery & *Skunk Piss* magazine), Brother Wayne Rollins (who gave me many of the ticket stubs sprinkled throughout the book), Peter Prescott, Tristram Lozaw, Richard "Dick" Vacca, Roxbury's legendary "Silver Shadow": DJ Bobby Taylor, Russ Gershon, Devon Davidson, Sarania Lazar (on behalf of her mom, Lynn), Gage One, the crew at the Cambridge Historical Commission (Emily Gonzalez and Meta Partenheimer), John Campoli, Patty Lederer, Mike Rivard and Chris Guttmacher.

Beyond my scanning sources, there are many more great people who have supported my efforts in various ways: Tony "DJ Flack" Flackett, Andrew Elder and Carolyn Goldstein at UMass Boston (with Andrew pulling double duty at The History Project), Duane Lucia, Jason Bitner, Mark Davis, Noah Schaffer, Bradley Jay, Larry Katz, "Big" Dan McCormack, Tony & Yvonne Rose, Prince Charles Alexander, Cha-Chi & Stephanie Loprete, James Sullivan, Joanie Lindstrom, Adam Zand, Christina Teves, Vivian and Mark Lefebvre, Tom Yaz, Ray Ortega, Chris Faraone, Sue O'Connell, Charles Giuliano, Peter Wolf, Dan McCarthy, the legendary Skippy White, Marc Siegel, Rayne Hoke, Sam Potrykus and Emma Leavitt at Dorchester Art Project, Paul "Blowfish" Lovell, "Miss" Lyn Cardinal, Kenne Highland, Wayne Marshall, Shaula Clark, Jennifer Sullivan, Chris Lovett,

Frank Rowe, Kathy Chapman, Greg Dalton-Kay, Tracy Harrington Kiddie, Jody Urbati-Moore, Dart Adams, Reed Lappin from In Your Ear, Henry Santoro, Jim Botticelli (Dirty Old Boston), Tim Devin, Bill Brotherton, Giordana Mecagni and Molly Brown at Northeastern, Cory O'Hayer, Clay Ferno, Tommy & Judy White, TJ Killilea, Erica Jones, Tom Faix, Drew Stone, Roger Miller, Clint Conley, Eric Green, Sean Quinn, Michael Marotta, Peter Levine, Adam Reilly, Peter Higgins and I assume many others I'm forgetting (sorry!).

Since the publication of the first volume I have had a lot of fun creating some Boston-centric events, many of them around the "Video Loft" branch of the *Buy Me, Boston* family tree, and I appreciate the venues who have hosted them: the Brattle Theatre (Ned Hinkle), the Coolidge Corner Theatre (Mark Anastasio), the Boston Public Library (Emily Todd, Gianna Gifford and Kristin Motta) and the Mass College of Art & Design.

There have been some great local retailers who helped get *Volume 1* out to the world: Newbury Comics (Larry Mansdorf and Terri Christopher), Brookline Booksmith (Russ Barker), Harvard Book Store (Rachel Cass), Bodega (Oliver Mak), Village Vinyl & HiFi (Jonathan Sadler), the Boston General Store (April Gabriel), the Book Rack in Arlington (Mike Buglio), Jason Faulkner, Million Year Picnic (Tony Davis) and Tres Gatos (Phil Wilcox). And a couple out-of-town pals: Max Ochester at Brewerytown Beats in Philly, and Ben Epstein at NOLA Mix in the Big Easy.

Finally, many mercis to my excellent designer Caryn Hirsch – it was a real honor to have her on board because she actually created some of the ads in these volumes, at the *Boston Phoenix* and through other freelancing in the 1980s. And reverberated props to designer and all-around good dude James Blackwell for helping get this *Buy Me, Boston* idea off the ground the first time around.

~ B.C.

FOR MORE INFORMATION ON THE PEOPLE AND ARCHIVES USED TO PUT TOGETHER *BUY ME, BOSTON, VOLUME 2:*

Willie "Loco" Alexander Archives [LOCO]
www.WillieLocoAlexander.com

David Bieber Archives [DBA]
www.DavidBieberArchives.com

Blue Bag Records/Chris Guttmacher [BBR]
www.Facebook.com/BlueBagRecords

Kay Bourne Archives at Emerson College: Iwasaki Library, Special Collections [KBA]
www.Emerson.edu/library/archives/special-collections

Cambridge Historical Commission [CHC]
www.CambridgeMA.gov/historic

Brian Coleman Archives [BCA]
www.BuyMeBoston.com
www.MassCult617.com

Mark Flynn Archives/Punkt Data [FLYNN]
www.PunktDataGallery.com

Reebee Garofalo Archives at UMass Boston: Joseph P. Healy Library [REEBEE]
www.Reebee.net
https://openarchives.umb.edu/

Russ Gershon Archives [GERSHON]
www.AccurateRecords.com

The History Project [THP]
www.HistoryProject.org

Erik Lindgren Archives/Arf Arf Records [ELA]
www.ArfArfRecords.com

Massachusetts Hip-Hop Archive at UMass Boston: Joseph P. Healy Library [MHHA]
https://openarchives.umb.edu/

Mike Rivard Archives [RIVARD]
www.ClubDelf.com

Richard "Dick" Vacca Archives [VACCA]
www.TroyStreet.com

Wayne Valdez Archives [VALDEZ]
www.Instagram.com/WayneValdez

Chuck White Archives at the David Bieber Archives [CWA]
www.Motherlode.tv
www.DavidBieberArchives.com

INDEX

1270 (club) ... 216
15 Lansdowne Street ... 225
3D Radio ... 25, 92
526 Leathers ... 113

A & P Supermarket ... 15
AAA Recording Studio ... 1
Abernathy, Ralph ... 161
Ade, King Sunny ... 23
Aerosmith ... 84
African Arts Folkloric Group ... 62
African Unity Dance Troupe ... 192
African Women's Day ... 213
Afrika Corps ... 59
Afro-American Institute (Northeastern) ... 139
Ahmed's Discotheque ... 65
Alexander, Prince Charles ... 278
Alexander, Willie "Loco" ... 35, 67, 112, 233
Allman Brothers ... 44
American Friends Service Committee ... 42
America's Soup Kitchen On Wheels ... 228
Ann Taylor ... 61
Arce, Jorge ... 208
Ark ... 69
Arlington Street Church ... 213
Armadillo ... 207
Atlantics ... 27
Atlantis Sound ... 58
Attache Mobile Telephone Co. ... 190
Aura ... 102
Avatar ... 31

B & D Deli ... 149
B Down Records ... 160, 194
Baby's Arm ... 59, 77, 222
Backstreet Bar (Provincetown) ... 64
Bagatelle ... 28
Bags ... 92
Bailey Rosenbaum, Margaret ... 181
Bank of Boston ... 255
Bank Sisters ... 206
Basin Street South ... 30
Bay State Banner ... 145
Beastie Boys ... 158
Beck, Jeff ... 44
Behind The Green Door ... 30
Belafonte, Harry ... 5
Bennett, Samm ... 32
Bentmen ... 71
Berklee College of Music ... 228
Berklee Performance Center ... 221
Berkley Disco ... 59
Berkley Street (club) ... 92
Berlin, Rick ... 71
Bertha Cool ... 237
Bicycle Peddler ... 63
Bieber, David ... 228, 262
Biff's Lounge ... 47
Big Mama Thornton ... 92
Birdsongs of the Mesozoic ... 74
Black Folks Theater Co. ... 192
Black Rose ... 232
Black Uhuru ... 23
Blue Hills Drive-In ... 52, 200
Blues Berry Jam ... 35
Bob Lee's Islander ... 39
Bob The Chef's ... 3
Bobbi Baker ... 33
Boesing, Martha & Paul ... 42
Boize ... 233
Bonzo Dog Band ... 44
Boston (band) ... 66
Boston Afro-American Arts Association (BAAA) ... 192
Boston Architectural Center ... 218
Boston Ballroom ... 173
Boston Beatmakers ... 110
Boston Black Repertory Company ... 127
Boston Bruins ... 12, 51, 253
Boston Celtics ... 255
Boston City Club ... 188
Boston Club ... 186
Boston Coalition for the Liberation of Southern Africa ... 151
Boston Comedy Club ... 141
Boston Daughters Of Bilitis ... 115
Boston Garden ... 5, 128, 152
Boston Gay Guide ... 156
Boston Globe ... 228
Boston Globe Jazz Festival ... 139
Boston Lobsters ... 46
Boston Magazine ... 226, 276
Boston Negro Artists Association ... 145
Boston Patriots ... 107
Boston Phoenix ... 91, 140, 193, 228
Boston Red Sox ... 106
Boston Rock (magazine) ... 34, 267
Boston School of Electronic Music ... 70
Boston Tea Party ... 28, 44
Boston Visual Artist's Union ... 32
Boutique de Optique ... 206
Bradford Hotel ... 104, 125
Brand X ... 28
Brandy's (bar) ... 212

Brattle Theatre 249
Brides of Funkenstein 87
Brigham's Ice Cream 63
Bright Spot 182
Bristols 71
Bromley Heath 248
Brother Blue (Dr. Hugh Morgan Hill) ... 53, 62
Brown Derby 182
Brown, Dennis 125
Brown, James 86, 104
Bullet LaVolta 71, 92
Bunratty's 178
Butterball Jr. 102
Byrd, Jimmy (Early) 159, 179

Cablevision 116
Café Yana 93
Caldor 14
Cambridge Imported Cars 229
Cambridge YWCA 29
Campisi, Ronn 1, 277
Candlelite Lounge 30
Cantabrigia Book Shop 89
Cantone's 57, 59, 222, 247
Cap'n Swing 140
Captain Freedom Haircuts Ltd. 18
Carl Hair Pieces 148
Carlin, George 141
Cars (band) 140, 188
Carvello, Joey 135, 241
Carver Auditorium 129, 221, 235
Casa Romero 232
Catalano, Deborah 228
Celebration 239
Celebrity Awards Show 170
Centre Street Café 24
Chambers Brothers 281
Chameleon (club) 55
Channel (club) 123, 141, 178
Charles River Tennis Club 166
Charles River Valley Boys 149
Charles Street Meeting House 42, 151, 223
Charlie's Tap 178
Chateau de Ville Dinner Theatre 191
Chez Vous Rollerway 154
Chico's News 273
Choice Dancers 119
Churches (various listings) 121
Ciddy Limitz 143
Cimarron 62
Cinema Brookline 242
Circus Theatre For Children 175
Citadel 193
Citymart 89
Clarke, Lenny 141, 279
Cliff, Jimmy 37
Cloud 69
Club 47 .... 149, 280, 281
Club Casablanca 83
Club Henry IV 263
Club, The 36, 233, 247
Cocker, Joe 44
Collier's Baby Sitting Service 273
Come On Strong Cola 82
Commonwealth Chevrolet 154
Connolly's Stardust Room 182
Continental Ltd 268
Coop 49
Cortee's 50
Court Street News 217
CPCS (Umass Boston) 90, 192
Cricket (venue) 44
Crimpers 196
Curtis, Darlene 148
Cxema 71
Cyclorama 246

D.Y.S. (band) 98
Dance Slam (TV show) 142
Dangerous Birds 158
Danny's His And Hers 24
Dating By Computer 139
Davis, Miles 139
Dead Boys 77
Dead End Kids 129
Decoders 36, 247
Deep Throat 30
Del Fuegos 158, 202, 247
Delaney & Bonnie 44
DeLoach, Brian 144
Denison House 119
Designers Display Competition 236
Devil In Miss Jones 30
Dickson Bros. Co. 252
DMZ 13, 77
Dodge Boys 253
Dogmatics 158, 202
Doherty, Dick 163
Don's Pub 247
Donut Hole 243
Down Avenue 237
Doyle, Martin 34
Doyle's 24
Dummy's 187
Durgin Park 155

E. M. Loews Theaters 52, 200
E. U. Wurlitzer 21
Earth Song (play) 42
East Side (bar) 212
Ebony Market 273
Either/Orchestra 92, 205
Eleganza 269
Ellis Hall Group 188
Emmanuel Church 175
Energetics.. 273
Erewhon Trading Company.............139, 227
Estes Boys 59
Etc Lounge 80
European (restaurant) 232
Everett Music 135
Eve's Garden 199
Exeter Street Theatre 263

F.U.'s 98
Fabulous Lords....................................... 161
Fag Rag 130
Fat Albert's Disco................................... 258
Felice, John 92
Fenway Community Health Center.......... 115
Fenway Park 214
Fifteen Lansdowne Street....................... 225
Filene's 168
Filene's Basement 16, 99
Final 4 Restaurant/Lounge..................... 178
Finast 51
Fine Arts Theatre 150
Finney, Mickey (MJ Finlan) 143
First Baptist Church (Cambridge) 4
Fleetwood Recording Studios 265
Fools 55
Fort Apache 247
Fournier, Jimmy 135
Fox Pass 233
Foxboro Racetrack 209
Francis, Elliott 184
Francis, Russ 78
Franklin Park Zoo 147
Fran's Place 68
Fred Woodard Jazz Quartet..................... 192
Freeze.. 158
Friends Social Club 217
Frisco East 35
Frolics Ballroom (Salisbury Beach)............ 13
Frye Boots 21
Fugs 150
Funkadelic... 86, 87
Future Dads 247

Galaxie 500 71
Gallery East....................................98, 202
Gang Green 71, 93
Gangstarr Posse 160
Garage (club) 186
Gardner, Hirsch 223
Gay Ways (radio show) 151
Gaynor, Gloria 33
Gene's Datsun 206
Geometric Cuts 174
Gilchrist's 147
Gillette...106, 146
Gorin's 60
Gospel Ebonetts 159
Gozbekian, Leo 26
Grand Master Woody 165
Grateful Dead 185
Green Street Grill.................................... 178
Green Street Station 71, 92
Greenberger, David 259
Gremies 91
Grice, Janet 32
Groggery 163
Guerra, Leon E. (hypnotist)....................... 48
Gulick, Jane 110
Guy, Buddy 92
Gwen's Hair Port East............................. 256

Hagler, Marvin 243
Hair Reflections 24
Hallucinations 28
Hancock Tower 153
Harlots 44
Harte, Rick 267
Harvard Book Store Café......................... 211
Harvey, Mark 32
Hat Off's 24
Havens, Richie 185, 281
Hawkeye 102
Head Of The Lion 24
Heart Punch Studio 247
Heinsohn, Tommy..................................... 14
Helldorado Productions............................. 71
Herbie's Cactus Room 182
Herbie's Ramrod Room 274
Hilliard, David 161
Hilltop Butcher Shop/Steak House 270
Hirsch, Caryn 108
Hitchhiking Day 1970 54
Hofbrau 59
Hood 244
Hoodoo Barbeque 276
House of Personality 24

Hubba Hubba ... 122
Human Sexual Response ... 57, 218
Hynes Auditorium ... 23, 102
Hypertension ... 221
Hypnosonics ... 124, 231

Infliktors ... 233, 265
Inn Square Men's Bar ... 237
Innis, Roy ... 161

J. Geils Band ... 40, 41
J. M. Fields ... 113
J. Mascis ... 125
J. P. Licks ... 204
Jack's (club) ... 124
Jack's Drum Shop ... 277
Jack's Trick & Joke Shop ... 83
Jackson, Wannetta ... 144
Jacques ... 65, 190
Jamaica Pond Open Door Theater ... 62
Jay Motors ... 89
Jazz Workshop ... 84, 118, 163, 169
Jerry's Kids ... 98, 158
Jimmy's Harborside Restaurant ... 240
Joe's Place ... 74
John Hancock Auditorium ... 170, 236
Johnson, Tom (Maverick Booking) ... 110
Johnstone, Magnus ... 245
Jo-Jo's Room ... 96
Jones, Grace ... 20
Jordan Hall ... 100
Jordan Marsh ... 101
Jumbo's ... 247

Kathy's Hair Plus ... 24
Katy's ... 84, 169, 203
Kennedy, Marie ... 90
Kennedy's Butter And Egg Store ... 24
Ken's Steak House ... 78
Kevin's Wharf ... 83
Kilslug ... 125
King Jr., Martin Luther ... 4, 5
Kiquote, Krispy and Kokie (clowns) ... 38
Kirk, Roland ... 44, 163
Knights of Columbus (Allston) ... 265
Kraftwerk ... 169
KUUMBA Singers ... 192
Kweskin, Jim ... 281

La Crepe ... 83
La Peste ... 265
Lamot, Dini ... 218
Land Of Oz ... 189
Landlubber ... 7
Lane Bryant ... 137
Lane, Robin & The Chartbusters ... 45
Lanes & Games ... 46
Lanes Of Mattapan ... 279
Last Poets ... 86
Last Stand ... 71
Le Papillon ... 108
Leather & Lace ... 133
Lechmere ... 195
Led Zeppelin ... 44, 128
Leeds ... 128
Left Nut ... 34
Lena Park Community Center ... 238
Lennie's On The Turnpike ... 163, 182
Leroy Smart ... 238
Lewis, Adam ... 262
Lilly Bros. ... 149
Lincoln, Abbey ... 139
Linehan, Joyce ... 110
Little Jimmy & The Home Wreckers ... 247
Little Walter ... 159
LL Cool J ... 235
Local 186 ... 178
Locke-Ober ... 263
Lodge ... 7
Logan, Lark ... 184
Los Bravos Band ... 266
Louie's Lounge ... 273
Louis (store) ... 162
Lucifer (club) ... 33
Lulu White ... 65
Luongo, John ... 117, 135
Lyres ... 71, 158

M.I.A.'s ... 247
Mad Angel ... 129
Maelstrom ... 92
Mail Box Disco ... 20
Makaha Restaurant ... 209
Mandrake Memorial ... 28
Manilow, Barry ... 127
Marley, Bob ... 118
Mason Dixon and the Line ... 163
Mason, Ray ... 92
Mass (band) ... 55
Mass College of Art ... 143, 259
Mass Records ... 8
Massachusetts Turnpike Authority ... 78
Massó, José ... 62
Maverick's ... 158
Mayflower (adult theater) ... 52
MC5, The ... 69, 128

McCord, Semenya 144
McLeod, Mackie 62
Meadow Glen Theater 52, 200
Medford Twin Drive-In 200
Medieval Manor 26
Mellen, Doug 34
Metro (club) 103
Miami, Lou (and Kozmetix) 124
Michael's Pub 59
Middle East Café 71
Mike's Custom Leather 166
Miller, Roger 71
Milton's 250
Minutemen 123
Mirage 241, 266
Miss Black Fox Beauty Contest 279
Mission Control 247
Mission of Burma 143, 266
Mississippi John Hurt 93
Mitchell, Paul 196
Mix Master Mike Rock 165
Modern Lovers 105
Modern Method Records 91
Molls, The 201
Montanas 232
Morphine 124
Morris, Joe 32
Morse, Steve 228
Mouse, Stanley 50
Movies To Go (store) 22
Moving Parts 57
Mr. Bartley's Burger Cottage 251
Mr. Butch 58
Mr. Curt 76
Mr. Sid 120
Muhammad, The Honorable Elijah 224
Mukasa Records 245
Murder In The Cathedral 175
Murphy, Eddie 141
Music Business Monthly 76
Music Hall 91, 127, 215
My Apartment 29

NAACP 144
Narcissus 239
Neats 71
Neighborhoods 59, 267
Nelson, Steve 50
Nervous Eaters 188
NESN (New England Sports Network) 94
New Alliance 76
New England Free Press 99
New England Mobile Book Fair 25
New England Performer 228
New England Teen Scene 97, 179
New England Telephone 88
Newbury Comics 22, 76
Newport Folk Festival 214
Newport Jazz Festival 214
Nightfall Magazine 117, 138
Nineties 257
Nixon, Richard 134
Nobby's Apparel 116
Noise 58
Nolan, Richard 76
Normandy Lounge 257
Normandy Sound 247
North Shore Coliseum 87
North Station Cinema 200
Now Shop 66

Odee's 163, 257
O'Halloran, Mickey 110, 129
Old Mole 199
Oliver's 163
Omarr, Dwayne 198
One People 62
Oona's 234
Orchestra Luna 129
Orpheum Theater 41
Orquestra Tropica 62
Orson Welles Cinema 37, 180
Out Of Town News 263
Outer Limits 178
Oxford Ale House 77

Pac-Man 22
Paine Furniture 271
Pallas Athene 24
Paperback Booksmith 11
Paradise (Boston) 188
Paradise (Cambridge) 95
Park Square Cinema 52
Parkway Plaza Cinema 242
Parliament Funkadelic (aka P-Funk) 86
Passim Coffeeshop 185
Passion 81
Paula Fontaine's 77
Paul's Mall 84, 118, 163, 169
People's Yellow Pages 2
Pesky, Johnny 154
P-Funk 86, 87
Phase 2 Dating Service 206
Phil In Phlash 9, 267
Phillips Books 89
Phobia 143

Pierce, Charles ... 96
Pierre's Continental Coiffures ... 157
Pilgrim Burlesk ... 52, 136
Pixies ... 92
Plan 9 ... 92
Playboy Club of Boston ... 257, 260
Plaza Twin Theaters ... 52
Plough & The Stars ... 231
Poco ... 44
Poitier, Sidney ... 5
Pony Room ... 182
Porter Square Dodge ... 134
Porter, Chris ... 178
Presto, Russ ... 135
Prime Movers ... 158, 202
Prince Charles & The City Beat Band ... 278
Prince Hall Masonic Temple ... 148
Project Place ... 259
Proletariat ... 158
Prudential Center ... 85
Psycho (band) ... 158
Punkt Data Gallery ... 9, 181, 218
Pussycat Cinema ... 242

Radio Hearts ... 67
Radio Shack ... 68
Ramblin' Jack Elliott ... 149
Ramones ... 13
Ramrod ... 274
Rat (Rathskeller) ... 13, 71, 77, 79, 124, 201
Raving Ron's Dancing Machine ... 193
Reading International ... 210
Real Kids ... 79
Real Paper ... 254
Record Garage ... 112
Red Auerbach's Basketball School ... 264
Red Book ... 184
Reef ... 30
Reflections Hair Design ... 73
Regency ... 80
Renay, Liz ... 136
Rhinoceros ... 275
Ribs On Wheels ... 273
Ripchord ... 57
Rivers, Sam ... 163
Roach, Max ... 139
Robell's Wig Service ... 24
Robert Todd Ltd. ... 261
Roberts / Neustadter Furs ... 170
Roberts, Tim ... 32
Robin, Ron ... 117, 135, 169
Rock & Roll Flea Market ... 77
Rock Against Racism ... 62, 103
Rock Against Reagan ... 164
Rods & Cones ... 55
Rogers of Harvard Square ... 172
Rondar Goode (Rent A Magician) ... 283
Roscoe's Lounge ... 273
Rose, Tony ... 24, 142, 170, 236, 278
Rose, Yvonne ... 170, 236
Route 114 Drive-In ... 52
Rowe, Frank ... 222
Ruane, Billy ... 71
Rudy Ray Moore ... 129
Rush, Tom ... 100, 149
Russell Auditorium ... 144
Russell, Bill ... 264
Rusty The Toe Jammer ... 248
Rykodisc ... 266
Ryles ... 59, 205

Sacred Mushroom ... 185
Sak's Fifth Avenue ... 252
Salem 66 ... 71
Salisbury Beach ... 38
Salvi Ford Sales ... 157
Sammy White's ... 163
Sanctuary ... 206
Sandman, Mark ... 124, 231
Sandy's Concert Club ... 72
Say Brother ... 75
Scarborough Fair ... 84
Scotch 'n Sirloin ... 232
Seventh Son ... 102
Shaheen's Fun-O-Rama Park ... 38
Shane, Gary ... 71
Shanty Lounge ... 182
Shear Croppers Room ... 155
Sheraton Boston Hotel ... 117
Shinehead ... 119
Short, Dick ... 144
Simeone's ... 263
Simon, Joe ... 221
Simone, Nina ... 109
Skippy White's Records ... 8, 135, 235
Skunk Piss Magazine ... 143
Skycap Plaza ... 165
Slaughter Shack ... 92
Sly & Robbie ... 23
Slyck ... 24
Smart, Syd ... 32
Smith, Elroy "R.C." ... 125
Somerville (Stand Up For Somerville) ... 176
Soothing Sounds For Baby ... 92
Souper Salad ... 232
Soylent Green ... 91

Spag's.......... 43
Sparky Dee.......... 235
Spectrum India.......... 227
Spencer Press.......... 171
Spin City.......... 235
Spingold Theater (Brandeis).......... 127
Spinoff.......... 216
Spoonie G (Gee).......... 119
St. Alphonse Hall.......... 127
Stark Reality.......... 29
Starr, Maurice.......... 279
Statler Hilton Hotel.......... 135
Stereo Jack's.......... 212
Steve's Ice Cream.......... 17
Stone Phoenix Coffeehouse.......... 105
Stoneham Theatre.......... 30
Store 54.......... 55
Strand Theatre.......... 198, 206
Straw Dogs.......... 71
Strawberries.......... 138
Stull, Rob.......... 119
Sugar Shack.......... 86, 104, 161, 279
Sun Ra.......... 28
Sure Shot Four.......... 248
Sweeney, Steve.......... 141
Sweet Sweetback's Baadasssss Song.......... 215
Sydney, Mr. Sylvia.......... 44
Sylvain Sylvain.......... 79
Sylvania.......... 152
Symphony Hall.......... 109

T Bone Walker.......... 74
T. I. C. 119
T. Max.......... 58
T. T. The Bears.......... 71, 178
Taang! Records.......... 194
Take It! Magazine.......... 230
Tape X (Complex).......... 133
Tasty Sandwich Shop.......... 257
Taylor, Bobby.......... 47, 144
Teddy Bear Lounge.......... 257
Teen Line.......... 183
Tello's.......... 251
Tennis-Up.......... 238
The Harder They Come.......... 37
Theatre Company of Boston.......... 175
ThermaSol.......... 132
Third Rail.......... 141, 233
Thor, Marc.......... 188, 233
Thunder, Margo.......... 203
Thundertrain.......... 77, 188
Tia's Seafood Restaurant.......... 244
Titanics.......... 71

Top Of The World Productions.......... 129
Tops N Bottoms.......... 114
Touraine.......... 167
Treat Her Right.......... 92
Tribe.......... 55
Trolley's.......... 232
T's Pub.......... 232
TV38.......... 12, 279
Two O'Clock Club.......... 198

Unicorn Coffee House.......... 185
United Fund.......... 146
Universal Productions.......... 198
Unnatural Axe.......... 143, 218
Upsidedown Cross.......... 125

V66 (TV station).......... 10, 262
Valdez, Wayne.......... 55
Van Peebles, Melvin.......... 215
Vaprin, Dinah.......... 62
Velvet Underground.......... 44
Viglione, Joe (Joseph).......... 76, 188, 262
Vild Records.......... 194
Villa Victoria Cultural Center.......... 208
Vinicio Paoli Leatherworks.......... 56
Vocations for Social Change.......... 2

WAAF.......... 203, 262
Wah Lum Academy.......... 24
Wailers.......... 118
Waits, Tom.......... 185
Walden Square Apartments.......... 153
Walker's (Western Wear).......... 21
Washington, Jackie.......... 149
WBCN.......... 40, 44, 103, 140, 159, 262, 272
WBUR.......... 151, 197
WBZ-TV4.......... 53
WCCM.......... 262
WCGY.......... 262
WCRB FM.......... 126
WCVB-TV.......... 103
WDJM.......... 262
WEEI.......... 6, 107
Wellfleet Pub.......... 67
West End Cinema.......... 52
West Newton Cinema.......... 242
Western Front.......... 65, 111
WFNX.......... 56
WGBH-TV (Channel 2).......... 75
Where It's At (club).......... 220
Whitch.......... 115
White, Chuck (Charles).......... 25, 34, 92
White, David Omar.......... 143

White, Sunny (Sonny) Joe........117, 135, 138, 184
Whitfield, Barrence & The Savages....................71
Who, The..44
WILD 1090 AM....8, 135, 138, 161, 179, 184, 224
Wildman Steve...50
Wilkins, Roy..161
Williams, Al...144
Wilson, Dave...93
Window To Watch...227
Windsor Cricket Club.....................................119
Winter, Johnny..128
WMBR...219
WMEX...61
WMFO...262
WMJX..131
WNAC-TV...177
Wolf, Peter...28, 40
WordsWorth...37
Working Women's Conference.........................223
World Wind I-Fi..238
Wreck Lounge..182
WRKO..108
WUNR 1600 AM...25
WZLX...262

Xanna Don't..71, 92

Your Mother's On The Roof (TV show).............116

Zayre...282
Zion Initation...111, 125
Zircon..65
Zulus...71, 92